■ Mercer Tillich Studies ■

Paul Tillich and Psychology

▪ Mercer Tillich Studies ▪

Paul Tillich and Psychology

Historic and Contemporary Explorations in Theology, Psychotherapy, and Ethics

Terry D. Cooper

MERCER
UNIVERSITY PRESS

ISBN 0-86554-993-1 MUP/P330

Paul Tillich and Psychology:
Historic and Contemporary Explorations
in Theology, Psychotherapy, and Ethics
Copyright ©2006
Mercer University Press
All rights reserved
Printed in the United States of America
First edition

The paper used in this publication meets the minimum requirements
of American National Standard for Information Sciences—
Permanence of Paper for Printed Library Materials,
ANSI Z39.48-1984.

Library of Congress Cataloging-in-Publication Data

Cooper, Terry D.
 Paul Tillich and psychology : historic and contemporary explorations in theology, psychotherapy, and ethics / Terry D. Cooper.-- 1st ed.
   p. cm.
 Includes bibliographical references and index.
 ISBN-13: 978-0-86554-993-7 (pbk. : alk. paper)
 ISBN-10: 0-86554-993-1 (pbk. : alk. paper)
   1. Tillich, Paul, 1886–1965. 2. Christianity—Psychology—History—20th century. 3. Psychotherapy—Religious aspects—Christianity—History—20th century. 4. Christian ethics—History—20th century. 5. Psychotherapy—Moral and ethical aspects—History—20th century. 6. New York Psychology Group. I. Title.
   BR110.C66 2005
   261.5'15092--dc22

2005028639

Contents

Acknowledgments vii

Chapter 1
Accepting Our Acceptance: Grace and Psychotherapy 1
    Tillich on Acceptance, 2
    Tillich and Luther, 7
    Theological and Psychotherapeutic Acceptance:
        Tillich and Carl Rogers, 15
    Incongruence and Estrangement, 17
    Acceptance and the "Demonic," 21
    Grace and Acceptance: A Conflation of Terms?, 25
    Acceptance and the Ground of Being, 31
    Summary, 35

Chapter 2
Anxiety and Its Treatment:
Psychotherapy and the "Courage to Be" 37
    Tillich's Own Struggle with Anxiety, 38
    Tillich's *The Courage to Be*, 41
    Distinguishing Fear and Anxiety, 43
    Anxiety's Three Major Threats, 45
    The Positive Side of Anxiety, 48
    Anxiety and the Limits of Psychotherapy, 51
    Limited Self-Affirmation, 52
    The Cognitive Therapy Challenge, 55
    A Tillichian Critique of Cognitive Therapy, 57
    Courage, Individuation, and Participation, 60
    Summary, 62

Chapter 3
Estrangement and New Being:
Sin and the Limitations of Psychotherapy 63
    Existence Itself Is the Problem, 64
    Existentialism and Depth Psychology, 65
    Created Goodness and Existential Estrangement, 69

Estrangement and Women's Experience:
    Plaskow's Critique, 76
Tillich, Marx, and Fromm
    on "the Fall" and Redemption, 80
The "Syndrome of Decay": Fromm's View of Estrangement, 84
Tillich's Three Characteristics of Estrangement, 91
Fromm's Vision and Tillich's Critique, 93

Chapter 4
The Psychology of Faith and Love:
The New York Psychology Group, 1941–1943 99
    First Year: Psychology of Faith, 100
    Reflections on the First Year of Discussion, 118
    Second Year: Psychology of Love, 127
    The Psychology of Love: Reflections on the Second Year, 140

Chapter 5
Ethics and Psychotherapy:
The New York Psychology Group, 1943–1945 147
    Third Year: Psychology of Conscience, 147
    Fourth Year: The Psychology of Helping, 168
    Ethics and Psychotherapy:
        Reflections on the Third and Fourth Years, 188

Chapter 6
Theology and Psychology:
Tillich's Ongoing Relevance 195
    Apologetic and Unapologetic Theology, 195
    From Tillich and Barth to Revisionists and Postliberals, 197
    Critical Hermeneutics: The Best of Both Worlds?, 203
    Browning's Development of Tracy and Ricoeur, 205
    Beyond Existential Anthropology:
        From the Individual to the Social, 208
    Tillich's Ongoing Relevance, 214

Index 219

Acknowledgments

Many people have been supportive conversational partners and have helped make this book possible. I thank Allison Stokes for sharing with me her materials from the New York Psychology Group. This book would not have been possible without Allison's gracious help. I also thank Britt-Mari Sykes, a colleague who shares a deep interest in Tillich and psychology, and who has been an invaluable consultant in this project as she has worked on her own book on Tillich.

I especially thank the members of the Armour Foundation for their generosity in helping make this book possible. I am deeply indebted to the late Dr. James Armour, whose influence inspired aspects of this book.

I also appreciate the support and encouragement I have received from Jane Owen, who was a warm host for my stay in New Harmony, Indiana, the home of the Paul Tillich Memorial Park, which Jane established.

I thank Guy Hammond, valued scholar of both Tillich and Erich Fromm, for carefully reviewing my manuscript and offering excellent suggestions. I also appreciate the support and conversational help I have received from Tillich scholar and friend, Don Arther. Both of these men have been very generous with their time and knowledge. Other colleagues, such as Marty Miller Maddox, Robert Asa, Dan Reynolds, David Johnson, Bud Peyton, Dennis Klass, Matthew Becker, and Steve May have offered valuable input concerning Tillich and psychology.

I would like to especially thank my family for their support in the making of this book. My wife, Linda, has listened to me talk about Tillich when I'm sure she thought I should be mowing the lawn or vacuuming the carpet. Her encouragement for all of my academic pursuits is matched by her own enthusiasm for learning. I also appreciate my parents, Don and Barbara Cooper, for consistently encouraging all my efforts.

Finally, I thank the person to whom this book is dedicated, Don S. Browning. For four decades, Don has been a pioneer in religion, ethics, and the social sciences. He is probably the most accomplished interdisciplinary thinker I know. But beyond that, he is a supportive friend and mentor. Working closely with Don on *Religious Thought and the Modern Psychologies* gave me an opportunity to come to an even deeper appreciation of his keen mind and generous spirit. So, with admiration and appreciation, I dedicate this book to Don.

For

Don S. Browning

with deep appreciation for a mentor and friend
who has helped so many of us
connect theology and psychology.

Chapter 1

Accepting Our Acceptance: Grace and Psychotherapy

Sometimes . . . a wave of light breaks into our darkness, and it is as though a voice were saying: "You are accepted. You are accepted, accepted by that which is greater than you, and the name of which you do not know. Do not ask for the name now; perhaps you will find it later. Do not try to do anything now; perhaps later you will do much. Do not seek anything; do not perform anything; do not intend anything. Simply accept the fact that you are accepted!" If that happens to us, we experience grace.
—Paul Tillich

Paul Tillich believed the heart of the Christian message revolves around the deep experience of "accepting our acceptance." He further believed it ironic that the rediscovery of this profound experience of grace, so deeply embedded in Luther, was largely lost until its re-discovery in psychotherapy. This emphasis on psychotherapeutic acceptance offers theologians a new framework for discussing the meaning of Luther's great discovery of grace. This new "grace language" of acceptance is perhaps the most significant reason Tillich remarked that "the theologian would do well to remain in contact with the psychotherapeutic movement."[1] While Tillich believed that theologians have much to say about the ontological grounding of this experience of acceptance, he also believed that theologians have much to learn from psychotherapy concerning the concrete experiencing of grace.

In this chapter, I wish to (a) highlight the significance of the term "acceptance" for Tillich's framework, (b) explore the link between the classic Lutheran understanding of the justification by grace and psychotherapeutic acceptance, (c) discuss the ways in which Luther functioned as a depth psychologist as well as theologian, (d) compare Tillich's theological understanding of "accepting our acceptance" with the psychotherapist who has probably most influenced the psychotherapeutic understanding of acceptance, Carl Rogers, (e) examine the concept of "the

---

[1]Paul Tillich, "The Impact of Pastoral Psychology on Theological Thought," in Hans Hofman, ed., *The Ministry and Mental Health* (New York: Association Press, 1960) 19.

demonic" and its relationship to acceptance, (f) investigate the charge that Tillich conflates the terms "grace" and "acceptance," thereby confusing the relationship between psychology and theology, and (g) explore the criticism that Tillich's view of God as the "Ground of Being" sabotages the highly personal language of psychotherapeutic acceptance.

Tillich on Acceptance

One of the most well-known and deeply appreciated writings of Tillich is his sermon, "You Are Accepted."[2] In this famous sermon, Tillich tells us that while there are no substitutes for words like "sin" and "grace," there *are* ways of rediscovering their meaning. This rediscovery will lead us down into the depths of human existence.[3] The word "sin" can be supplemented by the word "separation," which Tillich argues is a universal human experience. We are separated from ourselves, from each other, and from the ground of our lives. "This threefold separation constitutes the state of everything that exists; it is a universal fact; it is the fate of every life."[4] All of us know, in our depths, that we are separated from something to which we essentially belong. Our longing for reunion suggests to us that we *should* be united, and our guilt tells us that we are in part responsible for this separation. We actively participate in and perpetuate our condition. Thus, for Tillich, separation always means *both fate and choice*. While this combination seems most contradictory, it is the state of our existence from its beginning to its end.

> Such separation is prepared in the mother's womb, and before that time, in every preceeding generation. It is manifest in the special actions of our conscious life. It reaches beyond our graves into all the succeeding generations. It is our existence itself. *Existence is separation!*[5]

This conviction that existence itself necessitates separation will be explored more fully in chapter 3. For now, it is important only that we understand that estrangement means separation from that to which we essentially belong.

---

[2]Tillich, "You Are Accepted," in *The Shaking of the Foundations* (New York: Scribner's, 1948) 153-63.
[3]Tillich, "You Are Accepted," 154.
[4]Tillich, "You Are Accepted," 155.
[5]Tillich, "You Are Accepted," 155.

For Tillich, as for Luther, we could have no knowledge of sin or separation without the experience of grace. Our separation is clear to us because, however vague, we also have a sense of unity with that toward which we are separated. Conversely, we wouldn't really understand the experience of grace without the experience of separation.

> In grace something is overcome; grace occurs "in spite of" something; grace occurs in spite of separation and estrangement. Grace is the *re*union of life with life, the *re*conciliation of the self with itself. Grace is the acceptance of that which is rejected. Grace transforms fate into a meaningful destiny; it changes guilt into confidence and courage.[6]

Tillich is particularly eloquent about our separation or estrangement from ourselves. The influence of countless hours of conversation with psychotherapists is apparent in his description of self-estrangement. As Tillich puts it, "Life moves against itself through aggression, hate, and despair. We are wont to condemn self-love; but what we mean to condemn is contrary to self-love."[7] Following Fromm, Tillich believes that our real enemy is not so much self-love as it is selfishness and self-hate, neither of which should be confused with self-love. As he puts it, "He who is able to love himself is able to love others also; he who has learned to overcome self-contempt has learned to overcome contempt for others."[8] While Tillich, on other occasions, recoils from using the term "self-love," he clearly sees that the feelings of inadequacy associated with self-preoccupation are a greater problem than self-love.[9] Narcissism is rooted in a sense of inferiority, in spite of the fact that it appears quite grandiose.

---

[6]Tillich, "You Are Accepted," 156.
[7]Tillich, "You Are Accepted," 158.
[8]Tillich, "You Are Accepted," 158.
[9]Tillich appears to have grown progressively uncomfortable with the term "self-love" in his writings. This can be clearly seen, for instance, in his dialogue session with Carl Rogers. See "Paul Tillich and Carl Rogers: A Dialogue," in *Carl Rogers—Dialogues: Conversations with Martin Buber, Paul Tillich, B. F. Skinner, Gregory Bateson, Michael Polanyi, Rollo May, and Others*, ed. Howard Kirschenbaum and Valerie Land Henderson (Boston: Houghton Mifflin, 1989) 64-78. Also, a transcript of the Rogers-Tillich dialogue, recorded on 7 March 1965, was published separately: *Paul Tillich & Carl Rogers: A Dialogue* (San Diego: San Diego State College, 1966) 23 pages.

For Tillich, all Pelagian attempts to "muster up" self-love are doomed to fail. We cannot simply "will ourselves" into self-love. We cannot provide ourselves with the kind of love and acceptance necessary to break the power of our estrangement.

Self-contempt makes self-acceptance, through our own isolated efforts, quite impossible. As Jung put it, "no one is justified in boasting that he has fully accepted himself."[10] And our dilemma, for both Jung and Tillich, is that we are incapable of change without self-acceptance. This is the dilemma: we desperately want to change yet we cannot do so without first fully accepting and embracing ourselves. Yet we are incapable of offering ourselves this type of self-acceptance. So we turn to a therapist, but the therapist is only capable of offering us acceptance if he or she has accepted his/her acceptance. Self-condemnation inevitably spreads outward. Those dark, unacceptable regions within the therapist block the therapist from accepting the patient. And as Sheldon Kopp reminds us, "it is easier to see out of the shadows than into them."[11]

A larger experience of acceptance is necessary, then, before self-acceptance is possible. Just as this larger framework of acceptance was the source of Luther's self-confidence, so it is for Tillich.

> We cannot compel anyone to accept himself. But sometimes it happens that we receive the power to say "yes" to ourselves, that peace enters into us and makes us whole, that self-hate and self-contempt disappear, and that our self is reunited with itself. Then we can say that grace has come upon us."[12]

Thus, "accepting our acceptance" is never based on moral qualities, achievements, intellectual abilities, or any other human strength. It is transforming only when we realize we are unacceptable. In fact, the experience of *being* accepted is life-changing only when all of our own attempts at self-acceptance have miserably failed. All forms of "self-willed" acceptance are doomed to a self-preoccupying defeat. We simply cannot declare ourselves "okay." Popular notions in self-help literature often suggest that

---

[10]Carl Jung, *Modern Man in Search of a Soul* (New York: Harcourt, Brace, and World, 1933) 236.

[11]Sheldon Kopp, *Mirror, Mask, and Shadow: The Risks and Rewards of Self-Acceptance* (New York: Bantam, 1980) 34.

[12]Tillich, "You Are Accepted," 163.

we completely disregard another's opinion of us and decide, in the courtroom of our own autonomy, that we are acceptable. While this is well-intentioned advice, particularly to those of us who worry far too much about others' approval, it is ultimately impossible. We did not arrive at this state of feeling unacceptable on our own; neither can we heal it on our own.

It is here that Tillich drives home a point which greatly influenced later pastoral theology and counseling. Tillich insists that any discussion of acceptance, like any discussion of anxiety, desperately needs to be grounded in an ontological framework. An accepting therapist, whether conscious of it or not, points toward a Source of acceptance which transcends both therapist and patient. "Self-affirmation in spite of the anxiety of guilt and condemnation presupposes participation in something which transcends the self."[13] So while we each need to have our acceptance mediated by a particular person in a one-on-one encounter, the ability to accept this acceptance necessitates a transcendent Source.

> It is not the counselor as an *individual*, who really accepts—that is what I always tell my psychoanalytic friends: "Who are *you* to *accept* somebody?" But you can accept somebody if you realize that you both equally are accepted, so that the power of acceptance works through you and through him. And it is not you alone who accepts, you a questionable human being, who perhaps needs counseling and analysis as much as your patient does. You both stand in the need of acceptance-*in-spite-of*!! When this is realized, we have a relationship which in itself has the character of transformation.[14]

Also, as Tillich reminds us, being accepted does not mean that guilt has faded away or that a sense of unacceptability is now diminished. Trying to convince a patient that he or she is now completely innocent is not the task of therapy and would simply involve more denial. For Tillich, our guilt is no illusion. In fact, to pretend it is an illusion is to miss the whole "in spite of" dimension of acceptance. We are accepted *in spite of our guilt*, not because we *have no guilt*. While Tillich frequently recognized the problem of neurotic guilt *feelings*, he refused to deny the reality of guilt. This reality of guilt is one of the reasons that acceptance must be grounded in a

---

[13]Paul Tillich, *The Courage to Be* (New Haven CT: Yale University Press, 1952) 165.

[14]Paul Tillich, "Theology and Counseling," in *The Meaning of Health*, ed. Perry LeFevre (Chicago: Exploration Press, 1984) 121.

transcendent source. It must move beyond mere human acceptance. He puts it well.

> Here, however, is the point where the religious "acceptance as being accepted" transcends medical healing. Religion asks for the ultimate source of the power which heals by accepting the unacceptable, it asks for God. The acceptance of God, his forgiving or justifying act, is the only and ultimate source of a courage to be which is able to take the anxiety of guilt and condemnation into itself. For the ultimate power of self-affirmation can only be the power of being-itself. Everything less than this, one's own or anybody else's finite power of being, cannot overcome the radical, infinite threat of nonbeing which is experienced in the despair of self-condemnation. This is why the courage of confidence, as it is expressed in a man like Luther, emphasizes unceasingly exclusive trust in God and rejects any other foundation for his courage to be, not only as insufficient but as driving him into more guilt and deeper anxiety.[15]

It is in this eloquent statement that Tillich points toward the important contribution that theology can offer psychotherapy. While psychotherapy has greatly clarified the concrete experience of acceptance, theology can clarify the ontological foundation which makes the therapeutic experience work.

The early work of Don Browning and Thomas Oden helps us understand the importance of the relationship of ontological acceptance to the kind of psychotherapeutic acceptance which makes interpersonal healing possible.[16] While I will later return to their work in greater detail, I mention it now because of the significance of their central thesis, reminiscent of Tillich. There is a hidden or implicit ontological assumption of acceptance in secular psychotherapy which is made explicit and celebrated in the Christian community. While Browning and Oden approached this implicit assumption in psychotherapy from somewhat different frameworks, each found that effective therapy completely presupposes the patient's acceptability. In fact, it is precisely this assumption, often unrecognized in secular therapies, which makes the therapy process possible. It is hardly transforming that a particular human being, a therapist, accepts us. After all, we can easily find a rejecting voice soon after we leave the therapy session. It is a

---

[15]*The Courage to Be*, 166-67.

[16]Don S. Browning, *Atonement and Psycotherapy* (Philadelphia: Westminster Press, 1966); Thomas C. Oden, *Kerygma and Counseling* (Philadelphia: Westminster Press, 1966).

little more powerful when the therapist, as a representative of the mental health community, accepts us. Yet this, also, lacks the kind of transformational quality we need. But when a therapist communicates to us that we are acceptable period, acceptable before life itself, ontologically acceptable, this has enormous power. And again, all effective forms of psychotherapy make this assumption that the patient is ontologicially acceptable.

Tillich and Luther

In discussing Luther's impact on Tillich, James Luther Adams has said that "no writer of the twentieth century has been more successful and influential than Tillich in interpreting and disseminating the ideas of the great Reformer among the general public in the United States."[17] In a well-known passage in his autobiographical reflection, *On the Boundary*, Tillich proclaims his Lutheran heritage in a most explicit manner:

> I am a Lutheran by birth, education, religious experience, and theological reflection. I have never stood on the boundary between Lutheranism and Calvinism, not even after I experienced the disastrous consequences of Lutheran social ethics and came to recognize the inestimable value of the Calvinistic idea of the Kingdom of God in the solution of social problems. The substance of my religion is and remains Lutheran. It includes a consciousness of the "corruption" of existence, a repudiation of every kind of social Utopia (including the metaphysics of progressivism), an awareness of the irrational and demonic nature of existence, an appreciation of the mystical element in religion, and a rejection of Puritanical legalism in private and corporate life.[18]

While Tillich deeply appreciates the existential nature of Luther's experience, he believes that Luther's insights need to find a different vocabulary for our situation. The theological formulations of Luther's age need new expression. Yet the experience of grace and acceptance in Luther is most relevant to our dilemma.

Tillich believes that in Luther's time, the Roman Catholic Church had become a "system of divine-human management, represented and

---

[17]James Luther Adams, "Paul Tillich on Luther," in *Interpreters of Luther: Essays in Honor of Wilhelm Pauck*, ed. Jaroslav Pelikan (Philadelphia: Fortress Press, 1968) 304.

[18]Paul Tillich, *On the Boundary* (New York: Charles Scribner's Sons, 1966) 74-75.

actualized by ecclesiastical management."[19] Under these conditions, there could never be any certainty of Divine acceptance. The anxiety of guilt and condemnation could not be overcome no matter what one accomplished. The struggle was to find a merciful God.

> A tremendous amount of this anxiety was expressed in the art of the period, and also expressed in the demand for more and more pilgrimages, in the collection and adoration of relics, in praying many "Our Fathers," in giving of money, in buying indulgences, self-torturing asceticism, and everything possible to get over one's guilt . . . Luther was in the cloister with this same anxiety of guilt and condemnation. Out of this anxiety he went into the cloister and out of it he experienced that no amount of asceticism is able to give a person a real certainty of salvation in a system of relativities, quantities, and things. He was always in fear of the threatening God, of the punishing and destroying God. And he asked: How can I get a merciful God? Out of this question and the anxiety behind it, the Reformation began.[20]

Luther strongly objected to the notion that the sacraments, administered by the hierarchical authority of the church, were efficacious regardless of one's personal involvement. Luther believed this to be a magical view of the sacraments.

It is also helpful to understand Luther in reaction to Occamist anthropology, particularly the work of Gabriel Biel. For Biel, "doing what is in one" became the human will's necessary preparation for the reception of Divine assistance.[21] As David Steinmetz says in his fine work on Luther, Biel even suggested that human effort, unaided by the divine, has the natural power to love God supremely (at least temporarily) and achieve rather heroic moral standards.[22] While we are psychologically impaired by sin, humanity's capacity to love God more than ourselves has never been

---

[19]Paul Tillich, *A History of Christian Thought: From Its Judaic and Hellenistic Origins to Existentialism*, ed. Carl Braaten (New York: Simon and Schuster, 1967) 228.

[20]Tillich, *A History of Christian Thought*, 229.

[21]For an excellent account of Biel's theology, see Heiko Oberman, *The Harvest of Medieval Theology: Gabriel Biel and Late Medieval Nominalism* (Grand Rapids MI: Eerdmans, 1967).

[22]David C. Steinmetz, *Luther in Context* (Grand Rapids MI: Baker, 1995) esp. chap. 6.

destroyed. Like Pelagius, Biel believed that God would not have commanded us to do things for which we are incapable. Human beings thus have a natural inclination toward what is good, a condition not unlike what contemporary humanistic psychologists call a "self-actualizing tendency." God promises to respond to those who seek him, and the capacity to search for God is clearly within the parameters of human willing. Thus the theological concept of "election" refers only to God's foreknowledge of those who seek Him. Human choice, not Divine Sovereignty, makes salvation possible. God has bound himself to honor his own covenant with anyone who pursues him.

Luther's reaction to this type of anthropology is especially vivid in his disputation with Erasmus.[23] Luther detested the Aristotelian notion of acquired virtue, which Erasmus largely embraced. This perspective emphasized that we become righteous by *doing righteous acts*. For Luther, this ignored the fundamental plight of our existence, namely, that our will is bound and we are therefore not capable of "willing" righteousness. At the same time, however, the will is not forced to do anything against its own volition. Thus the will naturally "goes along with" sinful choices. This is why the Reformers could say that sin is inevitable, but not a compulsion. A compulsion always involves something outside the will forcing it against the will's own resistance.

For Erasmus, this notion of the will being in bondage eliminates human responsibility and villainizes God. Free will, for Erasmus, necessitates the possibility that the will can choose good, not just evil. Holding humanity responsible when we really do not have free choice creates a cruel picture of the Divine. Erasmus uses a parable of an apple to explain his position.[24] A child, he says, tries very hard, on his own, to reach an apple in a tree. The child's father sees the effort, knowing that the child will never be able to reach the apple without help. The father then lifts the child up and gently guides him to the apple. Aided by the father, the child grasps the apple and enjoys the reward. This is the way it is with God and his creation.

Both Luther and Calvin would say that the child could not even *see* the apple (due to the consequences of original sin), much less want to possess it. The will is irreparably "bent in on itself" and cannot repair its own

---

[23] *Luther and Erasmus: Free Will and Salvation*, ed. Rupp and Watson, Library of Modern Classics (Philadelphia: Westminster, 1969).

[24] *Luther and Erasmus*, 91.

damage. Freedom can only occur as a result of Divine benevolence, a grace that is mysteriously given to some and not to others. This grace is not based on merit, effort, or any human quality. It is instead based on God's choice. Any objection to this plan, for Luther, is built on the arrogance of a "theology of glory" which insists that God conform to all of our ideas and standards about justice and fairness. If our ethical sensitivities are insulted by such an image of God, it is because of our sinful insistence that God conform to our own standards. As Steven Ozment points out, Luther saw the dangers of making God into humanity's own ethical alter ego, a creation based on our demands as to what God must be.[25]

Erasmus insists that the will must remain neutral enough to choose, thus rejecting Luther's insistence that it is either bound to the Devil or to God's grace. Instead, we are morally neutral agents, filled with potential for both good and evil. Using a contemporary phrase, human beings are not biologically predisposed to act in a destructive or negative way. The deck is not stacked against us in advance. Luther, of course, believed that Erasmus should have been more honest and declared himself a full-fledged Pelagian. Perhaps in return, Erasmus might say to Luther that he should have been more honest and declared himself a full-fledged Manichaean.

The key theological differences between Luther and Erasmus, then, are a clear replay of the Pelagian controversy. As an Augustinian, Luther believes that salvation results exclusively from the grace of God. Human effort, readiness, or cooperation have nothing to do with it. As a semi-Pelagian, Erasmus believes that Luther leads us into a monstrously cruel, capricious God who unfairly passes over some and elects others. Erasmus insists that this God, on whom our very notions of justice and fairness exist, must not violate His own standards.

But for Luther, once again, salvation is not something we merit, not something God gives us because God has foreknowledge of our later accomplishments. It is pure gift. Yet because of our sinful pride, we resist the notion of imputed righteousness and instead insist on the power of our own works. Even the notion of faith is turned into a self-help form of salvation. We must somehow "dredge up" enough faith for salvation. Faith thus becomes an act of works. For Luther, faith is *not* based on intellectual

---

[25]Steven Ozment, *The Age of Reform* (New Haven: Yale University Press, 1980) 302.

struggle to believe in God nor on a psychological struggle to trust God. It is neither an intellectual nor a psychological achievement. Moralism will not provide salvation and rationalism will not supply salvific knowledge. There is no moral or cognitive redemption apart from the grace of God. The human will, as Luther frequently put it in his disputation with Erasmus, is like a corpse: it cannot resurrect itself, but instead, can only *be* resurrected by God.

Acceptance always means the reception of forgiveness. We cannot accept ourselves or God without the experience of forgiveness. And the greater our experience of forgiveness, the greater our capacity for love.[26] Love and rejection cannot co-exist. In fact, we are, of necessity, always hostile to that which rejects us. This hostility, as Luther knew so well, is also expressed toward a judging God. Tillich puts it this way:

> As long as we feel rejected by him, we cannot love God. He appears to us an oppressive power, as He who gives laws according to His pleasure, who judges according to his commandments, who condemns according to His wrath. But if we have received and accepted the message that He *is* reconciled, everything changes. Like a fiery stream His healing power enters into us; we can affirm Him and with Him our own being and the others from whom we were estranged, and life as a whole. Then we realize that His love is the law of our own being, and that it is the law of reuniting love.[27]

Without a deep sense of acceptance, our hostility toward life continues to expand. Life is perceived as critical, unfriendly, cold, harsh, and judgmental. We feel shamed by life. And after enough rejection, we usually develop strong, compensatory feelings of disregard for life. If we feel hated, we usually hate back. We perceive life as against us, so we are going to "act out" against life. Whether it is passive cynicism or active revolt, our own deep-rooted feelings of rejection drive us toward an aggressive rejection of life. There is woundedness beneath our aggression, yet because this woundedness brings up too much vulnerability and pain, we pretend to not need life. "To hell with the world" is the message of a person who feels deeply that the world has already rejected him or her. This may *appear* as arrogant defiance, but beneath the exterior is often a failure of acceptance.

---

[26]Paul Tillich, *The New Being* (New York: Scribner's, 1955) 10.
[27]Tillich, *The New Being*, 10.

For both Luther and Tillich, what is crucial here is that we understand that *God fully accepts even our hostile feelings toward God*. If God does not fully understand and accept our deepest feelings of contempt for him, then Divine acceptance is limited and shallow. The very darkest corners of our hostile feelings must be embraced. As Don Browning puts it, "God's acceptance is predicated on a complete and absolute empathic understanding of all our feelings, even our negative and hostile feelings toward him."[28]

Because of our raw vulnerability, this Divine empathy may at first be treated with reactivity and resistance. Because *we* cannot accept certain feelings, *God* probably can't either. We cling to our contrived standards that will "make us" acceptable. We must earn it. We are both suspicious and hostile toward unconditional acceptance. Yet unconditional acceptance *includes* our hostility toward it. Of course we resist it. It seems to good to be true. We'd rather hang on to familiar feelings of rejection than embrace a new world of grace. Yet clearly the cross represents God's capacity to take on even our most hostile feelings of rejection toward his love and acceptance.

> This freely given love contradicts these conditions of worth, and they, in turn, defend themselves with hostile rejection of this love. God makes this hostile defense useless and of no avail by *accepting it*. By still enduring, God demonstrates to man his ultimate acceptability in spite of these powers and their conditions.[29]

Our "conditions of worth," to use one of Carl Rogers's terms, are thus contradicted by unconditional acceptance. Our private and social standards for self-justification can easily hold us hostage. We become "bound up" in a vicious, self-defeating cycle of trying to achieve them. As we make these standards pivotal for our entire sense of worth, we turn finite goals into gods. This attempt to achieve these deified goals thus produces excessive anxiety because our entire sense of self-worth hinges upon them.[30] Idolatry always contaminates psychological health because the finite can never produce what we need from the infinite. Standards of self-justification thus take on the role of "the demonic," a concept I will explore later.

---

[28]Browning, *Atonement and Psychotherapy*, 204.
[29]Browning, *Atonement and Psychotherapy*, 206.
[30]For a more detailed elaboration of this point, see Thomas C. Oden, *The Structure of Awareness* (Nashville: Abingdon, 1969).

Tillich believes that Luther reversed the normal order of ethics and religion. In other words, Luther says that ethical behavior comes *as a result of acceptance* rather than leading one to acceptance. William Hordern puts this well: "Thus there is a causal relationship between repentance and forgiveness, but in God's case it is never our repentance that causes God's forgiveness; rather, it is God's forgiveness that causes our repentance.[31] If repentance becomes still another "work" necessary to win God's acceptance, then the question becomes how much repentance is necessary? As Hordern asks, how sorry must we feel? And for how long?

Luther's breakthrough came with the realization that nothing we do can *cause* God's grace to fall upon us. Practicing moral virtue will certainly not usher it in. The fact is that all moral virtue is highly ambiguous, still clouded by pride. Even when we succeed in doing the right thing, it is often not done for the right reason. Our motives are less pure than we would like to think. Luther's deep knowledge of what lies beneath virtue is an anticipation of Freud's undermining of Victorian morality.

Luther made his breakthrough of justification by grace against a background of the anxiety of guilt and condemnation. He tried desperately to escape the wrath of God, the angry Tyrant who was never pleased with even his best efforts. Luther could not get rid of his sense of guilt. Tillich argues that for our situation today, it is not primarily guilt, but meaninglessness, which is the primary dilemma. Doubt has replaced guilt as our central problem. The question is how Luther's transforming message of "accepting our acceptance" can be applied to our situation.

> Whereas Luther had interpreted the experience of justification as a religious-moral experience associated with the search for a righteous but merciful God, Tillich asserts the experience can occur also in the religious-intellectual sphere—for the doubter as well as for the "sinner." Precisely when the unbeliever is seriously concerned with how to maintain intellectual integrity to the point of radical doubt, divine grace is present. It is present in the experience of doubt, for it engenders participation in the very midst of meaninglessness. Thus the doubter is "justified." His doubting is a participation in truth. (Here one is reminded of Augustine's insight, "I doubt, therefore I am.").[32]

---

[31] William Hordern, *Living by Grace* (Philadelphia: Westminster Press, 1975) 78.

[32] Adams, "Paul Tillich on Luther," 316.

Again, Luther's experience reveals that the courage of confidence cannot be rooted in ourselves. In fact, Luther's confidence emerged only after his self-confidence had collapsed. This courage cannot be based on anything finite, even including the Church. Instead, it "is based on God and solely on God, who is experienced in a unique and personal encounter."[33]

Tillich believes that Luther's experiential discovery of the nature of grace is unprecedented.[34] One of the reasons that Luther was able to accomplish this task is that he was a "depth psychologist" as well as a theologian.

> Luther was a depth psychologist in the profoundest way, without knowing the methodological research we know today. Luther saw these things in nonmoralistic depths, which were lost not only in Calvinist Christianity but to a great extent in Lutheranism as well.[35]

Luther's mood-changes, struggles with despair, battles with self-contempt, inability to eliminate guilt, fear of Divine wrath, and relentless quest for assurance and acceptance all entered powerfully into his theology. While Luther may have struggled little with philosophical doubt about God's existence, he wrestled mightily with the psychological doubt concerning his own acceptability. For Luther, assurance was hard to come by.

Tillich understands Luther as a depth psychologist for obvious reasons. Luther was less concerned with the possibility that sin could be forgiven than with the more terrifying concern that he could never consciously name all his sin. Unrecognized, and hence unconfessed, sin produced a great anxiety in Luther. Sin had deep roots. It was not a mere behavioral problem.

Luther's mentor, Staupitz, introduced Luther to the German mystics with the hope that this would loosen Luther's destructive self-preoccupation and prompt a greater sense of connection with God. Yet for Luther, even the attempts to eliminate his pride were *acts of pride,* and hence, self-defeating. This was like a narcissist narcissistically trying to eliminate his narcissism. It was like fighting hard to get out of quicksand—the more he struggled, the deeper he sank.

Another problem was that mysticism encouraged giving oneself over to the love of God. But Luther found that his deepest feelings toward the

---

[33]*The Courage to Be*, 163.
[34]Tillich, *A History of Christian Thought*, 227.
[35]Tillich, *A History of Christian Thought*, 246.

Divine were ones of contempt rather than love. After all, how could he "warm up" to that critical, demeaning voice who declared him inadequate. He was ashamed of his own contempt for God, yet internally aware and courageous enough to admit it. A perfectionistic, demanding, authoritarian presence promoted hatred rather than love. What was Luther to do with these feelings? While the Almighty seemed disgusted with Luther, Luther knew, in his inner sanctum, that he was equally disgusted with God. Intrapsychic awareness had produced a theological crisis. His deep self-understanding unwittingly contributed to his theological woes and fostered a strong sense of anxiety and guilt. For Luther, the assumption that we can have conscious knowledge of all our sin is naïve. Sin blocks its own discovery. Sin censors itself, protects itself, and operates on the basis of self-defense. The battle between flesh and spirit is not as simple as a fight between bodily lust and spiritual matters.

"Flesh," instead, also includes the self's myriad attempts at self-justification, the clever trickery which can make us appear more righteous than we really are. Clearly, this anticipates Freudian thinking about the way in which the unconscious keeps itself in the dark. While Freud used psychological terminology and Luther used theological concepts, both pointed toward the fundamental human dilemma—the darker regions of the psyche have a multitude of maneuvers for keeping themselves unknown. If Luther had not been so self-aware, he would have had far fewer theological problems. Yet it would not have led to his great breakthrough on the nature of grace.

Theological and Psychotherapeutic Acceptance: Tillich and Carl Rogers

On March 7, 1965, in the radio/television studio of San Diego State College, Tillich appeared in a dialogue session with Carl Rogers, the humanistic psychologist who had made psychotherapeutic acceptance the very cornerstone of his life's work. Whatever their differences, these two individuals had enormously impacted the field of pastoral theology and counseling. Rogers spent most of his life trying to explicate the importance of the word "acceptance" as the key factor in psychotherapy. While Rogers explicitly distanced himself from the dogma of any theological language, he maintained a deep undercurrent of the "justification by grace alone" in his secularized version of interpersonal grace.

Rogers, like Rollo May, began preparation for ministry at Union Theological Seminary in New York; but Rogers, unlike May, dropped out of the program before completing it. Rogers instead moved across the street to Columbia University where he studied psychology. When Rogers left the world of theology, he severed his ties quite radically. Yet his work became one of the most influential resources of pastoral care in the twentieth century. He and Tillich were both passionately interested in human estrangement, though one saw it as merely an interpersonal problem and the other saw it as an ontological problem. Indeed, Rogers is perhaps the best representative of the humanistic psychology movement, a movement which longs to overcome self-alienation by releasing the hidden depths of human potential.

Brooks Holifield, in his comprehensive study, *A History of Pastoral Care in America: From Salvation to Self-Realization*, points out several reasons why Carl Rogers was so well received in pastoral counseling and clinical psychology circles in the 1940s, 1950s, and 1960s.[36] One reason had to do with a revolt against legalism, moralism, and advice-giving in pastoral settings. Postwar America was becoming more individualistic, more leary of institutions, more critical of mass culture, and far more concerned with individuality. A "growth-oriented" mentality seemed to be pushing out an older concern with adjustment or identifying psychopathology. Institutions, which had previously been seen as the channels through which personal development could take place, were gradually being regarded as the enemy of self-realization.[37] America, after the Second World War, became more and more intrigued with psychology's promise of personal growth.

> In 1940 there had been 3,000 members of the American Psychological Association; by 1957, there were 16,000, working alongside 9,000 psychiatrists. *Life* magazine reported in that year that the country had "more psychologists and psychiatrists, engaged in more types of inquiry and activity, than all the rest of the world together." In the entire world, moreover, there were only 1,400 psychoanalysts, and half of them were native-born Americans. Sigmund Freud's disciple and biographer Ernest

---

[36]Brooks Holifield, *A History of Pastoral Care in America: From Salvation to Self-Realization* (Nashville: Abingdon, 1983) chap. 7.

[37]Holifield, *A History of Pastoral Care in America*, 260.

Jones made a pilgrimage to this new Mecca in 1956, and he announced that in psychoanalytic work, too, the United States led the world.[38]

Even by 1951, Carl Rogers noted that nearly twenty percent of the members in the American Psychological Association were offering psychotherapy, making psychotherapy the fastest growing area in the social sciences.[39]

The Second World War had also convinced clergy that they needed far better skills in the "cure of souls." Counseling courses blossomed in most all the theological seminaries across the nation. In fact, as early as 1955, when H. Richard Niebuhr of Yale conducted an investigation of Protestant theological education, he expressed some concern that pastoral care and counseling in seminaries threatened to establish a separate existence from the rest of the theological curriculum.[40] Also, several major universities were offering Ph.D. programs in the area of Religion and Psychology, Pastoral Theology, or Pastoral Psychology. As Holified reports, by the end of the 1950s, there were 117 centers of clinical pastoral education which formed connections to more than forty theological schools.[41] In 1947, the *Journal of Pastoral Care* and the *Journal of Clinical Pastoral Work* began, followed in 1950 by *Pastoral Psychology*.

Paul Tillich and Carl Rogers were also both members of the New York Psychology Group, though rather disappointingly, Rogers indicates that the group had little impact on the development of his thinking.[42] Nevertheless, Tillich and Rogers were the two most influential thinkers on the post-World War II pastoral theology and counseling scene.

Incongruence and Estrangement

Rogers and Tillich both understand that a major problem of the human condition is that human beings are "at odds" or in conflict with themselves. As we have seen, Tillich frequently referred to this situation as estrangement. While Tillich's understanding of the dynamics of estrangement will be explored in chapter 3, it is important to briefly discuss its significance for

---

[38] Holifield, *A History of Pastoral Care in America*, 263.
[39] Holifield, *A History of Pastoral Care in America*, 264.
[40] Holifield, *A History of Pastoral Care in America*, 271.
[41] Holifield, *A History of Pastoral Care in America*, 271.
[42] Allison Stokes, *Ministry After Freud* (New York: Pilgrim Press, 1985) 125-26.

a comparison with Rogers. Estrangement, for Tillich, is a universal condition of separation and conflict. Estrangement moves in three directions: we are estranged from God as the Ground of our being, we are estranged from each other, and we are estranged from ourselves.

> Man as he exists is not what he essentially is and ought to be. He is estranged from his true being. The profundity of the word "estrangement" lies in the implication that one belongs essentially to that from which one is estranged. Man is not a stranger to his true being, for he belongs to it.[43]

This estrangement is manifest in a fundamental mistrust in the Ground and Source of our lives (unbelief), an elevation of ourselves as the center of the world (hubris), and excessive attachments or inordinate desires for finite things (concupiscence). All these problems arise out of our estrangement. Yet Tillich insists on also using the word "sin" to describe our predicament because sin communicates the personal responsibility involved in our estrangement. Thus, estrangement is not something which simply "happens to us" as passive victims. Instead, we participate in our own estrangement. We are not blameless. Thus, Tillich reminds us that

> Sin is a universal fact before it becomes an individual act, or more precisely, sin as an individual act actualizes the universal fact of estrangement. As an individual act, sin is a matter of freedom, responsibility, and personal guilt. But this freedom is imbedded in the universal destiny of estrangement in such a way that in every free act the destiny of estrangement is involved and, vice versa, that the destiny of estrangement is actualized by all free acts. Therefore, it is impossible to separate sin as fact from sin as act. They are interwoven, and their unity is an immediate experience of everyone who feels himself to be guilty.[44]

While Rogers speaks often about estrangement from others and ourselves, he says virtually nothing about an estrangement from our Source. Rogers's primary term for the condition of estrangement or self-alienation is "incongruence." Incongruence is basically acting inconsistently with our own experiencing process. It is experiencing life one way while symbolizing that experience to ourselves in quite another way. In other words, incongruence is a state of distorted awareness in which a gap exists

---

[43]Paul Tillich, *Systematic Theology*, vol. 2 (Chicago: University of Chicago Press, 1957) 45.

[44]Tillich, *Systematic Theology* 2:56.

between what we actually experience and what we tell ourselves and others we are experiencing. Thus we are strangers to ourselves.[45]

Again, this experience of incongruence emerges because of "conditions of worth" or what we might term "conditional acceptance." For Rogers, infants have no natural need to distort or deny their process of experiencing. They have not learned to hide, conceal, or pretend to be something other than what they are. If they are afraid, they show it; if they are angry, they reveal it; if they are curious, they stare. Again, there is a smooth continuity between what they feel and what they express. They have no need to "cut off from awareness" part of their experiencing process.

Sooner or later, however, even in healthy families, children understand that while some experiences or feelings are acceptable, others are definitely not. Thus, they realize that not all of their experience will be warmly received. As a consequence of these "conditions of worth," children learn to hide or deny certain experiences which are sure to bring condemnation. After all, the protection and approval of the parents is more crucial than the "truth" of what they are experiencing. So they begin to present to the parents only those things which will be acceptable. Only "part" of them, then, is perceived as "good." In addition to hiding certain feelings from their parents, children eventually internalize the conditions of worth and will not even admit to themselves these feelings. Consequently, children become strangers to themselves, the victims of incongruence. A gap now exists between their actual experience and the way in which they perceive themselves. This is precisely what Rogers means by incongruence and it has obvious similarities to Tillich's notion of estrangement.

Closely associated with the experience of incongruence is the unconscious experience of self-contempt. By ignoring certain dimensions of their experience, children reject particular feelings, and even learn to despise them. These feelings are not part of the self-concept. Instead, they are locked in a room of denial and unconsciously hated because they threaten the security of the dominant self-concept.

Because incongruence is the primary enemy of the human condition, Rogers believes that it desperately needs to be healed. This is accomplished by reversing the conditions of worth which created the incongruence in the

---

[45]Carl Rogers, "Toward a Modern Approach to Values: The Valuing Process in the Mature Person," in Carl Rogers and Barry Stevens, *Person to Person: The Problem of Being Human* (New York: Pocket Books, 1971).

first place. In other words, the incongruent person much experience a non-threatening therapeutic relationship, either professional or nonprofessional, in which empathy and unconditional positive regard encourage incongruent persons to embrace all of their feelings. Empathy necessitates one person nonjudgmentally entering the internal frame of reference of another. It is a deeply committed, perspective-taking exercise in which one person enters the phenomenological reality of another and sees life from his or her angle. Empathy affirms another person's experience without necessarily approving of the behavior. The helping person is open to the full range of the other's experience without denying, minimizing, or censoring part of their experience.

Unconditional positive regard, as Rogers frequently pointed out, is an attitude of deep respect and "prizing" of another person. Again, it attempts to reverse the conditional acceptance which caused the incongruence. It refuses to discriminate among feelings. Instead, *all* of the person's feelings are invited into awareness.

Finally, Rogers believed that the helper's own congruence is essential. The helper needs to be in touch with his or her own experiencing process and to be open about persistent feelings. The assumption here is that genuineness begets genuineness or that openness is contagious. If the helper is willing to be real or genuine in the relationship, perhaps the incongruent person can begin the risk also.

These, then, are the necessary Rogerian ingredients for effective therapy to occur: empathy, unconditional positive regard, and congruence. The pivotal assumption in Rogers's helping system is that if these conditions are offered, the incongruent person will move toward a healthy direction, both personally and socially. In other words, these individual recipients of the therapeutic triad will naturally become less aggressive, more self-actualizing, and more socially cooperative. This is a *natural, biological unfolding of the organism*, not unlike the blossoming growth of plants and other organisms. We actually have only one, not two, biologically given inclinations. It is called the actualizing tendency. All destructive impulses result from a frustration or distortion of this natural inclination toward growth. Rogers's similarities here with Rousseau are obvious. The "good" or healthy human organism is corrupted by conditions of worth, internalizes the social expectations, and falls way from the actualizing tendency. Stated more theologically, original creation is good, but then we fall into incongruence. Only a deep experience of acceptance—which we cannot offer ourselves, but must be mediated by another—offers a redemptive possibility. For Rogers, again, *acceptance is the key to psychological health.*[46]

Acceptance and the "Demonic"

In his dialogue with Tillich, Rogers seems very interested in Tillich's concept of the "demonic." After affirming the general content of Tillich's *The Courage to Be*, and agreeing with Tillich that humanity definitely has a "nature," Rogers pushes toward the issue of the demonic. Tillich suggests that his concept of the demonic refers to structures, both internal and external, which are stronger than the good will of the individual. Tillich's understanding of the demonic draws deeply from both Freud and Marx. Freud reinstated the psychological bondage of the will, which seems to reflect a kind of demonic activity. Marx, on the other hand, describes the undercurrents of class conflict and economic injustice which represent social demons. Tillich describes how he came upon the term "demonic."

> The only sufficient term I found was in the New Testament use of the "demonic," which is in the stories about Jesus: similar to being possessed. That means a force, under a force, which is stronger than the individual good will. And so I used that term. Of course I emphasized very much I don't mean it in a mythological sense—as little demons or a personal Satan running around the world—but I mean it as structures which are ambiguous, both to a certain extent creative, but ultimately destructive. I had to find a term which covers the transpersonal power which takes hold of men and society.[47]

Rogers seems concerned to eliminate any possibility that this description of the demonic applies to the natural state of the person. In other words, he dramatically parts company with Freud's view that human destructiveness is basic to our nature. As we have already indicated, Freud's insistence that the human organism has two fundamental drives—*eros* and *thanatos*—is in fundamental disagreement with Rogers's humanistic conviction that we have only one drive, the drive toward growth and self-actualization. While Rogers readily admits that human beings are capable of cruel and maladaptive behavior, he insists that those tendencies represent a deeper frustration of the force for growth. Stated in Freudian terms, than-

---

[46]Carl Rogers, *On Becoming a Person* (Boston: Houghton Mifflin, 1961).
[47]Tillich, "Paul Tillich and Carl Rogers: A Dialogue," 69.

atos is not natural to the human organism; it only comes about because eros has been blocked and distorted.

In a very interesting comment, which would no doubt make many Freudians skeptical, Rogers actually claims that a primary reason Freud ended up with such a gloomy portrait of the human condition is the fact that Freud, himself, did not experience the kind of empathic acceptance which tends to put the "dark side" of our psyches in perspective. Freud, because he refused to be psychoanalyzed himself, deprived himself of the deep experience of having another empathically stand with him in his journey through the "ugliness" of his own unconscious. Lacking this empathic partnership with a nonjudgmental person, Freud, like any other human being, could not adequately accept himself.

> It has been my experience that though clients can, to some degree, independently discover some of their denied or repressed feelings, they cannot on their own achieve full emotional acceptance of these feelings. It is only in a caring relationship that these "awful" feelings are first fully accepted by the therapist and can then be accepted by the client. Freud in his self-analysis was deprived of this warmly acceptant relationship. Hence, though he might come to know and to some extent to understand the hidden and denied aspects of himself, I question whether he could ever come to accept them fully, to embrace them as a meaningful, acceptable, and constructive part of himself. More likely he continued to perceive them as unacceptable aspects of himself—enemies, whom knowing he could control—rather than as impulses which, when existing freely in balance with his other impulses, were constructive. At any rate I regard this as a hypothesis worthy of consideration.[48]

Thus Freud, in spite of his genius, could not find the deep self-acceptance which comes not from self-knowledge, but from being known by another.

Tillich readily agrees with Rogers that the experience of *being accepted* is crucial before any self-affirmation can take place. As we have seen, Tillich believes that we can neither forgive nor accept ourselves. "If you look in the spiritual mirror," he says, "then you are much more prone to hate yourself and to be disgusted with yourself."[49] Yet while Tillich agrees

---

[48]Quoted in Howard Kirshenbaum, *On Becoming Carl Rogers* (New York: Delta, 1979) 251.

[49]Kirschenbaum and Henderson, "Paul Tillich and Carl Rogers: A Dialogue," 71.

that one person can help another toward self-acceptance, the actual experience of acceptance belongs to "another dimension: the dimension of the ultimate."[50] Nevertheless, interpersonal acceptance is the medium through which persons must go through in order for the dimension of the ultimate to be possible. But for Tillich, human beings do not merely live on the horizontal, finite plane of one person relating to another. Instead, we human beings also have a "vertical dimension" toward something which is not finite and transitory, but instead infinite, unconditioned reality.

While the exchange between Tillich and Rogers was friendly, humorous, and complimentary, I believe that the key issue raised—namely, the demonic—points toward some key differences between the two thinkers. As I have previously argued, this difference seems to revolve around the concept of ontological anxiety and its relationship to destructive behavior.[51] Rogers, though he has been influenced by Kierkegaard, appears to minimize the problem of ontological anxiety, the anxiety which emerges simply because of our capacity to step outside of ourselves, survey our own lives, and realize that we are going to die. This anxiety is an essential part of our being. It is also the springboard or precondition of destructive behavior. Flooded with the anxiety of nonbeing, we can move in very damaging directions, both for ourselves and society as a whole. We can become greedy, aggressive, extremely competitive, selfish, and compulsive as a result of the anxiety and insecurity which are simply part of being human. Anxiety, because it is built into our finitude, constantly tempts us to find sources of security which are not humanly available. Somehow we think we can "outsmart our finitude" by accumulating enough wealth, knowledge, or relationships to shield us from our own fragile existence.

In Rogers perspective, this anxiety arises from external or social pressure upon us and *not from within our own organism*. Why? Because our essential nature has only one, not two, inclinations. The tendency toward growth and self-actualization has no competitor. There is no death instinct, no destructive impulse, no overly anxious concern for our lives

---

[50]Kirschenbaum and Henderson, "Paul Tillich and Carl Rogers: A Dialogue," 71.

[51]Terry D. Cooper, *Sin, Pride, and Self-Acceptance: The Problem of Identity in Theology and Psychology* (Downers Grove IL: InterVarsity Press, 2003); Don S. Browning and Terry D. Cooper, *Religious Thought and the Modern Psychologies*, rev. ed. (Minneapolis: Fortress Press, 2004).

which is natural to us. We feel exaggerated forms of anxiety only when something is *done to us*. Anxiety is always an outside-in movement. External conditions of worth, social expectations, and oppressive forces beyond us prompt destructive forms of anxiety.

I would like to suggest that the discussion between Tillich and Rogers is indirectly continued in the correspondence between Rogers and Rollo May, seventeen years after Tillich's death.[52] May, I believe, accurately represents Tillich's concept of the demonic and offers an insightful continuation of the 1965 discussion between Rogers and Tillich.

In a sense, one might say that May does not think that Rogers is "existential enough" when it comes to the issues of anxiety and freedom. Rogers minimizes the struggle for authenticity by his insistence on the biological tendency toward self-actualization. In other words, for Rogers, if the therapeutic conditions are present, actualization seems to happen automatically. For May, even if all external threats are turned into nurturing influences, we are still tempted to act in destructive ways. Why? Because we still have the problem of ontological anxiety, an anxiety which continues even in a psychologically perfect environment. Just because we reduce, or could even eliminate, situational anxiety does not mean that a more basic type of anxiety will not emerge. Rogers, on the other hand, is clear about his disagreement with May:

> I suppose my major difference with Rollo is around the question of the nature of the human individual. He sees the demonic as a basic element in the human makeup, and dwells upon this in his writing. For myself, though I am very well aware of the incredible amount of destructive, cruel, malevolent behavior in today's world—from the threats of war to the senseless violence in the streets—I do not find that this evil is inherent in human nature. In a psychological climate which is nurturant of growth and choice, I have never known an individual to choose the cruel or destructive path. Choice always seems to be in the direction of greater socialization, improved relationships with others.[53]

Again, for Rogers, negative cultural influences are the primary factor in destructive behavior. There is absolutely no inherently evil inclination

---

[52]This correspondence appeared in the *Journal of Humanistic Psychology* in June and July 1982. The entire correspondence can be found in Kirschenbaum and Henderson, *Carl Rogers: Dialogues*, 229-55.

[53]Kirschenbaum and Henderson, *Carl Rogers: Dialogues*, 237-38.

within the human being. Ambiguous experiences with parents, the school system, and larger socio-economic realities provoke the destructive behavior we see around us.

May, one the other hand, points out that it is *individuals* who make up these schools, society, and larger cultural trends. The ambivalent mixture of good and bad or healthy and unhealthy in the social order reflects, or mirrors back, the ambivalence within each person. Negative inclinations from the social order attract the negative inclinations buried in our own psyches. To put it succinctly, May argues for dual inclinations within each person while Rogers insists on only one.

May reflects several key themes of his mentor and teacher, Tillich. The demonic is always a "live option" in our psyches because we can never eliminate ontological anxiety. To be alive is to be anxious. And to be anxious is to at least consider the possibility of doing destructive things *because of* that anxiety. Tillich, as we shall later see in more detail, disagreed with the neo-Freudians when they ceased to take Freud's death instinct seriously.

The reason that this discussion is important to our topic of acceptance can be stated as follows: While Rogers believed that Freud did not fully accept himself because of his ongoing claims about the darker regions of the psyche, Tillich insists that genuine acceptance can only take place when we have fully acknowledged our own demonic inclinations, our own psyche's dark regions. As we have seen in Tillich, acceptance always has a quality of "in-spite-of." For him, the right therapeutic conditions are not going to simply put us back on the right path of actualization, eliminate the dark regions in the psyche, and send us on our happy growth journey. Even with the right therapeutic conditions, we will have to face the ego-chilling effect of ontological anxiety and its many temptations to act in unhealthy ways.

Grace and Acceptance: A Conflation of Terms?

Deborah van Deusen Hunsinger, from a Barthian perspective, is critical of what she believes to be a collapse of psychological and theological terms in Tillich.[54] She wants to carefully distinguish symmetrical from asymmetrical relationships between psychological and religious constructs. A

---

[54]Deborah van Deusen Hunsinger, *Theology and Pastoral Counseling: A New Interdisciplinary Approach* (Grand Rapids MI: Eerdmans, 1995).

symmetrical relationship between two terms, one from psychology and one from theology, asserts the possibility of a reversible usage. In other words, we can alternate back and forth between a psychological term and a theological term without losing any content. For instance, we can smoothly move back and forth between the psychological language of healing and the theological notion of salvation. The two terms can collapse into one another. As a Barthian, Hunsinger believes this symmetrical process moves far too easily from the realm of the human to the realm of the Divine. It forgets the classic "ontological divide" between the Divine and human, and inevitably turns theology (which should rightly be focused on God's revelation) into anthropology. Put simply, Tillich has no business confusing the justification of grace with psychological acceptance. They belong to two different realms and two different disciplines—the first one theological and the second one psychological.

As a proponent of an asymmetrical relationship between psychological and theological constructs, Hunsinger insists that we cannot simply restate one term into the framework of another. Terms such as "salvation" and "health" or "grace" and "acceptance" should never be equated. "Respecting God's ontological otherness, as understood by Barth, would seem to require this kind of logical irreversibility."[55] There is no path from psychology to theology because this would involve a type of natural theology completely denied by Barth. The movement can only work one direction—from theology to psychology. Psychology can tell us nothing about God or God's relationship to the world. There is no analogy of being; only an analogy of faith.

Hunsinger's preference for an asymmetrical relationship between psychology and theology means that she opposes any unified system which attempts to integrate them. These two disciplines should remain separate units of discourse. For Hunsinger, we desperately need "methodological clarity about the relationship of the disciplines of psychology and theology to the overall task of the pastoral counselor."[56] Her suggestion is that the pastoral counselor become bilingual, knowing the language system of theology and psychology, but also knowing that a bridge cannot be built between them. The pastoral counselor simply does not need an overarching

---

[55]Hunsinger, *Theology and Pastoral Counseling*, xii.
[56]Hunsinger, *Theology and Pastoral Counseling*, 4.

systematic theory which pulls the two disciplines together. Psychology needs to be respected as psychology and *not* for making a contribution to theology. This sharp line of demarcation and impotence of psychology to tell us anything about the nature of Divine activity is no doubt one of the reasons that few psychologically oriented people have gravitated toward Barth. For Hunsinger, however, we should not "theologize" psychology any more than we "psychologize" theology.[57]

> [T]heology and psychology represent material that cannot be integrated into a unified whole. They are logically diverse; they have different aims, subject matters, methods and linguistic conventions. They do not exist on the same level. Both perspectives are fully a part of the pastoral counselor, that is, they are integrated into the *person*, but as a language and thought world, they are not to be integrated *with one another* in any systematic way.[58]

While there may be analogies between the disciplines, these analogies *always* come from the top (theology) down (psychology). It is never the reverse.

Hunsinger uses the example of what she calls a "negative mother complex" and a distrust in the providential care of God as a way to illustrate the differences between psychological and theological discourse. A "negative mother complex," she says, may indeed lead to difficulty experiencing one's "feminine" side, as well as difficulties trusting others. This is an important psychological diagnosis to understand and treat. Similarly, a distrust in the providence of God is a theological diagnosis which must be kept separate from the psychological assessment. We're talking here about two different levels of reality. One can be addressed naturally while the other requires a theological understanding dependent on God's revelation. These two experiences cannot be integrated because they do not refer to the same reality. We should not use psychological terms for understanding a distrust in the providence of God.

We must ask, however, whether this division of labor between psychology and theology adequately interprets the cross-over between theological convictions and psychological experience. Let's take the issue of trust. Clearly, our early experience with trust, neglect, and abandonment in our

---

[57]Hunsinger, *Theology and Pastoral Counseling*, 6.
[58]Hunsinger, *Theology and Pastoral Counseling*, 6.

families-of-origin greatly impacts our psychological reality. Yet it is this same "psychological reality" that we inevitably bring into the arena of theological discourse. Stated simply, if our biological mother or father cannot be trusted, then this psychological trust problem cannot be separated from the theological distrust in the providential care of God. If we have psychologically experienced the world as untrustworthy, this will indeed have theological ramifications. We do not begin our faith journey with a blank slate. In fact, Hunsinger's line between addressing psychological issues and theological ones may very well be blurred from time to time. Joseph Cooke, for instance, describes the relationship between the psychological experience of acceptance and the theological experience of grace.

> [I]f we happen to be in a situation where no single living person really knows us, or loves us just as we are, or reaches out to give of himself to meet our needs, it is almost impossible to find very much meaning in the idea of God's acceptance. The grace is all theoretical—off in the fantasy world of wish-fulfillment or empty intellectualization. But the legalism, the nongrace, the sense of worthlessness and rejection are real. They are what we experience and live with every day. It's hard to rest in God's uncondemning love and acceptance if we feel that the people around us are ignoring us, condemning us, criticizing us, putting us down. If grace is to mean anything to us, it has to have feet that run to meet us, hands that reach out to us, eyes that see us, a mouth that speaks to us, a heart that loves us and cares what happens to us.[59]

Like other pastoral theologians, Hunsinger is understandably worried that pastoral counseling has been in a state of identity crisis for several decades. It has uncritically accepted and operated from secular psychotherapeutic assumptions which have often not been theologically evaluated. An eagerness to win a strong clinical reputation has minimized the importance of a theological framework out of which to work.

Thus, many agree that this loss of theological identity is a crucial concern in need of much careful reflection. However, instead of simply chastising theology for not being *theological enough*, we should perhaps push various "secular" psychotherapies to expose their own hidden theologies. Don Browning and I have claimed that there are metaphors of ultimacy and ethical frameworks buried in the so-called nontheological

---

[59]Joseph R. Cooke, *Free for the Taking* (Old Tappan NJ: Fleming H. Revell, 1975) 184.

psychotherapies.[60] These "nonreligious" psychologies contain certain assumptions about the ultimate context of our lives. Perhaps the best way to deal with them is to do precisely what Barth would discourage, namely, put them on the table as competing visions of human life. Rather than saying to these psychotherapeutic perspectives that they cannot do *what they are in fact doing*, I believe that they should be seen as quasi-theological perspectives and approached as dialogue partners on that level. The horizon out of which they operate is not a modest, empirically tidy world of calculations. Psychotherapy, by its very nature, goes beyond the kind of tight empiricism one might find in neuroscience. Advocates of particular psychotherapeutic worldviews *begin with some type of faith assumptions* just as theological perspectives do. First principles are precisely *that*—first principles and not empirically verifiable, scientifically certain foundations. Pretensions of starting any thinking enterprise with complete neutrality or objectivity must be highly questioned. All of us begin our thinking having already been enormously influenced by the cognitive world out of which we have come. Even what we consider plausible or not plausible is, to a great degree, dependent on our context.

Yet even though all perspectives ultimately begin in a kind of faith, this does not mean that we cannot get some degree of critical distance from them and converse with others. This attempt to be self-consciously critical of our own perspective is what Ricoeur calls "distanciation."[61] Distanciation will never amount to "complete objectivity." That Enlightenment ideal is dead. Yet this does not mean we must "close shop" on all critical conversation.

Hunsinger is critical of Thomas Oden's highly creative study of Barth and Rogers, *Kerygma and Counseling*, which I have previously mentioned. In this work, Oden attempts to expose the hidden ontological assumptions in Rogers's framework, assumptions which are implicitly theological. Hunsinger believes that Oden won't let Rogers "stay a psychologist," but instead insists on his being a theologian. She says that Oden pushes Rogers into the role of theologian—which Rogers never claimed to be—then turns around and criticizes Rogers for not being a *better* theologian. Thus, she

---

[60]Browning and Cooper, *Religious Thought and the Modern Psychologies*.
[61]Paul Ricoeur, *Hermeneutics and the Human Sciences* (Cambridge: Cambridge University Press, 1981) 131-44.

accuses Oden of framing Rogers's thought into a conceptual world Rogers never intended to enter.

Yet Hunsinger's critique of Oden, in my view, misses the major purpose of what Oden is intending to do. Oden is interested in showing that Rogers's assumptions go far beyond "scientific psychology," make claims about the individual's ontological acceptability, and have hidden theological, or at least crypto-theological, assumptions. Hunsinger is too willing to take Rogers "mere" psychological claims at face value without exploring what is beneath them. Of course Rogers would say he's not a theologian. But Oden is insightfully pointing toward the assumptive world out of which he operates. It is this realm of metaphysical assumptions beneath his empirical psychology which is quasi-theological. Oden's service here is deeply valuable in so far as he exposes an ontological underworld which all too frequently passes as "scientific psychology." Again, I have no problem with Rogers moving beyond the limitations of pure empiricism. I simply believe that he, or any other psythotherapist, should be self-conscious when they do so. Rogers has definite assumptions about the ultimate context of our lives, and an ethical vision of the fully functioning person. Again, these beliefs clearly go far beyond empirical description. In fact, I would argue, along with Oden and Browning, that there is a deep Christian subsoil beneath Rogers's claims.

Hunsinger wants to preserve the integrity of each level of analysis, and keep psychological language quite distinct from theological language. She makes the following observation.

> Each discipline has relative autonomy; it can delimit its own sphere of inquiry to secure its self-defined integrity. Each discipline proceeds with the investigation of its subject matter according to the methods appropriate to it. A method of investigation based on God's self-revelation would arguably be quite different from the empirical observation of early childhood interpersonal relationships that form the basis for theories of psychological developments.[62]

---

[62]Deborah van Deusen Hunsinger, "An Interdisciplinary Map For Christian Counselors: Theology and Psychology in Pastoral Counseling," in *Care for the Soul: Exploring the Intersection of Psychology and Theology*, ed. Mark R. McMinn and Timothy R. Phillips (Downers Grove IL: InterVarsity Press, 2001) 221.

Yet, again, it is psychology, and particularly psychotherapy, which often does not play by its own rules. Instead, it spills over into the larger issues of ethics, meaning, human purpose, and the direction of the world. It takes on a metaphysical quality which becomes a competitor with traditional religious systems. As a person deeply influenced by Jung, surely Hunsinger is aware of the metaempirical claims frequently made by psychotherapy.

Thus, I disagree with Hunsinger's criticism of Oden's investigations into the theological substructure of Rogers thought. Hunsinger's view that Oden pushes Rogers into being a theologian does not adequately take into consideration that Rogers already functions as a theologian of sorts. Further, while both Oden and Hunsinger attempt to maintain a strict Barthian "analogy of faith" in which God's revelation sheds light on the human experience of acceptance, I believe, along with Browning, that the analogy works both ways.[63] In other words, the actual, concrete experience of acceptance in psychotherapy can genuinely inform us about the nature of Divine grace. This is obviously opposed to what a Barthian would allow.

Acceptance and the Ground of Being

Tillich believes that the experience of psychotherapy has the capacity to change our view of the human condition. But beyond that, he also believes it has the potency to help alter our image of God. For Tillich, basic insights into the nature of the human condition can also transfer to our notions of the Divine. Psychology can have an impact on theology, not just the other way around.

> One can say that psychotherapy has replaced the emphasis on the demanding yet remote God by an emphasis on his self-giving nearness. It is the modification of the image of the threatening father—which was so important in Freud's attack on religion—by elements of the image of the embracing and supporting mother. If I were permitted to express a bold suggestion, I would say that psychotherapy and the experiences of pastoral counseling have helped to reintroduce the female element, so conspicuously lacking in most Protestantism, into the idea of God.[64]

---

[63]Don S. Browning, *Atonement and Psychotherapy*.
[64]Tillich, "The Impact of Pastoral Counseling on Theological Thought," 15.

In this passage Tillich clearly states that the experience of psychotherapy has "softened" our image of the Divine.

But Don Browning asks a very important question about Tillich's image of God and his use of the personal language of psychotherapeutic acceptance: Does Tillich's discussion of God as the Ground of Being do justice to his important emphasis on Divine acceptance? Stated more directly, is the highly personal language of acceptance sabotaged by a portrait of God which is not personal? For Tillich, all we can say about God is that God is the Ground of Being. Nothing else can be said literally about God. God does not literally feel, love, or experience anything else associated with a "being," even a "Supreme Being." To call God a "being," for Tillich, is to place limits on the Divine. God, as the symbol for Being-Itself, must never be reduced to a Being.

In his early book, *Atonement and Psychotherapy*, Browning argued that while Tillich was right in his rejection of the monarchial image of God in much of theism, he went too far in rejecting *all* theism. Tillich's "God beyond God" does not offer a helpful analogy for the warmth of therapeutic acceptance.

> [A]lthough psychotherapeutic psychology helped Tillich understand the inadequacies of those religious symbols which depict God as the monarchial, threatening father, he did not understand the implications of psychotherapy which would render his own understanding of God as being-itself as inadequate. Psychotherapeutic psychology does not support Tillich in his banishment of the God of theism. When the psychotherapeutic relation is rightly understood and the anthropology and soteriology which it implies is comprehended correctly and applied analogically to the divine A Priori which revelation makes manifest, it drives toward a redefinition rather than an elimination of the God of theism.[65]

While Tillich frequently used the concept of therapeutic acceptance in reference to God's nature, we must remember that he did so *only symbolically*, not literally or analogically.[66] Browning believes that the concept of therapeutic acceptance, to be meaningful, must be applied *analogically*. In

---

[65]Don Browning, "Analogy, Symbol, and Pastoral Theology in Tillich's Thought," *Pastoral Psychology* (February 1968): 49-50.

[66]Browning, "Analogy, Symbol, and Pastoral Theology in Tillich's Thought," 50.

other words, human acceptance is genuinely similar to Divine acceptance, even though the later is perfectly expressed. If the parallel between Divine and human acceptance is emptied of any literal or cognitive content, how informative can it be?

Tillich proclaimed, of course, especially in *The Courage to Be*, that being-itself is encountered and experienced as an ontological acceptance.[67] But Browning raises an interesting issue.

> Let me suggest, though, that the experience of an immovable, absolute, and unconditioned ground and power of being would not convey a sense of acceptance. The experience and awareness of the *power* of being is not equivalent to a sense of being *accepted* by this power of being. We feel accepted by the divine only when we believe that the divine literally *knows* and *experiences* our distortions and yet accepts us in spite of them. Since being itself cannot literally be said to know or experience us (he has no destiny outside himself, and therefore cannot experience or know the uniqueness and individuality of my guilt and anxiety) it becomes impossible to know that one is accepted.[68]

The reality of deeply knowing and experiencing another's brokenness is always present in therapeutic acceptance. We learn to experience our own subjectivity and accept ourselves *because we are in a relationship with someone who understands our subjectivity*. Without this entry into our internal frame of reference, we would never have an assurance that we are accepted. It might be distant sympathy or detached acknowledgement, but it would not be the kind of empathic participation which will be life-transforming. As Browning puts it,

> [T]herapeutic acceptance necessitates that the healing agent experience us, receiving and therefore being moved by our subjectivity. In other words, the therapeutic agent must be *conditioned* by our subjectivity and, to some extent, be formed by it, without, of course, losing his own identity.[69]

Thus, this experiencing of the brokenness of another is a crucial aspect of healing. If the idea of Divine acceptance is to have any substance or power it must also include this dimension of empathic involvement in our brokenness. But the question becomes whether or not Tillich's uncondi-

---

[67]*The Courage to Be*.
[68]*The Courage to Be*, 50-51.
[69]*The Courage to Be*, 52.

tioned, Being-itself is adequate to convey this acceptance. Stated more forthrightly, is it appropriate to use the highly personal, involved language of therapeutic acceptance to describe the Ground of Being, when by definition, this ground is beyond all possible description, including anything personal? An extremely warm and highly personal experience is used to describe the rather aloof abstraction, being-itself. Again, if therapeutic acceptance is employed as a description of God's acceptance, then the elements of human acceptance must be present analogously in Divine acceptance. But, as Browning says,

> If this is done, it no longer becomes possible to talk about God as being-itself. Instead it becomes necessary to talk about God as a being—a supreme being. He can no longer be the philosophical absolute that is above time and space, completely determinative of his own destiny, unable to know, feel, or experience the contingencies of the world. Tillich's symbolic God must become eventually his real God.[70]

This, it seems, is a very important criticism of Tillich. Asked bluntly, does his view of the experience of grace match his image of God? A highly personal encounter is described, yet it is connected with a rather abstract principle quite beyond the human capacities of warmth, empathy, love, and positive regard.

Browning goes on to say that a revised theism could also be understood as the power of being who undergirds all of life. Nevertheless, "as God undergirds me and gives me the power to be, he also stands beyond me, transcending me and comforts me as a Supreme Being who heightens my awareness of my own subjectivity by experiencing me with unconditional positive regard and empathy."[71]

For Browning, there is nothing contradictory about saying that God is the Ground of all finite beings, on the one hand, and that he is the Supreme Being himself, on the other. "The God of Greek metaphysics and Latin scholasticism is dead and should not be resurrected no matter what the disguise, be it some newly developed form of Catholic Thomism or some variation of the Tillichian concept of God as 'being itself.' "[72] For

---

[70]*The Courage to Be*, 54.

[71]*The Courage to Be*, 54.

[72]Don Browning, *Atonement and Psychotherapy* (Philadelphia: Westminster, 1966) 223.

Browning, then, the Tillichian God is an immovable God who does not suffer, feel, or literally accept. Consequently, in his view, this God is not an appropriate description for what happens in the highly personal world of psychotherapy.

The controversy surrounding Tillich's notion of God as the Ground of Being will no doubt march on. I will revisit the issue through a discussion of the New York Psychology Group, where it came up often. It is not my purpose, and beyond the scope of my ability, to resolve that issue here. Nevertheless, I think it is odd to say, as Tillich does at times, that psychotherapy can be genuinely instructive for our understanding of God and Divine grace, then say, in more systematic statements, that all we can state about God is that God is "Being Itself." Being accepted by this Ground of Being does not seem to be nearly as transforming as being affirmed and accepted by a God who can literally love us, empathize with us, and understand the brokenness of our lives.

Summary

In this chapter I have examined the significance of acceptance in Tillich's view of Divine grace, noting especially how psychotherapy has resurrected the *experience*, rather than the conceptual system, of Luther. I have described ways in which Luther, as both "depth psychologist" and theologian, contributes to Tillich's dynamic view of sin and grace. I have contrasted Tillich with the humanistic advocate of psychotherapeutic acceptance, Carl Rogers, and investigated the issue of acceptance and the "demonic."

I proposed that in Rollo May's discussion with Rogers, which in many ways represents a continuation of the Rogers-Tillich dialogue, we can see the role of ontological anxiety in destructive behavior. For Rogers and other humanistic thinkers, there is only one, rather than two or more, competing inclinations within each person. A natural, biological tendency toward self-actualization is our only basic motivation. For Tillich and May, however, the very existence of ontological anxiety carries a temptation toward destructive tendencies. Thus, a "twin" motivation of potential destructiveness accompanies our self-actualizing tendency.

I then examined two of Tillich's critics. In reviewing Deborah van Deusen Hunsinger's claim that Tillich conflates theological and psychological language, I argued that many of the psychotherapies are *already functioning* at the level of descriptive theologies. They contain metaempirical assumptions about issues much larger than scientific psychology, assumptions which concern the ultimate context of our lives.

Finally, I examined a criticism that I believe carries a great deal of weight, namely, Don Browning's concern that Tillich's use of the highly personal language of psychotherapeutic acceptance does not match his view of God as the Ground of Being. I tend to agree with Browning that Tillich's view of God threatens to undermine his rich discussion of Divine grace and acceptance.

A major theme in Tillich's thought, and an issue of obvious importance to psychology, is the nature of anxiety. It is to this discussion that I now turn.

Chapter 2

Anxiety and Its Treatment: Psychotherapy and the "Courage to Be"

Neurosis is the way of avoiding nonbeing by avoiding being.
—Paul Tillich

The irony of man's condition is that the deepest need is to be free of the anxiety of death and annihilation; but it is life itself which awakens it, and so we must shrink from being fully alive. —Ernest Becker

Paul Tillich's best-known work is *The Courage to Be*.[1] In this important work, Tillich makes his classic distinction between neurotic and ontological anxiety. While neurotic anxiety can be effectively treated with psychotherapy, ontological anxiety, which is "built into" the human condition, can never be "conquered." Instead, it must be embraced. It is as much a part of our finitude as the air we breathe.

In this chapter, I will explore Tillich's understanding of anxiety as both a psychological and ontological problem. It is in dealing with the topic of anxiety that we can perhaps most clearly see Tillich's debt to existentialism, and particularly to Kierkegaard and Nietzsche. I will also explore Tillich's own experience with anxiety as a very important contributing factor to his overall view of courage in the face of great vulnerability. I will carefully examine *The Courage to Be*, and then contrast Tillich's views of anxiety with contemporary treatments of this psychological problem. I will especially focus on cognitive therapy, a very influential perspective on emotional distress which emerged after Tillich's death in 1965.

A dialogue between Tillich and psychology, which in this book I obviously am trying to promote, simply must include the crucial issue of anxiety. It is a pivotal concern for Tillich, a driving force in unhealthy behavior, and a major concern among both psychotherapists and theologians.

---

[1] Paul Tillich, *The Courage to Be*, Based on the Terry Lectures Delivered at Yale (New Haven CT: Yale University Press, 1952; Yale Paperbound, 1959).

Tillich's Own Struggle with Anxiety

Much like Luther, many of Tillich's theological themes grew out of his own existential struggles and life experience. Tillich was not simply a brilliant, abstract thinker who remained detached from the "up close and personal" dimensions of human agony. In fact, Tillich's experience, especially in World War I, seems to reaffirm Luther's rather famous comment that "a theologian is born by living, nay by dying and being damned, not by thinking, reading, and speculating."[2] As Tillich once wrote to a friend, "True experience has its roots in suffering, and happiness is a blossom which opens itself up only now and then."[3]

Rollo May, friend and biographer of Tillich, believes that Tillich's loss of his mother when he was seventeen years old greatly contributed to his anxiety. In fact, in his biography of Tillich, May devotes an entire chapter to the death of Tillich's mother and the impact it had on him.[4]

> At her death he felt the whole world disappear from under his feet. In all its concrete vividness he experienced the reality of nothingness. Where was the mother who furnished the rudder a strong love gives? He had depended upon her, and she was no longer there. Where there ought to have been someone, indeed the most important one, now there was no one. Shattered were the great confidence and the unconscious faith that behind all the vicissitudes of life there remained Mother. Not only did he experience a great bereavement, but he felt profoundly abandoned and betrayed. His orientation to the universe was gone; there was no longer any up or down.[5]

May then goes on to quote one of Tillich's poems written at the time of his mother's death:

> Am I then I? who tells me that I am!
> Who tells me what I am, what I shall become?

---

[2]Quoted in Erik Erikson, *Young Man Luther* (New York: Norton, 1958) 251.

[3]Quoted in Wilhelm and Marion Pauck, *Paul Tillich: His Life and Thought* (San Francisco: Harper & Row, 1976) 43.

[4]Rollo May, *Paulus: A Pesonal Portrait of Paul Tillich* (New York: Harper & Row, 1973) chap. 4.

[5]May, *Paulus*, 40-41.

What is the world's and what life's meaning?
What is being and passing away on earth?

O abyss without ground, dark depth of madness!
Would that I had never gazed upon you and were sleeping like a child.[6]

In this poem, the loss of anchorage is obvious. Tillich's mother represented a safe and friendly universe. Clearly, her death triggered the loss of what Tillich so frequently called "dreaming innocence." This movement into fuller consciousness was very painful. Ernest Becker, in his Pulitzer prize-winning book, *The Denial of Death*, vividly speaks to Tillich's experience.

> It can't be overstated, one final time, that to see the world as it really is is devastating and terrifying. It achieves the very result that the child has painfully built his character over the years in order to avoid: it *makes routine, automatic, secure, self-confident activity impossible*. It makes thoughtless living in the world of men an impossibility. It places a trembling animal at the mercy of the entire cosmos and the problem of the meaning of it.[7]

Thus, May believes Tillich's existentialism was not born on the battlefield, but instead was born the day his mother died. As an existential psychoanalyst, May therefore places enormous significance on Tillich's mother-loss, even suggesting that a search for mother lay behind Tillich's controversial fascination with women.

Dennis Klass, on the other hand, makes an interesting case that a major source of anxiety for Tillich was trying to define himself over against a strong, often authoritarian, father.

> Herr Pastor Tillich was not an easy parent from whom the boy could gain a separate identity; indeed he was a rather formidable man. He was a district pastor, a civil servant, related to upper class, and academically powerful—both intellectually and politically. We do not know the exact nature of the father-son relationship, that is, what Herr Pastor Tillich was expecting implicitly and explicitly of the boy, but we do know that Paul identified his father as his greatest obstacle to autonomy.[8]

---

[6]May, *Paulus*, 41.
[7]Ernest Becker, *The Denial of Death* (New York: Free Press, 1973) 60.
[8]Dennis Klass, "Beneath the Boundary Theme: An Inquiry into Paul Tillich's Autobiography and Theology," *Encounter* 34/3 (Summer 1973): 224.

Thus, this problem of autonomy, which typically emerges strongly in adolescence, was the "problem of being" during Tillich's teenage years and early adulthood. It is worth noting here that several years later, Barth accused Tillich of "still fighting the Grand Inquisitor."[9]

Less psychologically oriented, Wilhelm and Marion Pauck clearly believe the most significant anxiety-producing factor in Tillich's life was his experience as a military chaplain in World War I. In their biography of Tillich, the Paucks describe his war years this way: "These years represent *the* turning point in Paul Tillich's life—the first, last, and only one."[10] If he had not entered the war, Tillich's life would probably have taken a fairly normal path in academic circles. The war, however, threw him into extreme situations and diverse groups of people. Sleeping in trenches was a far cry from ivory-tower, polite conversation.

Entering the Fourth Artillery Regiment of the Seventh Reserve Division in 1914, Tillich served as military chaplain and soldier until January 1919. Much of this time was spent on the front lines of combat. On two occasions, Tillich was presented with the Iron Cross award for heroic service. Tillich watched many friends and excellent soldiers die. He literally dug grave after grave as he buried friends, many of them disfigured, without caskets. As Don Arther has reminded us, Tillich participated in three of the four largest and most destructive battles of World War I.[11]

> He did participate in the two most prolonged and bloodiest battles of the war—Verdun in Spring, 1916 and the Somme in the Fall, 1916. And he was involved in the second battle of the Marne in the Spring of 1918, when the Germans were close to capturing Paris again but were then pushed back and had their lines massively broken with the help of a large contingent of American forces. This was the last major battle of WWI and led to the German final defeat and armistice.[12]

---

[9]Paul Tillich, *My Search for Absolutes*, ed. by Ruth Nanda Anshen (New York: Simon and Schuster, 1967) 32-33.

[10]Wilhelm Pauck and Marion Pauck, *Paul Tillich: His Life and Thought*, 41.

[11]Don Arther, "Paul Tillich as a Military Chaplain," paper presented at the annual meeting of the North American Paul Tillich Society, Boston, November 1999.

[12]Arther, "Paul Tillich as a Military Chaplain," 2.

In spite of his courage and endurance, all the suffering pushed Tillich toward what were then called "nervous breakdowns." On three occasions, Tillich experienced acute traumatic stress disorder which hospitalized him. While he regained his stamina fairly quickly, these acute reactions led to an untreated posttraumatic stress disorder, a condition with which he probably struggled the rest of his life.

The mental health professions now realize that trauma needs desperately to be discussed, shared, processed, or psychologically "debriefed." While we as human beings are capable of enduring a great deal of trauma, we do not seem to be capable of repressing it for long periods of time. Tillich, in his war experience, seemed to be following a pattern of trauma-repression he had begun earlier. For instance, consider the way in which the Paucks describe Tillich's method of coping with loss.

> Tillich's loss of his mother took on an even more exotic turn: he repressed the fact of her death and did not speak of her to anyone. This was and would remain his way of dealing with the death of those he greatly loved.[13]

There is clear clinical evidence that posttraumatic stress disorder is greatly exacerbated by refusing to discuss the traumatizing experience. In his war situation, there may have been little time to have processed or psychologically debriefed this situation. However, based on his reaction to earlier losses, this emotional shutdown seemed to be Tillich's way of coping.

In a conversation with Don Arther, Tillich's daughter Mutie said that, after having read some key symptoms of posttraumatic stress disorder, she was certain her father suffered from this illness.[14] As has been widely reported, Tillich would frequently awake in the middle of the night, screaming, tossing, and twitching. These seem to be clear symptoms of the anxiety disorder, posttraumatic stress.

Tillich's The Courage to Be

Because *The Courage to Be* is probably the most widely read of all of Tillich's works, it is important to grasp the manner in which it relates anxiety and courage. While we normally think of courage as an ethical act such as performing a heroic duty in battle, for Tillich, "it must be consid-

---

[13]Pauck, *Paul Tillich: His Life and Thought*, 14.
[14]Arther, "Paul Tillich as Military Chaplain," 16.

ered ontologically in order to be understood ethically."[15] Tillich believes there is no adequate definition of courage as a virtue among other virtues, and consequently, the ethical question invariably leads to the ontological question about the nature of being.

> Courage as a human act, as a matter of valuation, is an ethical concept. Courage as the universal and essential self-affirmation of one's being is an ontological concept. The courage to be is the ethical act in which man affirms his own being in spite of those elements in his existence which conflict with his essential self-affirmation.[16]

Courage is the affirmation of one's own life in spite of the threat of death. This is what Tillich means when he describes courage as an "ontological" issue. It is not the courage to be a particular "thing"; instead, it is the courage to *be*, period. It is the courage to affirm one's life in spite of the fact that this life is constantly threatened by the possibility of nonbeing or death. And it is our own personal nonbeing, rather than some vague, universal threat, which prompts our anxiety.

The "courage to be," then, is a refusal to remain paralyzed, frozen, and afraid to move. It does not deny or minimize the constant threat of nonbeing. It fully embraces our vulnerability and finitude. It "takes into itself" the awareness that there may not be a tomorrow. It does not try to outmaneuver the precarious nature of life by finding a protective shield from the vicissitudes of being human. It acknowledges uncertainty and ambiguity as an ongoing part of the human situation. It knows that the attempt to escape this ontological anxiety leads to neurosis. In our frantic attempts to build a wall of safety around ourselves, we become the unwitting victims of our own defense mechanisms. It is here that Tillich makes a crucial point: *The attempt to flee ontological anxiety creates neurotic anxiety.*

This avoidance of anxiety is manifested in our refusal to experience our own depths or to know ourselves deeply. Tillich states this eloquently in his sermon, "The Depth of Existence."

> It is comfortable to live on the surface so long as it remains unshaken. It is painful to break away from it into an unknown ground. The tremendous amount of resistance against that act in every human being and the many

---

[15]*The Courage to Be*, 1.
[16]*The Courage to Be*, 3.

> pretexts invented to avoid the road into the depth are natural. The pain of looking into one's own depth is too intense for most people. They would rather return to the shaken and devastated surface of their former lives and thoughts.[17]

The human mind has endless tricks, maneuvers, and ploys to avoid staring into these depths. There is enormous pressure to pull us back into less-threatening and more-trivial concerns. Tillich, as we have already seen in chapter 1, was in profound debt to Freud's identification of the many defense mechanisms at work in our daily lives. Tillich would add that genuine self-knowledge is perhaps more related to courage than to intelligence. He would agree with Maslow's powerful statement about Freud's discovery.

> Freud's great discovery, the one which lies at the root of psychodynamics, is that *the* great cause of much psychological illness is the fear of knowledge of oneself—one's own emotions, impulses, memories, capacities, potentialities of one's destiny. We have discovered that fear of knowledge of oneself is very often isomorphic with, and parallel with, fear of the outside world. . . . In general this kind of fear is defensive, in the sense that it is a protection of our self-esteem, of our love and respect for ourselves. We tend to be afraid of any knowledge that could cause us to despair ourselves or to make us feel inferior, weak, worthless, evil, shameful. We protect ourselves and our ideal image of ourselves by repression and similar defenses, which are eventually techniques by which we avoid becoming conscious of unpleasant or dangerous truths.[18]

This fear of self-knowledge is very much like the fear of death. In fact, one might say that it *is* a fear of death—a death to the secure, stable, business-as-usual self. The plunge into self-consciousness requires dying to worn-out self-definitions. This journey necessitates a deep trust that we can live with whatever we discover.

Distinguishing Fear and Anxiety

Tillich believes that both depth psychology and existential philosophy have identified an important difference between fear and anxiety. Fear has a definite object which can be faced, examined, attacked, conquered, or at

---

[17]Tillich, *The Shaking of the Foundations* (New York: Scribner's, 1948) 59.
[18]Abraham Maslow, "The Need to Know and the Fear of Knowing," *Journal of General Psychology* 68 (1963): 118-19.

least endured. Fear is much more manageable because we *know* the object over which we feel apprehensive. This very ability to *name* it decreases its power. We know what we are "up against."

Anxiety, however, has no object. There is nothing to which we can point and say that *this* is the object of my fear. The fact that anxiety has no specific source makes the anxiety even stronger. As Tillich says, "The only object is the threat itself, but not the source of the threat, because the source of the threat is 'nothingness.' "[19] Fears are particular, focused, and subject to psychotherapeutic intervention. They can be managed, and in some cases, completely resolved. Anxiety, however, has to do with the preservation of our entire being. It is directed toward the unknown, and once again, the ultimate unknown is death itself.

The dynamics between fear and anxiety are quite similar to the dynamics between guilt and shame. Guilt, like fear, has a specific object. We have done something wrong and we can name the behavior. By making amends we can normally alleviate guilt. Shame, on the other hand, is a different story. Shame is not about anything specific. Instead, it is a generic feeling and self-judgment of inadequacy. *We*, not the behavior, are the problem. Its not that we simply did something wrong; instead, *something is wrong with us*.

We can do something about our guilt just as we can do something about our fear. Yet anxiety and shame are vague undifferentiated experiences which involve the totality of our being. They are all-encompassing and all-consuming.

Tillich makes the interesting observation that anxiety strives to become fear. The primary reason for this is that fear, with its specific object, can be met with courage. We can *do something* about a particular fear. Yet as much as we may want to transfer all our anxieties into fear, this cannot be done.

> But ultimately the attempts to transform anxiety into fear are vain. The basic anxiety, the anxiety of a finite being about the threat of nonbeing, cannot be eliminated. It belongs to existence itself.[20]

Life would be much more "manageable" if we could convert our existential anxiety into specific fears. We could simply call forth the ethical

---

[19]*The Courage to Be*, 37.
[20]*The Courage to Be*, 39.

courage to face each challenge. Yet anxiety raises the question of existence itself, not simply various aspects of our lives. It is our entire being which is called into question, particularly as we reflect on the ever-present possibility of nonbeing.

For Tillich, nonbeing can only be understood in terms of what it negates. In other words, nonbeing has no reality apart from being. It feeds off of being and can only exist through it. Put simply, without life, death would mean nothing. Death is only understandable when it is contrasted with the life it seeks to extinguish. In itself, death or nonbeing has no quality.

Anxiety's Three Major Threats

But how, exactly, does anxiety frighten us? How does nonbeing threaten being? Tillich identifies three different ways. First, nonbeing threatens the possibility of our self-affirmation through *fate and physical death*. This is the most obvious, universal, and inescapable threat of nonbeing. The anxiety of fate reminds us that our lives are contingent, unpredictable, and socially located. We live only in *this* time and *this* place. We are physically and intellectually limited to the contextual worlds we inhabit. This can be a stark reminder of our finitude. In spite of our experience of limited freedom, we eventually understand that our lives stand under the shadow of fate. We are contingent characters on an unpredictable journey. There appears to be no ultimate necessity for our lives.

Tillich adds that the anxiety of death is lurking beneath this anxiety of fate. In fact, he says "the anxiety of death overshadows all concrete anxieties and gives them their ultimate seriousness."[21] The anxiety of death propels the anxiety of fate. Dying is, after all, the ultimate reminder of our contingency. Yet full consciousness of our finitude is a kind of dying, also. We do not have endless possibilities; only the possibility of this situation. We do not have eternal understanding; only the knowledge of our own time and place.

The second type of threat of nonbeing is the anxiety of emptiness and meaninglessness. While the first threat concerns our literal, physical existence, this second threat concerns our spiritual self-affirmation. Tillich uses the term meaninglessness to describe the ultimate threat to our

---

[21]*The Courage to Be*, 43.

spiritual well-being. This refers to life without an ultimate concern, life void of all purpose. This meaninglessness shakes the foundation of everything. It raises Camus's suggestion that life is "absurd' and without any point whatsoever.

Just as the anxiety of death drives the anxiety of fate, so the anxiety of meaninglessness drives its less severe form, the anxiety of emptiness. Tillich states this beautifully.

> The anxiety of emptiness is aroused by the threat of nonbeing to the special contents of the spiritual life. A belief breaks down through external events or inner processes: one is cut off from creative participation in a sphere of culture, one feels frustrated about something which one had passionately affirmed, one is driven from devotion to one object to devotion to another and again on to another, because the meaning of each of them vanishes and the creative error is transferred into indifference or aversion. Everything is tried and nothing satisfied. The contents of the tradition, however excellent, however praised, however loved once, lose their power to give content *today*. And present culture is even less able to provide the content. Anxiously one turns away from all concrete contents and looks for an ultimate meaning, only to discover that it was precisely the loss of a spiritual center which took away the meaning from the special contents of their spiritual life. But a spiritual center cannot be produced intentionally, and the attempt to produce it only produces deeper anxiety. The anxiety of emptiness drives us to the abyss of meaninglessness.[22]

Doubt is thus an inevitable component of the spiritual life. Faith never tries to avoid doubt; instead, it takes doubt into itself. Specific doubts threaten us with emptiness; total doubt about our entire lives threatens us with meaninglessness and despair.

In describing how we often try to escape the threat of emptiness and meaninglessness prompted by doubt, Tillich is in agreement with Fromm's elaboration of how we attempt to escape from freedom.[23] We surrender our right to ask questions as we submit to an authority which eliminates the burden of our freedom and its accompanying anxiety. We "turn in" our freedom in exchange for some form of factual certainty.

> Fanaticism is the correlate to spiritual self-surrender; it shows the anxiety which it was supposed to conquer, by attacking with disproportionate

---

[22]*The Courage to Be*, 47-48.
[23]*The Courage to Be*, 48.

violence those who disagree and who demonstrate by their disagreement elements in the spiritual life of the fanatic which he must suppress in himself. Because he must suppress them in himself he must suppress them in others. His anxiety forces him to persecute dissenters. The weakness of the fanatic is that those whom he fights have a secret hold upon him; and to this weakness he and his group finally succumb.[24]

The frantic effort to escape all doubt only makes the doubt worse. The anxiety of emptiness underlying doubt must be acknowledged and embraced as part of the life of faith.

The third way in which the anxiety of nonbeing threatens us is through guilt and condemnation. This threatens our moral self-affirmation. Tillich believes that all human beings feel a certain accountability as to what they have made of themselves. As Tillich says, "This situation produces the anxiety which, in relative terms, is the anxiety of guilt; in absolute terms, the anxiety of self-rejection or condemnation."[25] Guilt is an inevitable component of recognizing that all of our deeds, even those which seem to be our most moral ones, are actually riddled with mixed motives and ambiguous intentions. Even our noble efforts lack absolute purity.

We often try to escape from the anxiety of guilt in one of two ways. First, we may defy our own negative self-judgments, attempt to "unplug" our own guilt, and lead lives of normlessness and wrecklessness. "No rules, no guilt." This becomes the rebellious anomism out of which we function. This is, of course, quite destructive and does not really eliminate the undercurrent of our guilt.

The second way we may try to escape our guilt is through an airtight legalism. This approach seeks to drown out anxiety with scrupulosity. Moral rules are tenaciously upheld with an utter disregard for differing circumstantial factors. Yet the rigorous attempts to follow the letter of the law, rather than its spirit, cannot eliminate the anxious guilt pulsating just beneath our "upright" behavior. Also, it takes enormous psychological energy to repress all the darker elements of our psyches and convince ourselves that we are morally "pure."

The anxiety of guilt is pushed along by the more desperate feeling of total condemnation. This is the dreaded verdict which is always in the background of specific guilt concerns.

---

[24]*The Courage to Be*, 49-50.
[25]*The Courage to Be*, 51-52.

For Tillich, all three types of anxiety contribute to our overall situation. They can lead to a situation of existential despair. As Tillich says, "The pain of despair is that a being is aware of itself as unable to affirm itself because of the power of nonbeing."[26]

Tillich believes that each type of anxiety has been prominent in different historical periods. The anxiety of fate and death was felt most acutely during the turbulent times of the collapse of ancient civilization. The anxiety of guilt and condemnation dominated the end of the middle ages and the period of the Reformation. It was, as we saw in chapter 1, the background of Luther's struggle to find grace. And at the end of our modern period, the primary threat is the anxiety of emptiness and meaninglessness. None of these types of anxiety, however, are very far from each other. Where one dominates, the other two are in the background.

The Positive Side of Anxiety

Tillich believes that in spite of their potential damage, these three types of anxiety can have productive purposes. The anxiety of fate and death, for instance, can produce nonpathological efforts to find safety. While no absolute or final security is possible, there *are* things we can do to reduce the dangers of life.[27] A basic need for some sense of security appears to be a permanent feature of the human condition. For Tillich, if we have the power to reduce some aspects of fate and death, we should by all means do so.

Pathological anxiety, however, seeks a type of security which is not humanly possible. The demand for security ends up making the insecurity worse. Further, the security to which the neurotic clings forces his life within narrow parameters. Tillich uses the metaphor of a prison.

> Pathological anxiety about fate and death impels toward a security which is comparable to the security of a prison. He who lives in his prison is unable to leave the security given to him by his self-imposed limitations. But these limitations are not based on a full awareness of reality. Therefore the security of the neurotic is unrealistic. He fears what is not to be feared and he feels to be safe what is not safe.[28]

---

[26]*The Courage to Be*, 55.
[27]*The Courage to Be*, 74.
[28]*The Courage to Be*, 75.

Tillich goes on to say that the anxiety which we are unable to take on ourselves manifests itself in unrealistic concerns. By not facing our realistic anxiety, it emerges again in strange, unrealistic ways. Consequently, we work overtime on imaginary fears while we neglect the real anxiety of nonbeing. This displacement of our fears serves the important function of reducing our existential anxiety. By being preoccupied with our neurotic anxieties we dodge ontological anxiety.

Tillich believes we can see this same dynamic in pathological forms of guilt and condemnation. Normal, existential anxiety about guilt pushes us toward moral self-discipline and responsibility. While we know that we'll never be able to remove all of our imperfection, we can nevertheless strive toward higher ethical living.

Neurotic anxiety, on the other hand, drives us toward fixed, rigid, and unrealistic self-expectations. As Tillich says, "The anxiety of becoming guilty, the horror of feeling condemned, are so strong that they make responsible decisions and any kind of moral action almost impossible."[29] Consequently, we feel defensive and guilty even about trivial matters. Genuine guilt, which is connected to our estrangement, is repressed as we focus on surface level concerns.

This structure can also be seen in the anxiety of emptiness and meaninglessness. The anxiety of doubt can serve the productive function of motivating us toward "the creation of certitude in systems of meaning, which are supported by tradition and authority."[30] Anxiety is reduced through our attempts to be clear, reasonable, and as certain as possible. In spite of this attempt to be certain, however, some degree of ambiguity still exists. Neurotic anxiety seeks to silence all doubt and refuses to ask any questions. This refusal to deal with our genuine uncertainty "comes back around" in unrealistic concerns. Tillich, who loved to build sandcastles on the beach, once again uses a castle metaphor to describe the neurotic.

> Neurotic anxiety builds a narrow castle of certitude which can be defended and is defended with the utmost tenacity. . . . However the castle of undoubted certitude is not built on the rock of reality.[31]

---

[29] *The Courage to Be*, 75.
[30] *The Courage to Be*, 76.
[31] *The Courage to Be*, 76.

The neurotic person doubts the smaller details of life, which in fact do not appear doubtful, as a way of maneuvering around those larger concerns of life he or she refuses to face. Again, the neurotic displaces his or her doubts onto something less threatening in order to avoid an encounter with full reality. The inevitable doubt built into the human condition of estrangement is dodged as the neurotic fixates on trivial concerns. The point, again, is that *any attempt to avoid existential anxiety re-surfaces as neurotic anxiety.*

Tillich believes that his analysis concerning the differences between existential and pathological anxiety points toward five important principles.[32] First, existential anxiety has an ontological character which cannot be eliminated. Consequently, it must be absorbed into the courage to be. Second, pathological or neurotic anxiety always represents a failure to embrace existential anxiety. Third, pathological anxiety can only lead to a limited self-affirmation. This self-affirmation will be based on a rigid, fixed, unrealistic self-understanding which will in time have compulsory defenses. Fourth, pathological anxiety produces an insatiable need for security, an unrealistic expectation for perfection, and a misguided need for certainty. Fifth, pathological anxiety is primarily an object of medical healing or psychotherapy and existential anxiety is in need of ministerial help. Neither the medical nor the ministerial function is completely bound to its professional identity. The minister sometimes functions as a medical healer and the medical healer (psychotherapist) functions as minister. However, these functions are limited, and should not involve an official change of vocation. We need them both. They each contribute to reaching a full self-affirmation—*the courage to be.*

Tillich believes that both physicians and clergy often fail to recognize this important distinction between existential and pathological anxiety. It is possible, however, to develop some principles for the cooperation of physicians and clergy in dealing with the problem of anxiety. First, existential anxiety is not the concern of the physician *as physician*. While physicians need to be *aware* of existential anxiety, they need not pretend that their methods can heal it. And second, the minister needs to be aware of neurotic anxiety just as the physician is aware of existential anxiety, but the minister, *as minister*, is not normally designated to cure neurosis. As

---

[32]*The Courage to Be*, 77-78.

Tillich puts it, "The minister raises the question concerning a courage to be which takes existential anxiety into itself. The physician raises the question concerning a courage to be in which the neurotic anxiety is removed."[33] Yet Tillich goes on to say that neurotic anxiety always involves the inability to take our existential anxiety upon ourselves.

Neither profession is the sole possessor of its function, however. There may indeed be some cross-over. The psychotherapist may genuinely help a patient toward ultimate self-affirmation, toward the courage to be. But this doesn't automatically change his/her primary function of treating neurotic anxiety. He or she can "function ministerally" without officially changing professions. The same is true for clergy who help neurotic persons with their anxiety. They can "function psychotherapeutically" while remaining clergy.

Just as nothing is ever "merely spiritual" or disconnected from the body, nothing is ever "merely biological" or disconnected from the human spirit. Like Niebuhr, Tillich believes that even in the most lofty, spiritual or aesthetic concerns we are bodily creatures, and even in the lowest forms of biological behavior we are still spirit.

Anxiety and the Limits of Psychotherapy

It is beyond the scope of *The Courage to Be* to provide therapeutic suggestions for neurotic or nonexistential anxiety. Tillich wants to provide an ontology of anxiety, not a treatment plan for anxiety disorders. Nevertheless, he speaks insightfully about various theories of neurotic anxiety.

> There is, however, one common denominator in all the theories: anxiety is the awareness of unsolved conflicts between structural elements of the personality, as for instance conflicts between unconscious drives and repressive norms, between different drives trying to dominate the center of the personality, between imaginary worlds and the experience of the real world, between trends toward greatness and perfection and the experience of one's smallness and imperfection, between the desire to be accepted by other people and society or the universe and the experience of being rejected, between the will to be and the seemingly intolerable burden of being which evokes the open or hidden desire not to be. All these conflicts, whether unconscious, subconscious, or conscious, whether

---

[33]*The Courage to Be*, 73-74.

unadmitted or admitted, make themselves felt in sudden or lasting stages of anxiety.[34]

Attempts are often made to find the fundamental cause of anxiety, the primary anxiety on which all other psychological distortions are based. This attempt to locate a specific cause of anxiety carries with it an assumption that anxiety can then be treated. But for Tillich, the problem is that these attempts lack a clear criterion for distinguishing what is primary and what is secondary. One theorist recognizes one element of anxiety while another theorist suggests another. But the deeper problem is that psychotherapy, in its confused state, *lacks a clear distinction between existential and pathological anxiety.*[35]

This is understandable, however, because depth psychology analysis, in itself, is not capable of investigating such a distinction. This can only be supplied by an ontological investigation. As Tillich puts it, "Only in the light of an ontological understanding of human nature can the body of material provided by psychology and sociology be organized into a consistent and comprehensive theory of anxiety."[36]

Courage can never eliminate ontological anxiety. It can only take the anxiety "into itself." In other words, ontological anxiety cannot be conquered any more than we can eliminate our finitude. We can only affirm ourselves "in spite of" our ontological anxiety. Again, this is what Tillich means when he says that being takes nonbeing into itself. Anxiety is a part of self-affirmation in the same manner that doubt is a part of faith. We don't wait for a world devoid of doubt before we have faith; similarly, we do not wait on all anxiety to be negated before we affirm ourselves. Anxiety turns us toward courage, but courage can never completely get rid of anxiety.[37] Just as Luther believed we are *both* saint and sinner, Tillich believes we are *both* courageous and anxious.

Limited Self-Affirmation

Tillich believes it *is* possible to affirm ourselves even if we refuse to face our existential anxiety. The problem with this, however, is that we are only

---

[34]*The Courage to Be*, 64-65.
[35]*The Courage to Be*, 65.
[36]*The Courage to Be*, 65.
[37]*The Courage to Be*, 66.

affirming a reduced, partial self. It is not *full self-affirmation*. We are affirming something less than our essential or potential being.[38] We forfeit part of our potential and focus only on the less threatening aspects of ourselves.

> [T]he neurotic personality, on the basis of his greater sensitivity to nonbeing and consequently of his profounder anxiety, has settled down to a fixed, though limited and unrealistic self-affirmation. This is, so to speak, the castle to which he has retired and which he defends with all means of psychological resistance against attack, be it from the side of reality or from the side of the analyst. And this resistance is not without some instinctive wisdom. The neurotic is aware of the danger of a situation in which his unrealistic self-affirmation takes its place. The danger is that he will fall back into another and much better defended neurosis or that with the breakdown of his limited self-affirmation he will fall into an unlimited despair.[39]

Let's break this highly packed paragraph down. Tillich believes that neurotic individuals have a greater sensitivity to nonbeing which pushes them toward higher levels of anxiety. As a consequence, they erect a rigid, limited, and unrealistic view of themselves. A great deal of psychological energy is poured into the maintenance of this skewed view of reality. As anxiety threatens to emerge, the self-image tightens into a more restricted portrait. At some level, the neurotic person knows that the falsely built fortress could crumble, so there is enormous pressure to keep the fort strong. If the neurotic does not maintain the limited, distorted self-conception, he or she could spiral into an encompassing despair. At best, the neurotic will retreat back into another, even more entrenched, neurotic defense. The "limited self" which flees anxiety thus has only two options: (a) a strong defense of a distorted self-image, or (b) a breakdown into despair.

Nearly every school of psychotherapy addresses this important issue of disjunction between one's genuine and false self. We've already witnessed this distinction in Carl Rogers, who describes this discrepancy as "incongruence." Karen Horney offers a brilliant analysis of the differences between the "idealized self" and the actual self.[40] Perls, in his development

---

[38]*The Courage to Be*, 66-67.
[39]*The Courage to Be*, 68.
[40]Karen Horney, *Neurosis and Human Growth* (New York: W. W. Norton, 1950).

of Gestalt psychotherapy, frequently describes this alienation between authentic and inauthentic selfhood as the major psychological problem.[41] Jung described the problem of the "shadow" which results from a refusal to acknowledge and embrace the full range of our experience.[42] And many other theorists would agree.

Again, neurotic self-affirmation is only partial affirmation. It is born out of an internal conflict it often will not admit. By refusing to embrace our entire being, we can only acknowledge the least-threatening dimensions of our selfhood. We are thus forced to live out of a highly restricted world of our own creation. Anxiety keeps us within these narrow parameters.

> The neurotic is sick and needs healing because of the conflict in which he finds himself with reality. In this conflict he is hurt by the reality which permanently penetrates the castle of his defense and the imaginary world behind it. His limited and fixed self-affirmation both preserves him from an intolerable impact of anxiety and destroys him by turning against reality and reality against him, and by producing another intolerable attack of anxiety. Pathological anxiety, in spite of its creative potentialities, is illness and dangerous and must be healed by being taken into a courage to be which is extensive as well as intensive.[43]

Liberation and healing will require the dissolution of these narrow borders of self-awareness. Parts of the psyche which remained closed off from awareness will simply not heal on their own.

But again, psychotherapy sometimes *claims* that it can heal *all* anxiety. Anxiety is viewed as a sickness for which the therapist provides a "cure." From this standpoint, there is no recognition of the ontological root of anxiety. "Medical insight and medical help—this is the conclusion—are the way to the courage to be; the medical profession is the only healing profession."[44]

But, Tillich asks, if anxiety is *only* a sickness, then why is it universal? Who doesn't struggle with finitude, doubt, guilt, vulnerability, and the ever-present threat of death. It is precisely here that the medical profession needs

---

[41]Fritz Perls, *The Gestalt Approach and Eyewitness to Therapy* (New York: Bantam, 1976).

[42]Carl Jung, *Modern Man in Search of a Soul* (New York: Harcourt, Brace, and World, 1933).

[43]*The Courage to Be*, 69.

[44]*The Courage to Be*, 71.

the assistance of other professions (including the theologian) in order to "understand and to actualize man's power of being, his emotional self-affirmation, his courage to be."[45] Philosophy is inescapable for even the most scientifically rigorous medicine. The reason is that all treatment assumes a view of human nature.

The Cognitive Therapy Challenge

Since Tillich's 1950 Terry Lectures, and even since his death in 1965, a new paradigm within the psychotherapy community has been very influential. This new framework is cognitive therapy. Cognitive therapy believes that the source of all disturbed feelings, including anxiety, is distorted, irrational thinking. The cognitive process itself is the focus of treatment. Behind psychological disturbance there is mental distortion, exaggeration, and misinterpretation. We *feel* badly because we *think* crookedly. Dealing directly with the emotional or affective dimension of our lives does not "get at" the underlying cause. Instead, we must move behind the feeling state and expose the thinking process which is propelling it. This thought process may be automatic and very difficult to pinpoint. Nevertheless, a cognitive appraisal of some sort always underlies our emotional states. Referring to anxiety, Aaron Beck, a pioneer in the area of cognitive therapy, makes the following claim.

> The crucial element in anxiety states, then, is a cognitive process that may take the form of an automatic thought or image that appears rapidly, as if by reflex, after the initial stimulus (for example, shortness of breath), that seem plausible, and that is followed by a wave of anxiety. When the missing link is identified, then the "mysterious" arousal of anxiety can be understood. Of course, a specific thought or image is not always identifiable. In such cases it is possible, however, to infer that a cognitive set with a meaning relevant to danger has been activated.[46]

Traditionally, anxiety has been seen by the majority of psychotherapists as an emotion out of control.[47] Beck believes that this view has probably emerged because the *feeling* of anxiety and terror are the most dramatic

---

[45]*The Courage to Be*, 72

[46]Aaron Beck and Gary Emery, *Anxiety Disorders and Phobias* (New York: Basic Books, 1985) 5-6.

[47]Beck and Emery, *Anxiety Disorders and Phobias*, 6.

aspects of the disorder. Yet this preoccupation with feelings has led psychiatrists and psychologists away from anxiety's source—the cognitive dimension. While it may not at first be easy to tap the underlying thought process, it *is* occurring. And focusing on this cognitive element is the crucial factor.

Beck's perspective does not acknowledge Tillich's distinction between fear and anxiety. As the reader may recall, Tillich believes that fear has a specific object whereas anxiety does not. According to Beck, this distinction breaks down for a couple of reasons. First, fear is always a matter of appraisal, a cognitive estimate of potential threat. Fear is primarily a thought process, a mental alarm system. Anxiety, on the other hand, is an emotional reaction *based upon the preceding cognitive appraisal*. Again, fear is cognitive and anxiety is emotional. Because this issue is important in relationship to Tillich, it is important to quote Beck directly.

> Anxiety may be distinguished from fear in that the former is an emotional process while fear is a cognitive one. Fear involves the intellectual appraisal of a threatening stimulus; anxiety involves the emotional response to that appraisal. When a person says he fears something, he is generally referring to a set of circumstances that are not present but may occur at some point in the future. At this point the fear is said to be "latent." When a person has anxiety he experiences a subjectively uncomfortable emotional state characterized by physiological symptoms like heart palpitations, tremor, nausea, and dizziness. A fear is *activated* when a person is exposed, either physically or psychologically, to the stimulus situation he considers threatening. When the fear becomes activated, he experiences anxiety. Fear then, is the appraisal of danger; anxiety is the unpleasant feeling state evoked when fear is stimulated. In addition to anxiety, a variety of symptoms referable to the autonomic and the somatic nervous system may be provoked concurrently.[48]

Beck's disagreement with Tillich can be stated forthrightly: while it may *seem* that there is no object involved in our anxiety, there actually is. It may be a vague image or it may be a rapid, reactionary thought, but we are *fearing something* or our anxiety would not even be possible. Anxiety is not, as the existentialists contend, objectless. It may be hard to pinpoint, but an object is always present.

For Beck and Emery, terms such as "realistic," "unrealistic," "rational," or "irrational" should be used to describe our fears and not our anxieties.

---

[48]Beck and Emery, *Anxiety Disorders and Phobias*, 9.

Why? Because these words all refer to a cognitive process, an assessment and evaluation. Anxiety is simply a feeling. As a feeling it is completely dependent upon the fear analysis which precedes it. Anxiety does not evaluate reality; rather it is an emotional response to a previous evaluation (fear). Again, to quote Beck:

> Anxiety, however, is not *the* pathological process in so-called anxiety disorders any more than pain or fever constitute the pathological process in an infection or injury. We should not allow nature's mechanism for dramatizing the feeling of anxiety to mislead us into believing that this most salient subjective experience plays the central role in the so-called anxiety disorders.[49]

Beck draws an interesting analogy between anxiety and physical pain. Pain is not the primary problem; instead, it is a symptom of the problem. Pain alerts us that we need to do something about the source of our illness, but pain itself is not that source. Similarly, anxiety itself is not the problem. Instead, it points back toward an evaluation of danger. Anxiety is never the *cause* of psychological disturbance.

Thus the key to treating anxiety is to address the exaggerated appraisals (fears) beneath it. Automatic thoughts and hidden images need to be clarified in order to be challenged. In some cases, we must infer the thought because it is simply too quick to be directly "caught." Even though we cannot directly challenge it while it is occurring, we can see where the thought has been. The emotional reaction provides the evidence and clues concerning the cognitions which caused it. For Beck, we can then describe, after the fact, the rapid-firing thought process which occurred and challenge this interpretation in the future. Thus, "free-floating anxiety" is in reality not diffuse. Instead, there are specific, subtle thoughts underlying it. "Using a 'cognitive analysis,' the therapist may establish even more precisely that the anxiety is not 'diffuse' but is related to specific fears."[50]

A Tillichian Critique of Cognitive Therapy

I strongly suspect that Tillich would applaud much of the work of Beck, Ellis, and other cognitively oriented thinkers who have dealt with the ever-present possibility of distorting and exaggerating everyday events, and

---

[49]Beck and Emery, *Anxiety Disorders and Phobias*, 14.
[50]Beck and Emery, *Anxiety Disorders and Phobias*, 94.

consequently, causing unnecessary emotional upheaval. However, I also suspect that Tillich would argue that finite human reason, however determined it may be, can never resolve the issue of ontological anxiety. Death, the possibility of despair and meaninglessness, the ambiguities and uncertainties which haunt all of our commitments—these are not issues which can be resolved by "thinking correctly." Tillich would see any such effort as a hopeless Pelagianism, a self-willed, stubborn attempt to resolve our deepest questions of meaning, purpose, and ultimate significance through a reliance on the power of individual selfhood. As finite creatures, we are not "built" to resolve infinite questions. Left to our own devices, anxiety floods us, overwhelms us, and shows us our smallness in the face of ultimate reality. Human reason, on its own, cannot calm these waters. In fact, it easily drowns in a frenzied self-preoccupation. It attempts to find a place of permanent security, an anchor, a "hold" on reality which can only be offered by our Source or Ground.

Beck makes an overly optimistic jump from believing we can identify the faulty thinking lying beneath all our anxiety—a monumental task when we consider the power of the unconscious and the multiple ways we are capable of deceiving ourselves—to believing we can challenge and change our irrational processes. Through cognitive restructuring, we can live calm lives. All of our destructive behavior, all our self-preoccupations, and all frantic attempts to find security, are based on our crooked thinking. In fact, evil is completely tied to exaggerated thinking.

Tillich would no doubt point out that while cognitive therapy *appears* to be operating from historic stoicism, in reality it is *not*. Historic stoicism grounded each individual's rationality in a submission to the Logos, or cosmic principle of rationality which governs all things. Beck and fellow Rational-Emotive Therapy leader Albert Ellis make no such claims. There is only the single, isolated individual who "thinks correctly." Yet this individual activity may not be matched by a larger rational framework. Stated simply, reality itself may not be rational. We may be islands of reason surrounded by an ocean of chaotic irrationality. Beck and Ellis support individual rationality but have no place for an ontology of reason.[51]

---

[51]For a fuller critique of Beck and Ellis on this point, see Browning and Cooper, *Religious Thought and the Modern Psychologies,* esp. chap. 10.

Tillich would surely argue that cognitive therapy can deal with many aspects of *neurotic* anxiety. However, the minute finite reason tries to resolve the question of existence itself, particularly without a trust in its Source and Ground, it will not be successful. Reason is not that strong, not that "pure," not that capable of resisting the undercurrents of self-deception. Changing anxious thoughts into nonanxious ones, particularly concerning life's crucial issues, is simply not that easy. Tillich would not agree that human destructiveness is only a cerebral problem. It is more than an issue of distorted thinking.

Beck believes that cleaning up our fears will get rid of our anxieties. Anxiety *results* from specific fears, some of which are not conscious. Tillich argues the opposite point. He says, "It is the anxiety of not being able to preserve one's own being which underlies every fear and is the frightening element in it."[52] The specific, concrete fear always has the backdrop of anxiety.

Tillich would no doubt reject the Pelagianism inherent in cognitive therapy's strong-willed attempt to "conquer" our anxiety and affirm ourselves. The "courage to be" necessitates "accepting our acceptance" in spite of our unacceptability, an experience outlined in chapter 1. Accepting acceptance stands outside of moral, intellectual, or religious preconditions. Just as we cannot "save" ourselves, we cannot ultimately "calm" ourselves, particularly in the face of ontological anxiety. Instead, self-acceptance and self-affirmation presuppose that we participate in a reality which transcends the individual "self." Tillich states this eloquently.

> The divine self-affirmation is the power that makes self-affirmation of the finite being, the courage to be, possible. Only because being-itself has the character of self-affirmation in spite of nonbeing is courage possible. Courage participates in the self-affirmation of being-itself, it participates in the power of being which prevails against nonbeing. He who receives this power in an act of mystical or personal or absolute faith is aware of the source of the courage to be.[53]

Tillich would also question the cognitive therapy assumption that correct thinking will lead to ethical behavior. Clear rational capacities do not necessarily free us from the demonic. Reason has biases, defenses, subjec-

---

[52]*The Courage to Be*, 38.
[53]*The Courage to Be*, 180-81.

tive tugs of which it is not always aware. It cannot free itself from the grip of ontological anxiety. As Tillich's colleague Reinhold Niebuhr puts it,

> Faith in the providence of God is a necessity of freedom because, without it, the anxiety of freedom tempts man to seek a self-sufficiency and self-mastery incompatible with his dependence upon forces which he does not control.[54]

The answer to the problem of ontological anxiety is in trust rather than in self-control or self-mastery. Only grace can ultimately calm our anxious self-preoccupations. Conscious reason, contrary to Beck, can never identify all the "objects" which trigger anxiety. Reason, also, needs help when it is in the deep waters of existential anxiety. It cannot save itself.

Courage, Individuation, and Participation

One of the richest aspects of Tillich's analysis of courage is his distinction between "the courage to be oneself as an individual" and "the courage to be a part of community." One dimension, of course, refers to individual self-affirmation as an individual—a separated, unique, and incomparable self. This is the path toward authentic selfhood which Jung frequently called "individuation." It is not "self-centered" in the sense of being selfish. Instead, it is "self-centered" in that it involves a centered self. As Tillich puts it, "The theological assertion that every human soul has an infinite value is a consequence of the ontological self-affirmation as an indivisible, unexhangeable self. It can be called 'the courage to be as oneself.' "[55]

But Tillich knows that the self cannot be a self without a world to which it both belongs and is separated.

> Self and world are correlated, and so are individuation and participation. For this is just what participation means: being a part of something from which one is, at the same time, separated. Literally, participation means "taking part."[56]

Tillich recognizes that the courage to participate or "to be a part" may *appear* to be a form of weakness or lack of courage. Conformity, after the destructiveness of Nazi Germany, did not seem to be a favorable word.

---

[54]Reinhold Niebuhr, *The Nature and Destiny of Man*, vol. 1 (New York: Scribner's, 1964) 271.
[55]*The Courage to Be*, 87.
[56]*The Courage to Be*, 88.

Bowing down to authoritarianism and forfeiting autonomy appeared to be the cardinal sin. Tillich clearly understands and argues that this is a dangerous pattern. Yet the refusal to "be a part," to participate in the world, is also a failure of courage. Self-affirmation is individual, but it is not solipsistic. It should not preclude a connection with community life.

> We are threatened not only with losing our individual selves but also with losing participation in our world. Therefore self-affirmation as a part requires courage as much as does self-affirmation as oneself. It is *one* courage which takes a double threat of nonbeing into itself. The courage to be is essentially always the courage to be as a part and the courage to be as oneself, in independence.[57]

We affirm our own being by participation in the world. And more particularly, we become persons through an encounter with other persons. Community and individuality are not enemies.

But Tillich is quick to say that there is no such thing as a "group self," "group anxiety," or "group courage." There is no authentic "we-self." The enlargement of the individual self to a group level is always an inaccurate description. Selfhood refers to a centered self, and there is no central "self" in a group. There may be a central power, a particular person in charge of the group, but there is no group ego.

> There is no collective anxiety save an anxiety which has overtaken many or all members of a group and has intensified or changed by becoming universal. . . . The courage to be as a part is like all forms of courage, a quality of individual selves.[58]

Tillich's insistence on discussing "the courage to be a part," as well as the courage to be, matches the insights of several key twentieth century psychologists. To mention only a few, Alfred Adler spoke often about "social interest" as a central feature of mental health; Otto Rank frequently described the anxiety of "connecting with others" as well as the anxiety of affirming autonomy; Karen Horney based much of her theory on the interpersonal anxiety of relating to others; and family-systems theorist Murray Bowen highlights the importance of "differentiation," which is never isolated from others, but always involves an ongoing connection. Autonomy does not mean one lives out of a vacuum. Tillich offers a

---

[57]*The Courage to Be*, 89-90.
[58]*The Courage to Be*, 92.

corrective to the singular, isolated existentialist who only battles the anxiety of interiority.

Summary

Tillich's discussion of anxiety draws on both his own tragic experiences in life as well as the depth of his philosophical and psychological analysis. Tillich's life was *both deeply lived and deeply interpreted.* The early loss of his mother and the horrendous experiences in World War I clearly pushed him out of any sort of "dreaming innocence."

Tillich provides all discussions of anxiety with a much-needed philosophical substructure. He moves courage from the strictly ethical to the ontological level. His analysis of the three major forms of anxiety (fate and death; guilt and condemnation; emptiness and meaninglessness) are surely insightful. He greatly expands our understanding of everyday fears by showing the element of anxiety lurking behind then.

But Tillich also insightfully understands the character of neurotic, as well as existential, anxiety. His analysis of the limited self-affirmation inherent in neurosis is of great clinical interest. He functions as *both psychological and philosophical diagnostician.* Few theologians could have both digested the amount of psychology Tillich did, and yet remained capable of critiquing psychotherapy's limits, particularly when therapies take the form of Pelagian self-salvation.

The issue of anxiety, so central to a discussion in religion and psychology, leads quickly to an issue which propels our anxiety—human estrangement. It is to this important Tillichian contribution that we now turn.

Chapter 3

Estrangement and New Being: Sin and the Limitations of Pyschotherapy

Sin is separation from one's own essential being and its divine ground. Salvation is the healing of this split in the healing power of that which transcends man and gives him the courage to accept himself.
—Paul Tillich

Sin is not primarily sin against God but sin against ourselves.
—Erich Fromm

Paul Tillich spent a great deal of time in conversation with Erich Fromm. They knew each other in Germany before the Nazi regime forced them to leave their native land, and also spent time together in New York. Both were influenced by Marx and Freud. And both were very regular members of the New York Psychology Group which, as we shall see in the next chapter, met during World War II. In fact, even a casual acquaintance with the New York Psychology Group materials reveals that Tillich and Fromm were probably the two central figures in this important group of distinguished intellectuals. In many ways, Tillich and Fromm represent two very different approaches to the human condition. Tillich believes it is impossible to understand human nature apart from its Ground and Source. Stated differently, we can never understand *human* being without reference to the *Ground* of being. Fromm, on the other hand, wanted to emancipate his humanism from any need for God-talk.

In this chapter I will explore some of the similarities and differences between Tillich and Fromm as representatives of theological and secular humanism. Again, as a psychoanalyst and Marxist, Fromm is one of the most eloquent spokespersons for the position that humanity must heal itself and not rely on a transcendent Source to provide its redemption. Tillich obviously disagrees. In arriving at a comparison between Tillich and Fromm, I will rely in part on Guy Hammond's fine study of these two men, *Man in Estrangment: A Comparison of the Thought of Paul Tillich and Erich Fromm.*[1] I will also (a) examine the contributions that existentialism

---

[1] Guy Hammond, *Man in Estrangment: A Comparison of the Thought of Paul Tillich and Erich Fromm* (Nashville: Vanderbilt University Press, 1965).

and psychoanalysis offer a theological understanding of sin, (b) look at Reinhold Niebuhr's critique of Tillich's "fall from essence to existence," and (c) explore the extent to which psychotherapy can heal the problem of estrangement. The hope is that through an examination of Tillich and Fromm, the two major leaders of the New York Psychology Group, we may come to a deeper understanding of the human condition and its remedy.

Existence Itself Is the Problem

According to Tillich, while the content of the Christian message is not *derived* from an analysis of the human predicament, any meaningful theological response must address the issues raised by this philosophical analysis. For Tillich, the philosophical analysis is thus allowed to set the stage for the theological responses. Tillich trusts that we human beings know how to ask the right questions. Further, he trusts that a philosophical analysis of the human condition will reveal that it is *existence itself* which is the problem. Put another way, philosophy naturally leads us to the conviction that we are estranged. Something is not right. We are somehow separated from life, from each other, and from ourselves. As Guy Hammond suggests, "This means that in Tillich's view the analysis of the human predicament is a task for philosophy rather than theology, and that in this task the philosopher must draw upon interpretive materials from all realms of culture—art, literature, drama, etc.—as well as upon philosophical insight per se."[2] This analysis of the human predicament, of course, is existential analysis. And while it offers a rich investigation into the questions of being human, it offers little in the way of "answers." Existential analysis can safely arrive at the conclusion that human existence is estranged. It can further describe that estrangement. But it is helpless in understanding the ultimate causes or the cure for that estrangement.

Relying on David Tracy's revised correlational approach and a hermeneutical perspective, I will later critique this Tillichian position that philosophical analysis only raises questions and does not provide answers. I believe that many philosophical analyses do indeed suggest their own ultimate answers to the problem of being human. But we will get to that later.

In Tillich's view, estrangement is total. Every aspect of the human condition is affected by it. We cannot rely upon some "nonestranged" part of

---

[2]Hammond, *Man in Estrangment*, 12.

ourselves to rescue the parts which are estranged. It is precisely because *all* of human existence is estranged that human beings cannot provide an answer to the problem of estrangement. This is Tillich's way of talking about "total depravity." We are too sick to prescribe our own healthy treatment. We are not too sick, however, to contribute to our diagnosis. Yet the healing of our sickness is not something that humanity can provide itself. Tillich would never agree with Marx, for instance, that we can isolate a specific "cause" of estrangement, such as class-conflict, and by eliminating that specific problem, get rid of the entire dilemma of estrangement. Estrangement is much deeper than that. For Tillich, such a hopeful belief is utopian nonsense. Thus, all naturalistic anthropologies which seek to identify *the* fundamental, finite cause of human estrangement are doomed to fail. What is needed is an answer beyond estranged existence, an answer which transcends our predicament.

There is, then, no particular aspect of the human predicament which causes the rest of it to be estranged. We cannot identify and locate a human source of estrangement and thereby rectify that condition. As we shall see, this is where Tillich parts company with many neo-Freudian and humanistic psychologists, as well as Marxists, who believe that estrangement can be overcome by human effort. Stated simply, we cannot "clean up" our estrangement problem.

Existentialism and Depth Psychology

Tillich believes that existentialism and psychoanalysis offer theology important contributions concerning estranged existence. In an important essay entitled "The Theological Significance of Psychoanalysis and Existentialism," Tillich argues that psychoanalysis belongs to the general currents of existentialist thought.[3]

> Everybody who has looked into the works of existentialist writers from Dostoyevsky on to the present will immediately agree that there is much depth-psychological material in the novels, the dramas, and the poems, as

---

[3]Paul Tillich, "The Theological Significance of Existentialism and Psychoanalysis," in *The Meaning of Health*, ed. Perry LeFevre (Chicago: Exploration Press, 1984). This essay was first published in *Faith and Freedom* 9/25 (Autumn 1955), then was slightly revised for inclusion in Tillich's *Theology of Culture*, ed. Robert C. Kimball (New York: Oxford University Press, 1959) 112-26.

well as the visual arts—modern art being the existentialist form of visual arts.[4]

Existentialism and psychoanalysis share a common revolt against the "philosophy of consciousness." The "philosophy of consciousness" takes human thought at face value. Existentialism and psychoanalysis, on the other hand, view consciousness as governed by the impulses and irrational urges beneath it. One view embraces human consciousness as a straightforward, what-you-see-is-what-you-get phenomenon while the other wants to look beneath "obvious" awareness and expose the undercurrents which unconsciously shape it. One view prizes the primacy of intellect, believing that conscious reason can master the world. The other view is suspicious of conscious reason and wants to know what irrational dimensions are influencing it. Tillich believes this conflict has gone on for centuries: Aquinas vs. Duns Scotus, Erasmus vs. Luther, Descartes vs. Pascal, Hegel vs. Kierkegaard, and so on. The philosophy of consciousness reached its zenith in Hegel, who provoked a rebellion in such masters of suspicion as Nietzsche, Marx, and Freud. Tillich, as we might suspect, highlights Schelling as a very important player in this revolt against the finality of finite reason.[5]

Freud is especially important because he offered empirical, methodological procedures for demonstrating the power of the irrational unconscious.[6] While previous thinkers had offered insightful intuition, Freud attempted to provide these intuitions with a scientific foundation.

While existentialism and psychoanalysis are concerned with our estrangement, Tillich believes they can talk about estrangement only when they assume a particular vision of our *essence*.[7] Otherwise, how would we know we are estranged? And from *what* are we estranged? Some notion of a straight line is necessary to understand that a line is crooked. Thus, Tillich does not believe the existentialist Sartre when he says that human beings have no essence, but instead they create their essence ("existence precedes essence"). Tillich quickly adds that if human beings go about

---

[4]"The Theological Significance of Existentialism and Psychoanalysis," 83.
[5]"The Theological Significance of Existentialism and Psychoanalysis," 85.
[6]"The Theological Significance of Existentialism and Psychoanalysis," 85.
[7]"The Theological Significance of Existentialism and Psychoanalysis," 90.

creating their essence, then this *is* their nature or essence—they create themselves. An implicit belief in human essence is inescapable.

Existentialism points toward universal, inescapable struggles of the human psyche. Nathan Scott, in his excellent book on existentialism, describes these beautifully:

> [T]he existentialists do all tend to agree that we do not begin to discover what it means to be human until we are brought up against the great limiting realities of suffering and guilt, or sorrow and disappointment and death. For it is only when we know what it means to be "shipwrecked," it is only when we have felt the sting of some radical failure, of blighted hopes and foundered purposes, of some misfortune that it is sheer, unmitigated woe—it is only then that we begin, in any deep way, to appreciate our human finitude, how frail and unsheltered and vulnerable we are before the vicissitudes of life. And to be without any experience of extremity is to lack a certain necessary equipment (of wisdom and maturity) apart from which no really authentic life can be achieved.[8]

As universal characteristics of the human psyche, anxiety, guilt, and estrangement cannot be "therapized" away. They are part of the structure of self-conscious finitude. To be a human being is to wrestle with them. They are not psychological disorders in need of treatment; they are conditions of estrangement in need of salvation. They must be faced by everyone, yet we have endless maneuvers for trying to dodge them. The existential conditions of our estrangement do not represent psychological disturbance; instead, it is the attempt to by-pass or escape them which leads to psychological disturbance. This is what Jung knew when he said that "neurosis is always a substitute for legitimate suffering."[9]

Tillich, like Reinhold Niebuhr, believed that Freud failed to separate humanity's existential and essential natures. Freud only dealt with our estranged condition and called it our essential nature. Maintaining the traditional Judeo-Christian belief that creation is good, both Tillich and Niebuhr insist that our essential nature is not distorted. Because Freud failed to make this important distinction, he concluded his thinking with a very gloomy view of both the individual and culture.

---

[8]Nathan A. Scott, *Mirrors of Man in Existentialism* (New York: Collins, 1978) 22.

[9]Carl Jung, *Collected Works*, vol. 2, trans. R. F. C. Hull (Princeton NJ: Princeton University Press, 1973) 75.

His dismay of culture shows that he is very consistent in his negative judgments about man as existentially distorted. Now if you see man only from the point of existence and not from the point of view of essence, only from the point of estrangement and not from the view of essential goodness, then this consequence is unavoidable. And it is true for Freud in this respect.[10]

Tillich goes on to clarify this point by making reference to the similarities between the Freudian concept of libido and the traditional Christian understanding of concupiscence, or disordered desire. Concupiscence is not part of humanity's essential nature. Yet unfortunately, because we have fallen from this essential nature and lost our centeredness in God as our ultimate concern, we try to infuse finite things with infinite significance. Our desires turn into cravings as we elevate finite things to the status of gods. This is addiction, not love. Without a centeredness in God, we try to turn other things into deities. This invariably throws our lives out of balance. We can no longer love finite things *as finite things*. Instead, because we have deified them, we love them in distorted and unhealthy ways. Stated differently, there is always a psychological "payoff" for worshipping finite things. Nothing finite is "built" to be the center of our lives.

Freud's description of libido, then, is extremely helpful in describing humanity's estranged existence, but it tells us nothing about our *essential* condition. Tillich, however, thinks it fortunate that Freud was inconsistent. His pessimism about the human condition does not match his optimism about therapeutic outcome.

Nevertheless, says Tillich, Freud's understanding of estranged existence is a great gift to Christian theology.[11] It is particularly helpful in moving theologians away from static and moralistic views of sin. Tillich basically says the following: Make no mistake, the human condition, in its estranged existence, is just as bad as Freud indicates it is. In fact, Tillich believes that some of Freud's followers (including Tillich's friends, Fromm and Horney) have lost some of the depth of Freud's analysis because they have minimized the severity of the human condition by their optimistic, naturalistic hopes for human improvement.

---

[10]"The Theological Significance of Existentialism and Psychoanalysis," 88-89.
[11]"The Theological Significance of Existentialism and Psychoanalysis," 89-91.

They have rejected the profound insight of Freud about existential libido and the death instinct, and in so doing they have reduced and cut off from Freud what made him and still makes him the most profound of all the depth psychologists. . . . But Freud, theologically speaking, saw more about human nature than all his followers who, when they lost the existential element in Freud, went more to an essentialist and optimistic view of man.[12]

Neo-Freudians who describe the human situation in more optimistic terms often believe we can correct, on the basis of natural intervention, our fundamental predicament. These approaches, which are assumed by Horney, Fromm, and others, ultimately argue for a kind of self-healing about which Tillich and the Christian tradition is most skeptical. Healthier forms of parenting, the right sort of environment, greater education, or more equal distributions of wealth, for Tillich, will not "end" our problem of estrangement. It is much too deep for that.

They try with their methods to overcome existential negativity, anxiety, estrangement, meaninglessness, or guilt. They deny that they are universal, that they are existential in that sense. They call all anxiety, all guilt, all emptiness, illnesses which can be overcome as any illness can be, and they try to remove them. But this is impossible. The existentialist structure cannot be healed by the most refined techniques. They are objects of salvation. The analyst can be an instrument of salvation as every friend, every parent, every child can be an instrument of salvation. But as analyst he cannot bring salvation by means of his medical methods, for this requires the healing of the center of the personality.[13]

Put straightforwardly, the great existential struggles of human life cannot be "therapized" away. While psychotherapy can greatly aid us in clearing away neurotic elements of our lives, the larger questions of meaning, value, purpose cannot be "resolved" by psychotherapeutic technique.

Created Goodness and Existential Estrangement

Clearly, one of the most disputed areas of Tillich's theology is his understanding of humanity's "fall from essence to existence." Many of Tillich's critics believe he has moved away from a Christian understanding of the

---

[12] "The Theological Significance of Existentialism and Psychoanalysis," 89-90.
[13] "The Theological Significance of Existentialism and Psychoanalysis," 91-92.

goodness of creation in his position. These critics argue that Tillich presents "the Fall" of humanity into estranged existence as ontologically necessary, a matter of fate. Yet if this is the case, they ask, then how can humanity be held responsible for the condition in which it finds itself? Before we move into the more psychologically oriented comparison of Tillich and Fromm, it might be helpful to look briefly at this controversial theological issue.

Langdon Gilkey, in his excellent book on Tillich, recalls a rather humorous incident at Union Theological Seminary when Reinhold Niebuhr and Tillich exchanged views on this issue. Niebuhr and Tillich were both mentors of Gilkey and, although the narrative is lengthy, it is worth quoting in detail.

> On another occasion Tillich got the better of Reinnie. It was some meeting at Union, again sometime in 1947–1949, where methods in theology were under discussion. Reinnie had been chiding Tillich for deserting a "mythical" account of Creation and Fall, which kept Creation and Fall clearly separate, and for embracing a philosophical interpretation ("the impersonal and necessitating abstractions of ontology"), which inevitably "identified" Creation and Fall, the ultimate and baleful evidence of a philosophical pantheism. . . . Tillich smiled, recognizing a familiar argument in their continuing debate, and then stood up. Pushing back the sleeve on his suit jacket, Tillich looked carefully at his watch and then up at Reinnie. . . . "Alright, Reinnie. You wish to separate the Creation and Fall. Good. *Zen* how long vas it, Reinnie?" Tillich pointed to the face on his watch: "*Vas* it from twelve noon to five after twelve, Reinnie, or perhaps a little longer? How long did *ze* good Creation, separate from *ze* Fall, last? And, Reinnie, if you do not know, in fact cannot, say to me how long it lasted, then how long can we *separate zem* as you wish to do? And what does it *mean* to try to separate *zem* in myth if *zey* cannot be separated? Must we not hold *zem* together as one event, even if we distinguish *zem* as different aspects of that event of coming to be? But that is ontology united to myth, is it not Reinnie?" . . . Niebuhr may not have understood clearly how Tillich escaped pantheism, but he clearly understood how someone had gotten the better of him! Thus he laughed that delighted if somewhat embarrassed laugh that appeared naturally whenever he realized the joke was on him, shrugged his shoulders, and muttered something about the obscure labyrinths of philosophy.[14]

---

[14]Langdon Gilkey, *Gilkey on Tillich* (New York: Crossroad, 1990) 203.

Indeed, Tillich "wins" the exchange. Yet I wish to ask whether Tillich, in his seeming identification of Creation/Fall, does not embrace an unavoidable form of Manichaeism. Granted, Reinold Niebuhr and every other theologian is left with a strange paradox concerning the "timing" of the Fall. Yet I question whether or not Tillich's solution of equating Creation and Fall preserves the notion of created goodness that has been foundational for the Judeo-Christian tradition. Gilkey appears to be on Tillich's side in this debate, though he readily acknowledges that "there has been no more controversial area of Tillich's thought than his interpretation of what in theology is called "the Fall."[15] While Tillich won this exchange, I'm not so sure he won the argument. In order to look carefully at this issue, we need to revisit Niebuhr's best-known critique of Tillich, "Biblical Thought and Ontological Speculation in Tillich's Theology."[16]

Pelagius frequently argued that Augustine had not successfully stripped himself of his old Manichaean thinking. Similarly, Niebuhr, whom we normally associate with Augustine because of his penetrating analysis of original sin,[17] argues that Tillich sounds much too close to Manichaeism in his discussion of the fall from "essence to existence." For Niebuhr, Tillich's "fall" involves a sense of ontological fate that ends up eliminating personal responsibility for sin. While Tillich tries to distinguish the words "estrangement" (fate) from "sin" (our personal responsibility in our estrangement), Niebuhr does not think his distinction holds. This becomes very problematic for a Judeo-Christian tradition that wants to assert the goodness of Creation. If the very structure of our existence pushes us into sin, then we live in a world in which *existence itself is evil*. In fact, by making the Creation and Fall two sides of the same coin, Tillich sounds very similar to Origen, who understood the Adamic story as symbolic of a preexistent Fall.[18]

Actualizing our freedom, for Tillich, means falling into sin. Niebuhr thus thinks that Tillich falls into the trap of thinking of sin as "ontological

---

[15]Gilkey, *Gilkey on Tillich*, 114.

[16]Reinhold Niebuhr, "Biblical Thought and Ontological Speculation in Tillich's Theology," in *The Theology of Paul Tillich*, ed. Charles W. Kegley (New York: Pilgrim Press, 1982) 252-63.

[17]See Reinhold Niebuhr, *The Nature and Destiny of Man*, 2 vols. (New York: Scribner's, 1964).

[18]Origen, *On First Principles*, trans. G. W. Butterworth (Gloucester MA: Peter Smith Press, 1973).

fate."[19] Humanity's actualization of freedom is equated with estrangement from undifferentiated being. Sin is a disruption of unity between God and humanity. This disruption is fully located in the actualization of human freedom. We cannot exist without separation from God; therefore, merely being in existence brings on sin. Stated differently, to exist is to sin. Yet if actualized freedom inevitably means sin, then how is our creation good? Niebuhr's objection, then, is that Tillich speaks only of Adam's created goodness as a goodness *before* creation. Goodness is thus *mere potentiality, not actuality*. This involves a world of discreet essences or Platonic "forms" which anticipate creation.

Niebuhr frequently describes sin as inevitable but not necessary. The possibility of trusting God is ever-present, yet we human beings seem to invariably distrust God and place ourselves at the helm of our lives. This placing of ourselves at the center may not appear as puffed-up pride, which Niebuhr described so well in *The Nature and Destiny of Man*. Instead, it may take the form of an insecure self-preoccuaption or the attempt to "fix" our anxiety by complete self-avoidance. Yet for Niebuhr, it is always a self-designed solution to the problem of anxiety, a proudful God-replacement in that we substitute our own strategies for depending on God.

But this condition is not "fated" by the simple fact that we have entered human existence. Like Augustine, Luther, and Kierkegaard, Niebuhr is convinced that we bring this condition on ourselves. It is not built into the very structures of finitude. Put differently, *finitude itself is not the problem*. It is instead our refusal to embrace our finitude or contingent existence that creates our problem.

Tillich, on the other hand, suggests that we are ontologically fated by powers much larger than ourselves. For Niebuhr, Tillich's mistake in discussing Creation and Fall is that he makes one story out of two. The first story, Creation, must be held separately from the second, the Fall. Creation is the beginning of history; the Fall has to do with the corruption of history. Niebuhr admits that there are problems and unanswered questions in his view, but Tillich's attempt to solve the dilemma *ends up saying that temporal existence is itself evil*. Again, this makes existence good only when it is potential, and not when it is actual.

---

[19]Niebuhr, "Biblical Thought and Ontological Speculation in Tillich's Theology," 256.

> [I]t symbolizes the fact that every act of estrangement, or isolation, or of imperialism is a "fall" from a more ideal possibility of relating life with life in terms of love.... Such a formulation makes history more real, for it does not set it in contrast to some symbolic period before creation when all particular things were not yet separated existences. Rather it sets every historical act, achievement, and event in contrast to the primordial and the eschatological, that is, to innocency and perfection. Thus, every historic decision, which must be either for the self or for God and the other, has a historic urgency and reality which it cannot have if its fate of self-seeking is identified with its fate of being a self.[20]

Niebuhr's accusation, in a nutshell, then, is this: Tillich identifies Creation and Fall, and in so doing, makes sin necessary. Sin, in spite of Tillich's attempt to describe it as personal responsibility, is enveloped in ontological fate. To exist is to be estranged.

Note that this does not mean, however, that Tillich does not develop a strong undersanding of personal sin. Indeed, he does. The quarrel is not with the manner in which sin is described but with the manner in which it comes about. As Gilkey points out, Tillich is no optimistic liberal on the issue of sin.

> [D]espite the unconventionality of his method with regard to the Fall, Tillich's emphasis on the universality and weight of sin is unqualified; his sense of its utter inescapability and oppressive burden is unmatched; and his picture of the despairing suffering resulting from sin rivals that of even the most realistic of his theological colleagues, and most any contemporary piece of existentialist literature. As in his emphasis on the necessity of revelation, so in the depth and pervasiveness of "estrangement" or "alienation" in his system, Tillich can hardly be described as a "liberal," however much his thinking on other grounds is correlated throughout with cultural experiences and categories. On the contrary, as he always claimed, his theology belongs and here especially, strictly in the Pauline, Augustinian, and Reformation line of theologians of "sin and grace," rather than among the liberal theologians of continuity.[21]

Tillich clearly understands that sin is "already there" as a universal condition before anyone makes his or her first choice. He also believes that

---

[20]Niebuhr, "Biblical Thought and Ontological Speculation in Tillich's Theology," 260-61.

[21]Gilkey, *Gilkey on Tillich*, 114-15.

many of the biblical theologians have emphasized the issue of personal responsibility at the expense of understanding sin as part of the human condition. Nevertheless, Tillich speaks frequently about our participation in this estranged condition, our adding our own choices and actions to the predicament. For Tillich, we *are* responsible.

But along with Niebuhr and many others, we may want to know *how we can possibly be held responsible whenever existence itself is estranged.* Whether or not our sin throws gasoline on the fire, we are *already in the fire* as ontologically fated creatures, are we not? How, then, can we possibly maintain the traditional Judeo-Christian claim that creation is good?

Gilkey, as an appreciative student of *both* Tillich and Nieubhr, and one who has written excellent books on each of them,[22] offers an insightful clue for understanding how Tillich's view of the Fall might be maintained. Not everyone, of course, will think the issue is therefore resolved, but it is worth investigating his suggestion.

Gilkey argues that it is helpful to keep Kierkegaard in mind when we explicate Tillich's notion that the road to "existence" is through finite freedom. In other words, biological existence, for Tillich, does not mean "existence" in a genuinely human sense. We "achieve" existence through "choosing ourselves." This is an act of freedom which gives shape and form to our lives. Prior to this we have only "potential" existence, not real existence. Gilkey puts this issue quite nicely.

> We *are* when we actualize ourselves by choosing ourselves, that is, by accepting our destiny as "ours," our projects as our own future, and our actions as our responsibility . . . the movement into actuality is already a movement of creaturely freedom as well as of destiny; this is the crucial point. Our freedom does not become active only when we are, so to speak, already here, created and active in our environment; on the contrary, it is our freedom, which, together with our destiny, in fact in *choosing* our destiny, ushers us *into* full existence. Here the work of freedom is very much a creative part of our coming to be, even a part of our "creation."[23]

Thus, we are only "fully created" when we, in part, create ourselves. This necessitates moving out of "dreaming innocence" or the state of pure

---

[22] In addition to his book on Tillich, Gilkey also provided an outstanding study of Niebuhr: *On Niebuhr: A Theological Study* (Chicago: University of Chicago Press, 2001).

[23] Gilkey, *Gilkey on Tillich*, 120-21.

potential. This movement from potential essence to actual existence is only possible with a self-creating freedom. As Gilkey puts it, "finite actuality, therefore, comes to be in part through a principle of nonnecessity: freedom in union with destiny and self-constitution of the self which is also a 'choosing of the destined self.' "[24]

So the key here is the question, "What does it mean to really *exist*?" We can only "exist" as a person when we employ our finite freedom. This involves a sense of personal responsibility. Thus, Creation can be seen as good while existence is possible only as a result of finite freedom, the movement out of "dreaming innocence" and toward selfhood. Thus, Tillich, like Niebuhr, wants to claim that sin is inevitable but not ontologically necessary. It is not a requirement of finitude but it inevitably occurs as we choose our existence.

Not all, of course, will be convinced by Gilkey's argument and I seriously doubt that this debate between philosophical and biblical theology is over. I leave it to more agile theological minds to resolve it. Many will argue that Tillich is much better at describing sin than discussing how it comes about.

I would suggest, however, that no matter how hard we may try, it is probably not possible to get beyond the simple confession *that* sin is to the mysterious question of *why* sin is. The point of the narrative of the Fall seems to disclose to us the nature of our predicament in the here-and-now. Both the inevitability of sin and the personal responsibility for sin seem to paradoxically manifest themselves in our experience. This is as true in the social sciences as it is in theology. Tillich says, "Man's predicament is estrangement, but his estrangement is sin."[25] Or as Gilkey puts it, "We are willing participants in estrangement as well as unwilling victims in it."[26] The paradox is that sin is both destiny and personal choice. To exist is to be estranged and yet we each add our own contribution to estrangement.

---

[24]Gilkey, *Gilkey on Tillich*, 121.

[25]Tillich, *Systematic Theology*, vol. 2 (Chicago: University of Chicago Press, 1957) 47.

[26]Gilkey, *Gilkey on Tillich*, 124.

Estrangement and Women's Experience: Plaskow's Critique

In her insightful book, *Sex, Sin, and Grace: Women's Experience and the Theologies of Reinhold Niebuhr and Paul Tillich*, Judith Plaskow raises questions about the capacity of Tillich's understanding of estrangement to describe the experience of many women.[27] While she believes that Tillich appears to offer a broader understanding of sin than that of his colleague, Reinhold Niebuhr, who was preoccupied with the sin of pride, Tillich's approach is nevertheless riddled with problems because of the nature of his ontology. Plaskow's problem with Tillich's ontology is much the same as Niebuhr's objection, even if for different reasons. By equating the actualization of freedom with the fall into estrangement, Tillich indirectly encourages a passivity which is already a major problem for many women. By making self-actualization and estrangement part of a single act, Tillich does not adequately address the issue of self-abnegation and implicitly suggests that to *not* actualize one's freedom is to remain closer to God, one's Ground and Source.

> His many individual statements concerning sin as self-abnegation and grace as reconstitution of the self tend to be undercut by the monistic tendency of the ontology which underlies them . . . his specific remarks relevant to women, in other words, are not supported by the context in which they are set.[28]

Let's explore her claim.

Unlike Niebuhr, who focused on the more typically male-dominated sin of pride and self-assertion, Tillich seems to include the issues of self-abnegation, self-loss, and "uncreative weakness" as part of estrangement. Tillich seems willing to explore issues of self-contempt, the ambiguities of self-sacrifice, the need for self-love and self-justice, and the obligation to actualize one's potential—all issues highly important to women. These issues, argues Plaskow, hold promise in describing the experience of many women who are troubled less by self-assertion and much more by a failure to "be" a self. Yet Tillich's "follow through" is disappointing. Even though he

---

[27]Judith Plaskow, *Sex, Sin, and Grace: Women's Experience and the Theologies of Reinhold Niebuhr and Paul Tillich* (Lanham MD: University Press of America, 1980).

[28]Plaskow, *Sex, Sin, and Grace*, 95.

wants to create a new and more inclusive understanding of estrangement, he falls back into very traditional categories to describe it: unbelief, hubris, and concupiscence. And while Tillich does not want to equate hubris and pride, as Niebuhr seems to do, all of his examples of hubris point toward prideful self-exaltation. The notion that hubris can also be expressed in humility, which Tillich acknowledges, is completely undeveloped.

While Tillich wants to broaden his concept of estrangement, his use of traditional language gets in his way. Plaskow can understand his use of classical language *if* he breathes new life into it. But she believes he doesn't just use classical language; instead, he falls back into classical ways of thinking about sin—ways which do not speak to women. Tillich needs a much more thorough reinterpretation of the language.[29] While Tillich realizes *both* the self's obligation toward self-realization and its *failure to move in that direction*, his focus is clearly on the former. Consequently, he says little to women who avoid their obligation toward self-actualization. Like Niebuhr, his focus is far more on the problems associated with self-assertion than with the dilemma of selflessness.

Again, while Plaskow does not agree with Niebuhr's theological anthropology, she *does* seem to find the same problems that Niebuhr found with Tillich's ontology. More specifically, Tillich's view of the fall from essence to existence, ends up equating self-actualization with estrangement. Actualizing our potential means accentuating our sin. Moving out of an undifferentiated state with our Ground and Source means that we are now estranged. There is no "healthy separation," no positive individuation, no pure self-actualization. Instead, it is the other side of estrangement. Plaskow is thus concerned that this identification of freedom and estrangement will unwittingly promote passivity, dependence, and the failure to self-actualize. Tillich states it straightforwardly: "Actualized creation and estranged existence are identical."[30]

For Plaskow, this view of estrangement leaves no room for the sin of refusing to actualize one's freedom. By equating self-actualization with sin, Tillich implicitly suggests that nonactualization may leave us less sinful.

> Indeed, it raises the question as to whether and how failure to be self-actualizing can be considered sinful at all. . . . Tillich's identification of

---

[29]Plaskow, *Sex, Sin, and Grace*, 111.
[30]Tillich, *Systematic Theology* 2:44.

the choice for self-actualization with the fall provides no way of explaining how or why uncreative weakness is not, so to speak, a "fall back" toward essence or reunion with the divine ground. It provides no way of explaining why uncreative weakness is sin at all.[31]

Again, Tillich's invitation to actualize our potential is undermined by his ontological equation of sin and differentiation. If actualizing one's potential also means actualizing one's estrangement, then there is a subtle suggestion to remain passive.

Another way of putting this is that while Tillich speaks of the polarities of separation and union, his emphasis is clearly on union. In fact, reunion with our Divine Ground permeates his theology. To exist separately from this Divine Ground is to fall into estrangement.

> Tillich cannot dwell on the ambiguities of uncreative weakness, despite his recognition of their prevalence, because his ontology provides him no basis for doing so. But this also means that much in his thought which is applicable to women's experience is thrown into question by its broader context. Though Tillich certainly never says this, the underlying message of his ontology is right in the tradition which sees women as more religious than men. Insofar as self-actualization is associated with sinfulness, the relative "naturalness" of women, their less highly differentiated sense of self, and their failure to pursue self-actualization may all be viewed as marks and guarantors of a close and fervent God-relation throughout life. To subscribe to this tradition is, of course, to favor retention of these characteristics and oppose change. . . . "Women's sin" would be a virtue. The female destiny of estrangement, as compared with the male, would entail less separation from the original unity of God's life. To the extent that this is the hidden message of Tillich's ontology . . . his theology reinforces the status quo.[32]

Further, doesn't Tillich's solution of reunion with the Ground of our being effectively eliminate our self-actualization, individual personhood, or autonomy? The parallel with Buddhism is obvious. If self-affirmation created our estrangement, then the solution seems to be a return to a nonactualized unity with our Source. Unity swallows individuality. Participation conquers selfhood.

---

[31]Plaskow, *Sex, Sin, and Grace*, 118.
[32]Plaskow, *Sex, Sin, and Grace*, 119-20.

Plaskow raises an extremely interesting issue concerning the "Great Mother" qualities of Tillich's conception of God. Issues of separation and unity become paramount as one relates to this Great Mother image. Tillich, himself, mentions this. In describing the symbolic nature of the Ground of being he says that it "points to the mother-quality of giving birth, carrying, and embracing, and, at the same time, of calling back, resisting independence of the created, and swallowing it."[33] Plaskow believes that Tillich's image of God is very well captured in Erich Neumann's portrayal of the archetype of the Great Mother.

> As *elementary character* we designate the aspect of the Feminine that as the Great Round, the Great Container, tends to hold fast to everything that springs from it to surround it like an eternal substance. Everything born of it belongs to it and remains subject to it; and even if the individual becomes independent, the Archetypal Feminine relativizes this independence into a nonessential variant of her own perpetual being.[34]

While Tillich's emphasis on the Mother-image of God seems to move away from the more hierarchical problems associated with God as "stern father," the mother-image is not without its problems. In fact, on a symbolic level, Plaskow believes that Tillich's thought contains two contradictory images of God's "mothering." On the one hand, Tillich seems to suggest that God as mother encourages autonomy, individuality, and self-actualization. Yet on the other hand, there is an image of a Mothering God whose children have "left home" without her permission, who have alienated themselves from her, and who need to be brought back into reunion with the Great Mother. Plaskow then makes a very interesting observation about this image: "If a hierarchal model is stunting to human selfhood, a part/whole model does not allow for the genuine independence of the self at all."[35] She goes on to say that Tillich's mother-image points toward a resistance to human independence, a desire to maintain a nonautonomous unity between children and mother.

Let's take this imagery one step further. At a symbolic level, does this image of the Divine-human relationship not describe what has been called

---

[33]Tillich, *Systematic Theology* 3:293-94.

[34]Erich Neumann, *The Great Mother: An Analysis of the Archetype,* Bollingen Series XLVII (Princeton NJ: Princeton University Press, 1972) 25.

[35]Plaskow, *Sex, Sin, and Grace,* 166.

a schizophrenic-creating "double-bind" message? "Be independent but do not leave." "Be autonomous but it's a sin." "Actualize your potential but you'll be estranged." "Move toward selfhood but if you do, you'll fall into sin." These are no-win scenarios, double-binding communications which leave one in profound confusion and ambivalence. In psychotherapy, they would clearly be seen as health-impairing messages from a neurotic parent to a struggling child. These messages point to a Mother-figure whose need to live through her children constantly violates the possibility of their own growth and maturity. While they seem to encourage autonomy, they equally suggest that differentiation from the Great Mother leads to disharmony and chaos. It must be better to remain a child at home than take the risk of differentiation from the Cosmic Mother.

In summary, then, we can restate Plaskow's concern as follows. Even though Tillich is a champion of "the courage to be" and speaks to many existential issues surrounding self-actualization, his larger ontology is at odds with these themes. His preoccupation with the God-human unity eclipses his emphasis on the dilemmas of selfhood. By equating self-actualization with fall into estrangement, his ontology indirectly chastises the movement toward personal freedom and independence. He therefore concentrates too much on the *active* sin of striving for selfhood and not enough on the *passive* sin of refusing the journey to selfhood. His ontology leaves no room for healthy self-actualization. Instead, to assert oneself is to fall into sin.

This criticism of how Tillich's ontological equation of separation and sin creates problems for self-actualization is somewhat similar to an earlier criticism: Tillich's use of the personal language of psychological acceptance is obscured by his understanding of God as "Being Itself," about whom we can say nothing which is nonsymbolic. The ongoing question is whether many of Tillich's richest insights in his theological anthropology are sacrificed at the altar of his ontology. Again, while this issue is beyond the scope of this book, I hope that it provokes, even in a small way, continued discussion by Tillich scholars and psychologists interested in Tillich.

Tillich, Marx, and Fromm on "the Fall" and Redemption

Tillich believes that Marx has provided an important service for humanity by indicting the pretensions of society and pointing toward an underworld of class conflict. Yet he also believes that Marx did not adequately grasp the fallenness of the human condition. Marx failed to recognize that today's oppressed, if liberated, would inevitably become tomorrow's oppressors. Marx, and later Fromm, end up with a utopian perspective, an overly optimistic eschatology.

Mary Thelan has insightfully analyzed Marx's thought as a secular version of "the Fall."[36] Marx's theory of human estrangement is a story about economics, not a story about the corruption of freedom. The "garden of Eden,' for Marx, is the stage of economic development in which primitive communism had no division of labor, and consequently, no class conflict. This was the period in which humans produced only enough goods for their own consumption. This was the "golden age" of equality and cooperative personal relationships. The pursuit of one's own interest did not involve the oppression of someone else.

Eventually, however, human beings began to produce more goods than they actually needed. This accumulation of surplus goods led to the disintegration of society by introducing a division of labor. Different "classes" emerged out of differing access to available goods. This division of labor produced self-alienation as persons became part of the economic machine. A vicious competition for more and more goods set human beings at odds with each other. As this alienation from one's neighbors emerged, the poor became alienated from both their own freedom and a larger sense of social meaning. Thelan puts it well.

> Finally, the original harmony between men and reality was lost. Instead of cooperating unconsciously with the changing techniques of production, man felt the course of history as a power alien to himself which holds him, helpless, in bondage to its external necessity.[37]

Thus "original sin" is described in the Marxist system of salvation. However, this diagnosis is not permanent.

The revolution of the poor (proletariat) will change this problem of alienation. In Marx's eschatology, healing from alienation will occur as persons are once again equal. We human beings will become masters of our society by controlling the economic factors which have alienated us. We will live in a classless society where brotherhood/sisterhood will reign.

---

[36]Mary Frances Thelan, *Man as Sinner in Contemporary American Realistic Theology* (Morningside Heights NY: King's Crown Press, 1946) 34-41.

[37]Thelan, *Man as Sinner in Contemporary American Realistic Theology*, 36.

Cooperation will rule the day. Such is Marx's apocalyptic vision, a very optimistic view of the future. The utopian ideal is on its way.

What is important to see here is that the notion of "ideology" is limited to the ruling class. In other words, ideology is a tool used by the ruling class to maintain the sickness of the social order. It is tainted, biased, and self-serving reason. It spins out elaborate theories to justify its own oppressive existence. Ideologies attempt to sanction the exploitation of the poor. Again, Thelan is insightful on this point.

> The ruling class succeeds in establishing and maintaining itself only by publishing the fiction that its rule is the common interest of all classes; thus the modern bourgeoisie employs the shibboleths of free trade and sacredness of property rights as instruments for keeping the proletariat in bondage and dispossessed. Its "freedom" is freedom to enslave, and its "property" is power to exploit.[38]

Unlike theologians, Marx does not blame "the Fall" on any sort of moral failing. This is simply the way economic production developed. Evil did not push humanity into this situation, and therefore, it cannot serve as a "cause." Instead, evil is a consequence of this social evolution. The correction of the problem *will* happen, and this redemption will not involve humanity's repentance and internal change. For Marx, all individual problems are in reality social and economic problems. There is nothing "wrong" with our psyches. Once the social and economic demons are cast out, the intrapsychic demons will disappear also. Again, the problem is not *within* us. It is this claim which places Marx at great variance with both the Christian tradition and the thought of Freud. Both will see Marx's view of the "redeemed" proletariat as quite naïve.

It is hard to overestimate the impact of Marx on psychoanalyst, Erich Fromm. Fromm's frequent label as a "psychoanalytic social psychologist" points toward his indebtedness to both Freud and Marx. Having a strong background in the dynamic views of psychoanalysis, Fromm is equally at home in a Marxist understanding of the social dynamics which undergird human behavior. Fromm clearly believes that familial relationships are significantly influenced by surrounding social structures. The parent-child world is not a universe unto itself. It is limited to, and shaped by, social reality. In fact, the family becomes the instrument by which the society

---

[38]Thelan, *Man as Sinner in Contemporary American Realistic Theology*, 39.

communicates and instills its basic values. Family reactions are a reflection of larger social relationships. As Guy Hammond puts it in describing Fromm's thought, "the family in a certain society tends to produce in its offspring a character structure desired or approved by that society."[39] This is what Fromm meant by social character. This is not to say that there are not important individual differences in personality formation. This is the value of psychoanalysis. But there is also room for a psychoanalytic social psychology which examines the patterns of society that shape a particular core of common character traits. This emphasis on the social factors in character formation leads to a study of sick societies. Again, Hammond states it clearly.

> When the role of the society in character formation is emphasized, the attention of the social psychologist is turned from individual pathology to social pathology, or, more specifically, to the "socially patterned defect" in individual character structure. Fromm's work in contrast to Freud's is therefore characterized by a prevailing interest in social pathology and in the possibility of social health or "the sane society."[40]

Thus, the Marxist impact on Fromm is obvious. To a large extent, consciousness is a social product. Yet Fromm did not go as far as Marx in reducing humanity's conscious ideas (ideology) to economic conditions of production. As we have seen, in Marx's thought human consciousness is an epiphenomenon or by-product of economic realities. Pocket books determine mental life. This even includes humanity's perception of itself and its own needs. Other than very few basic physiological needs, our understanding of our own human needs and drives is a social construction. Marx's materialism is the all-determining factor.

Fromm, on the other hand, believes this economic determinism is exaggerated. Marx correctly diagnoses "false consciousness" but unfortunately believes that this can be corrected by strictly economic means. For Fromm, Marx did not adequately consider the nonphysical needs of humanity. Some basic human needs simply transcend the physical.

Before examining Tillich's three primary characteristics of estrangement, I wish to turn our attention to Fromm's description of humanity's alienation, a description which also contains three primary ingredients. This

---

[39] Hammond, *Man in Estrangement*, 27.
[40] Hammond, *Man in Estrangement*, 27.

will be followed by a comparison of "remedies" for our condition offered by Tillich and Fromm.

The "Syndrome of Decay": Fromm's View of Estrangement

In a short, but very important first chapter of his book, *The Heart of Man: Its Genius for Good and Evil*, Fromm exposes some of his significant assumptions about the human condition.[41] He raises the question of whether or not human beings can best be understood as "wolves," "sheep," or a combination of both.[42] Fromm believes that this question concerning the essential goodness or evil of humanity has, of course, been debated for centuries in philosophy and religion.

Having been raised Jewish with a strong exposure to the Hebrew Scriptures, Fromm is convinced that the Hebrew Bible, or Christian Old Testament, does *not* teach that humanity is corrupt. In fact, says Fromm, Adam and Eve's disobedience is not understood as sin. Further, "the disobedience is the condition for man's self-awareness, for his capacity to choose, and thus in the last analysis this first act of disobedience is man's first step toward freedom."[43] This disobedience was a necessary part of human development.

What makes a person evil, in Fromm's view, is *doing* more and more evil. When the Hebrew Bible refers to the "hardening" of Pharoah's heart, for instance, this is a reference to the accumulated evil which can take a person over. As humanity *behaves* in evil ways, it *becomes* more evil. There is no notion here of evil or sin being a "condition," as in much of Christian thought.

This is consistent with the Jewish understanding of dual inclinations toward goodness and evil: *yester ha-rah* and *yester ha-tob*. The Hebrew understanding is that both these capacities reside within the human condition. It is a human being's responsibility to choose between these two options. As Fromm puts it, "Man is left alone with his "two strivings," that for good and for evil, and the decision is his alone.[44]

---

[41]Erich Fromm, *The Heart of Man: Its Genius for Good and Evil* (New York: Harper & Row, 1964).

[42]Fromm, *The Heart of Man*, 17-23.

[43]Fromm, *The Heart of Man*, 20-21.

[44]Fromm, *The Heart of Man*, 20.

Fromm acknowledges that Christian thought moves in a different direction with its concept of original sin and the bondage of the will. While Fromm objects to this pessimistic line of thought, he does not want to be perceived as a naïve optimist. He states this directly:

> As one whose views have often been misrepresented as underestimating the potential of evil within man, I want to emphasize that such sentimental optimism is not the mood of my thought. It would be difficult indeed for anyone who has a long clinical experience as a psychoanalyst to belittle the destructive forces within man.[45]

Nevertheless, Fromm does not believe that the mere existence of destructive forces within humanity indicates that those destructive forces are *primary*. They may well represent a distortion of deeper, more positive inclinations. Also, the presence of destructive inclinations does not mean that they cannot be overcome. They are not necessarily a permanent fixture of the human condition.

As I shall discuss later, one can see a clear difference between Fromm and Tillich on this issue. Fromm holds onto the possibility that humanity can overcome its situation *without any outside help* and manage to sustain a good life. Stated simply, we can overcome our alienation. For Tillich, on the other hand, we are much too alienated or estranged to be able to accomplish this on our own.

Fromm's first symptom of the syndrome of decay is a form of lifelessness. He makes the following extremely interesting statement: "There is no more fundamental distinction between men, psychologically and morally, than the one between those who love death and those who love life, between the necrophilous and the biophilous."[46] Fromm goes on to say that very few are totally life-affirming or death-affirming. We are a mixture. But the crucial issue is which one is dominant within us. Fromm uses the term "necrophilous" as an expansion of the type of paraphilia often called necrophilia, a desire for intercourse with corpses. But he expands the notion to include all forms of lifelessness—psychologically as well as physically. While many necrophiles are literally preoccupied with corpses, sickness, burial, and destruction, others are fascinated with psychological control, dominance, and the extinguishing of another's liveliness. They

---

[45]Fromm, *The Heart of Man*, 21.
[46]Fromm, *The Heart of Man*, 38.

"kill" another's spirit. They seek to transform a lively partner into a robotic, "dead" person. They enjoy the denial of another's freedom. They love "force" because this involves the ability to kill and dominate another. The necrophile wants nothing to grow, expand, or exhibit signs of life. Further, the necrophile's joy comes from control and draining the life and independence from another. The necrophile is literally a "kill joy."

> Necrophilia constitutes a fundamental orientation; it is the one answer to life which is in complete opposition to life; it is the most morbid and the most dangerous among the orientations to life of which man is capable. It is true perversion: while being alive, not life but death is loved; not growth but destruction.[47]

By contrast, the biophilous person is very similar to Maslow's self-actualizing person or Rogers's fully functioning person. It is expressed in what Fromm calls the "productive orientation." This is the person who loves life, growth, and expansion, the person who prefers adventure in new territory rather than the rut of familiarity. He or she enjoys loving, reasoning, pulling things together rather than pushing things apart.[48] The motivation is to live fully, experience deeply, and affirm human existence.

As we have seen, Fromm believes that we are all a mixture of biophilous and necrophilous tendencies. However, he differs from Freud in that he does *not* think these two inclinations are ineradicable, biological instincts (which Freud called *eros* and *thanatos*) in constant battle. Fromm instead believes that the death instinct is a secondary, rather than primary, tendency. It emerges as an outgrowth of the frustration of the life-instinct. In other words, it is the blocking and distorting of the life instinct which makes the death instinct possible. Stated differently, the "death instinct" is not natural. "Most living beings," says Fromm, "seem to fight for life with an extraordinary tenacity, and only exceptionally do they tend to destroy themselves."[49]

> In this view the "death instinct" is a *malignant* phenomenon which grows and takes over to the extent to which Eros does not unfold. The death instinct represents *psychopathology*, and not, as in Freud's view, a part of *normal biology*. The life instinct thus constitutes the primary potentiality

---

[47]Fromm, *The Heart of Man*, 45.
[48]Fromm, *The Heart of Man*, 47.
[49]Fromm, *The Heart of Man*, 49.

in man; the death instinct a secondary potentiality. The primary potentiality develops if the appropriate conditions of life are present, just as a seed grows only if the proper conditions of moisture, temperature, etc., are given. If the proper conditions are not given, the necrophilous tendencies will emerge and dominate the person.[50]

Fromm goes on to describe the important conditions which are necessary for the emergence of biophilia. These conditions include loving, encouraging, consistently affectionate contact with others. They also include an absence of conditional threats to one's acceptance. In short, this context sounds very much like the kind of therapeutic atmosphere described by Rogers and other humanistic psychotherapists.

A second ingredient in what Fromm calls the "syndrome of decay" is malignant narcissism. By specifying "malignant" narcissism, Fromm is indicating that some forms of narcissism are benign. Further, he believes that a certain degree of narcissism is functional in that it aids survival. After all, if we had little interest in our own lives, survival would be more problematic.

Benign narcissism involves a pride in our own efforts and achievements. This pride, however, is not based merely on the fact that *we* have produced the work. If that were the case, anything we did would be considered "wonderful" without any sort of reality check whatsoever. While the motivation for our work may be narcissistic in nature, benign narcissism is able to critically evaluate that work and check it with other achievements. The mere fact that we are relating our work to that of others helps keep our narcissism at bay. We have a "reality check" with the world outside our own awareness.

With malignant narcissism, however, the elevated self-evaluation is based on nothing external to our own awareness. Put simply, it doesn't matter if we have "nothing to show for it." The achievement is great because *we did it*, not because it stands as something important. In fact, it doesn't matter that we don't really achieve or produce. Our self-inflation is simply based on being who we are—special, unique, entitled. There need not be any *reason* for us to be proud. Our exaggerated pride simply *is*. Justification is unnecessary. Unlike benign narcissism which is able to

---

[50]Fromm, *The Heart of Man*, 50-51.

check itself against external forms of achievement, malignant narcissism has no such checks in reality.

> If I am "great" because of some quality I *have*, and not because of something I *achieve*, I do not need to be related to anybody or anything; I need not make any effort. In maintaining the picture of my greatness I remove myself more and more from reality and I have to increase the narcissistic charge in order to be better protected from the danger that my narcissistically inflated ego might be revealed as the product of my empty imagination. Malignant narcissism, thus, is not self-limiting, and in consequence it is crudely solipsistic as well as xenophobic.[51]

Thus, for malignant narcissists, other people are simply instruments who can serve as an adoring audience. The capacity to love, or to be emotionally available, are all enormously distorted. As malignant narcissists, we love out of a delusional world in which we are the center of the universe. We will also highly elevate anything or anyone connected to us. Our spouses are wonderful simply because they belong to *us*, our children are fabulous simply because the kids are *ours*, the town we live in is spectacular because it is an extension of *us*, and so on. Thus malignant narcissists, as Fromm suggests, have greatly impaired rational judgment. They are unable to look at the objective merits or value of anything. If it is connected to them, it is great. Reason becomes egocentrically biased. As Fromm tells us, however, this is hard for the narcissist to see.

> Usually the person is convinced that there is no bias, and that his judgment is objective and realistic. This leads to a severe distortion of his capacities to think and to judge, since this capacity is blunted again and again when he deals with himself and what is his. Correspondingly, the narcissistic person's judgment is also biased against that which is not "he" or not his. The extraneous ("not me") world is inferior, dangerous, immoral. The narcissistic person then, ends up with an enormous distortion. He and his are overevaluated. Everything outside is underestimated. The danger to reason and objectivity is obvious.

Social narcissism is not as easy to recognize as individual narcissism, but it is very real and dangerous. The features are the same except that a group further reinforces each other's elevated status. The "sense of reality" is strengthened by collective support. The sense of superiority is rampant.

---

[51]Fromm, *The Heart of Man*, 77.

The essence of this overestimation of one's own position and the hate for all who differ from it is narcissism. "We" are admirable; "they" are despicable. "We" are good; "they" are evil. Any criticism of one's own doctrine is a vicious and unbearable attack; criticism of the other's position is a well-meant attempt to help them return the truth.[52]

The irony is that even religious groups, which would seem to have their narcissism checked by the concept of God, often find their narcissism fueled because they are playing on the "right team." Instead of recognizing their own limitations and finitude in contrast to a Deity who represents omniscience and omnipotence, they instead identify with God's absoluteness in a manner which further inflates their narcissism. Fromm states this pointedly.

[W]hile the concept of an indefinable and indescribable God was the negation of idolatry and narcissism, God soon became again an idol; man identified himself with God in a narcissistic manner, and thus in full contradiction to the original function of the concept of God, religion became a manifestation of group narcissism.[53]

A third ingredient within what Fromm describes as the "syndrome of decay" is what he calls "incestrous fixation on mother."[54] As was the case with his description of the necrophile, so here, too, Fromm expands what we consider incestuous fixation. While he believes that Freud correctly focused on the problem of a little boy's libidinous attachment to mother (Oedipus complex) and the little girl's fascination with father (Electra complex), a previous, prelibido fixation is more significant. This preoedipal attachment to mother can be found in *both* girls and boys. This pregenital connection is a natural outgrowth of a person's desire for protection, certainty, and the freedom from responsibility. Initially, of course, the infant is helpless and needs precisely this kind of caretaking. The problem is that we can become fixated here and the desire for certainty, security, protection, and unconditional love can push us toward seeing "mother" everywhere, even after our biological mother may not be available. The search for "mother" reveals a desire for a life without risks. In fact, there may be a strange longing for lifelessness, or life back in the womb. This

---

[52]Fromm, *The Heart of Man*, 82.
[53]Fromm, *The Heart of Man*, 89-90.
[54]Fromm, *The Heart of Man*, 95.

desire involves a complete identification with the mothering figure, a symbiotic attachment which eliminates personal freedom and responsibility. Insofar as being human means deciding, choosing, and taking risks, this womb-return hides a desire for a kind of death. Womb and tomb seem strangely similar.

Fromm admits that while various human beings have different levels of mother-fixation, some forms are much more benign than others. All of us struggle to be independent persons and the desire to be part of our "mothers," particularly during stressful times, is probably always present. In severe cases, however, there is a complete symbiotic attachment. This goes beyond dependency because dependency assumes that two people are separate. There is an inseparability here, an attachment which is deeper than dependency. As Fromm says, "it is a desire to lose completely one's individuality, to become one again with nature."[55] This, again, is a deeply regressive retreat from life, a desire to psychologically cease to exist.

It is interesting to think about the implications of Fromm's view for pantheism. Is it, too, a sort of psychological regression in which one fuses again with mother-God as a way to avoid the fear of aloneness and autonomy? While many would immediately take issue with such a claim, it is worth some thought. Does a desire to merge with God in a symbiotic attachment expose a deep fear of being a "self?"

The desire to merge with any mothering ideology, group, or nation, can be so strong that we may want to eliminate the burden of individuality. We seek escape through a return to a symbol for mother.

> If I fail to cut the umbilical cord, if I insist on worshipping the idol of certainty and protection, then the idol becomes sacred. It must not be criticized. If "mother" cannot be wrong, how can I judge anyone else objectively if he is in conflict with "mother" or disapproved by her? This form of impairment of judgment is much less obvious when the object of fixation is not mother but the family, the nation, or he race. . . . The tendency to remain bound to the mothering person and her equivalents—to blood, family, and tribe—is inherent in all men and women. It is constantly in conflict with the opposite tendency—to be born, to progress, to grow. In the case of normal development, the tendency for growth wins. In the case of severe pathology, the regressive tendency for symbiotic union wins, and it results in the person's more or less total incapacitation.

---

[55]Fromm, *The Heart of Man*, 105.

> Freud's concept of the incestuous strivings to be found in any child is perfectly correct. Yet the significance of this concept transcends Freud's own assumption. Incestuous wishes are not primarily a result of sexual desires, but constitute one of the most fundamental tendencies in man: the wish to remain tied to where he came from, the fear of being free, and the fear of being destroyed by the very figure toward whom he has made himself helpless, renouncing his independence.[56]

Fromm's experience with the authoritarianism of Nazi Germany and the manner in which so many persons gave up their freedom to be protected by the "motherland" is clearly behind much of his insight here. The craving for a thoughtless, unruffled, perfectly secure world can seduce persons away from the rigors of personhood.

So these, then, are the three elements in Fromm's syndrome of decay: necrophilous tendencies, malignant narcissism, and an incestuous mother fixation. They represent lifelessness and destruction, radical self-centeredness, and a dehumanized craving for security. They distort their opposing tendencies to be life-affirming, to care for others, and to be open toward life as an adventure.

Tillich's Three Characteristics of Estrangement

Like Fromm, Tillich also describes three features of estrangement. While he offers much insight into each of these characteristics, he is careful to insist that none of these characteristics represents the *cause* of our estrangement. Instead, these characteristics are manifestations of our condition.

The first characteristic is unbelief, or better, "unfaith." This has less to do with the rejection of particular beliefs and more to do with distrusting or "turning away" from the Ground of our being. Tillich has been deeply influenced by both depth psychology and the Protestant reformers on this issue of distrust or "unfaith." From his background in depth psychology, he is convinced that much of the distrust process is unconscious. We cannot always consciously control our level of trust in the Divine. The command to "have more faith" often overlooks this psychological reality. Tillich has also been influenced by the Reformers in that he sees "unfaith" as a distrust stemming from our whole being than a rejection of certain doctrinal notions. "Unfaith" is far more than a lack of cognitive assent. The

---

[56]Fromm, *The Heart of Man*, 106-108.

acknowledgment of outdated theological positions which have been rigidly upheld for centuries does not represent a dynamic faith. Faith is an existential enterprise, not a mere cognitive exercise.

The loss of a trust in the Ground of our Being also affects our relationship with others and with ourselves. We have forfeited our centeredness in God and our lives are now out-of-balance. Without a trust in our Source, our anxiety often becomes so severe that it completely preoccupies us. We have nothing to offer others because we feel lost at sea, ungrounded, desiring some form of comfort and security. This anxious world robs us of our ability to care for others and to love. Our anxiety arrests our attention and holds us hostage.

Distrust leads to the next manifestation of estrangement, which Tillich calls "hubris," pride, or self-elevation. The main factor in hubris is a refusal to see our finitude. We become the center of the universe. Hubris is the "flip side" of distrust or unbelief. With God removed as the center of our being, something has to fill God's place. That something quickly becomes us. This self-elevation is true of individuals and groups alike. Tillich puts it this way.

> [T]he self-elevation of a group happens through the self-elevation of individuals. Every individual within and outside the group falls into moments of *hubris*. All men have the hidden desire to be like God, and they act accordingly in their self-evaluation and self-affirmation. No one is willing to acknowledge, in concrete terms, his finitude, his weakness and his errors, his ignorance and his insecurity, his loneliness and his anxiety. And if he is ready to acknowledge them, he makes another instrument of *hubris* out of his readiness. A demonic structure drives man to confuse natural self-affirmation with destructive self-elevation.[57]

Note the deceptive nature of human self-elevation. Even if we "catch ourselves" in our pride, we become quite prideful about this recognition. We are more internally aware, more insightful, more spiritually sensitive than all of the other intrapsychically uninformed people around us. Hubris, then, with its prison of self-preoccupation, is very similar to Fromm's malignant narcissism.

Tillich's third characteristic of estrangement is "concupiscence," which is inordinate desire, craving, or lust for finite things. As Tillich says, con-

---

[57]Tillich, *Systematic Theology* 2:51.

cupiscence has the quality of trying to pull the whole world into oneself.[58] While this word has frequently been associated with sexual lust, it is important to recognize that it can involve any sort of finite thing or experience. In fact, concupiscence is very close to our contemporary understanding of addiction. It is also associated with the notion of idolatry. As an inordinate desire for finite things, concupiscence deifies its object. Its object (money, power, sex, social status, and so on) becomes pivotal for our entire existence. We become convinced that we simply cannot live without it. Stated simply, *some*thing becomes *every*thing.

Tillich's three characteristics of estrangement feed off of each other. Distrust or "unfaith" creates a vacuum in the center of human life which is taken over by the self. The self is not designed to be its own ultimate concern. Once the self has been elevated to the center of the universe (hubris), it desires things disproportionately (concupiscence). Having lost our centeredness in God and pridefully placed ourselves at the center of our existence, we then attempt to satisfy our deep need for communion with God by fixating on finite objects. We remain unsatisfied as we move from object to object in an attempt to satisfy our hunger for relationship with our Source and Ground of Being. Augustine's influence on Tillich is obvious here.

There are some similarities between the descriptions of distorted human nature in Fromm and Tillich. Tillich's "hubris" and Fromm's "malignant narcissism," as we have seen, bear many similarities. The most obvious difference, however, is that "unbelief," or "distrust" does not play a major role in Fromm's naturalistic humanism. For Fromm, "God" is a symbol for human potential. He reduces all theological language to psychological or anthropological language.

Fromm's Vision and Tillich's Critique

Fromm understands the human condition through a three-stage evolutionary process. He believes that human beings were originally one with nature, unencumbered by the burden of self-consciousness. Indeed, our unity with nature was a prehuman state characterized by harmony with the basic rhythms of nature.

---

[58]Tillich, *Systematic Theology* 2:52.

Eventually, however, a break with nature occurred because of the dawning of self-consciousness. We human beings became self-reflective, self-transcendent, and capable of understanding our separateness from the natural world. Of course we were still embedded in nature, but higher thought processes pushed us toward a self-reflective transcendence. This self-transcendence, however, should in no way be confused with a Divine realm. It is a purely human process. We once only had instincts; now we can reflect on those instincts. Hammond provides a helpful description of Fromm's understanding of the evolution of human consciousness.

> He must go out from his "home" in nature and see himself as a distinct and separate entity before he can be reunited with nature, his fellow man, and himself, on a higher conscious level. He must, in a word, become alienated; full realization lies on the other side of alienation.[59]

Clearly, in this view, alienation is a necessary step toward full human consciousness. It is worth noting Fromm's similarity with Tillich in claiming that alienation or estrangement is a basic component of actualizing human consciousness. Both Fromm and Tillich seem to say that alienation is a necessary price paid for the emergence of human freedom.

According to Fromm, previous societies did not offer a situation in which humanity could experience full consciousness. Modern society, on the other hand, offers such a world, though no one has completely achieved it.[60] But the important thing for Fromm is that *both* alienation and reconciliation are naturalistic concepts. Alienation is part of the journey toward full humanity, a necessary step without which full consciousness could never be achieved.

It is important to recall Tillich's basic conviction that the alienation process is *total*. This means that we are estranged from all dimensions of life, including ourselves. As Hammond points out, Tillich was well aware of two divisions of thought among existentialists: those who see estrangement as total and those who see it as partial, and hence, humanly curable. Hammond offers a helpful way of labeling these two divisions: the "radical existentialists" and the "utopian existentialists."[61] The radical existentialists believe that reconciliation is not possible. To be human is to be alienated.

---

[59]Hammond, *Man in Estrangement*, 65.

[60]Hammond, *Man in Estrangement*, 76.

[61]Hammond, *Man in Estrangement*, 117.

And this alienation is tragic. Humanity cannot resolve its alienation problem. In this group, Tillich places Nietzsche, Heidegger, Jaspers, Bergson, and Sartre. Healing or salvation is simply not going to happen. Freud, also, would be in this group.

The more optimistic group, the "utopian existentialists," argue that alienation is indeed a present reality but that it can be eventually overcome. Through psychological and social development, the alienation problem will eventually be rectified. Tillich puts both Jung and Fromm within this group. This group does not hold a tragic view of human existence. For Tillich, they have minimized the human predicament. And again, when we deny that estrangement is total, we are saying that some "unestranged" or "unalienated" part of ourselves must salvage or heal the estranged part. This is the only way a naturalistic view of redemption can work. The healthy dimension within us must heal the unhealthy part. Estranged existence cannot produce its own cure.

For Tillich, all views of estrangement, including the most tragic ones, necessitate a concept of humanity healed. We cannot understand something as "sick" unless we have a vision of health. This is why Tillich believed that even the essence-denying wing of existentialism (including Sartre) actually has an implicit understanding of human essence. Lurking beyond the dark images of existentialism is a perception of what humanity is in its essence, fullness, or healthiness. Again, if we assume we are alienated, we must be working with an assumption about what we are alienated *from*. Often these same existentialists who beckon us toward some type of healing are also telling us that alienation can never be overcome.

The third part of Fromm's evolutionary process is an eschatological vision in which we will once again be unified with nature. But this will not be a simple return to preconscious days. Once we have tasted self-consciousness we can never go back. In his *The Sane Society*, Fromm puts it this way.

> The problem of man's existence, then, is unique in the whole of nature; he has fallen out of nature, as it were, and is still in it; he is partly divine, partly animal; partly infinite, partly finite. *The necessity to find ever-new solutions for the contradictions in his existence, to find ever-higher forms of unity with nature, his fellowman and himself, is the source of all of all*

> *psychic forces which motivate man, of all his passions, affects and anxieties.*[62]

So, on the one hand, we are "freaks of the universe," yet on the other hand this is a necessary part of our becoming fully human. We cannot remain in limbo, kicked out of nature and standing isolated and naked with no direction. Instead, we seek a reunion with nature but this must come through the development of full human consciousness and productivity. The analogy of being expelled from the Garden of Eden (nature) is obvious. Yet his process of being kicked out of nature's garden has the benefit of helping us find our human potential. Of course, we are vulnerable, helpless, and "alienated," but it is part of the road to fulfillment.

So human nature has a goal—full human consciousness or the turning of the unconscious into consciousness. Once full consciousness is achieved, humanity will once again be reunited with nature. The estrangement will be overcome. The salvific agent, then, is greater self-awareness.

The actualities of the potential inherent in human nature is called the "productive orientation." The productive orientation, which seems quite similar to the humanistic concept of self-actualization, overcomes our separation with each other and ourselves through the use of reason, love, and creativity. However, for Fromm, this does not become a biologically unfolding or "blossoming" process. It requires some struggle as we wrestle with conflicting tendencies to move forward or to regress. Regardless of how much progress we have "under our belts," we still have a tug toward regression. The lure of destruction may never completely go away but it can be overcome.

In spite of this tug toward regression, Fromm clearly understands human "redemption" as a self-healing process. Humanity must save itself. In fact, for Fromm, the whole notion of God's grace is a symbolic way of talking about what humanity gives itself. It is *our* love, not God's love for us, which is healing. All theological statements are reduced to anthropological ones.

> The human reality behind the concept of man's love for God in humanistic religion is man's ability to love productively, to love without greed, without submission and domination, to love from the fullness of his

---

[62]Erich Fromm, *The Sane Society* (Greenwich CT: Fawcett Publications, 1955) 31.

personality, just as God's love is a symbol for love out of strength and not out of weakness.[63]

For Fromm, then, "God" does not refer to a power beyond humanity, but is instead, a symbol for humanity's own power. God represents the "higher self" of humanistic religion. "God" is what human beings ought to become.

Tillich is predictably critical of what he considers to be Fromm's utopian perspective. In his review of Fromm's *The Sane Society*, he finds Fromm to be deeply insightful in his description of alienation.[64]

> The description of this alienation is carried through with passion and profound insight. One is fascinated page after page by the incisiveness of the analysis, the concreteness of the presentation, and the beauty of the style.[65]

Nevertheless, while Fromm's diagnosis of the human condition is strong, his prognosis is too optimistic. Tillich argues that the fundamental difference between theological estrangement and Fromm's alienation is the latter's assumption that humanity can heal itself. Fromm, like Marx, ends us with a utopian world in which alienation is conquered. There is nothing outside, beneath, or beyond humanity which helps this healing process. Humanity is on its own. And much like Feuerbach, Fromm believes that projecting our own strength onto a "God" who rescues us is a form of self-sabotage. Tillich questions any possibility of humanity overcoming its own alientation.

> How can alienated man overcome alienation by himself? How can the "dead" man of the twentieth century revive himself? Without an answer to these questions Fromm's description of communitarian humanism sounds utopian.[66]

Though he writes a great deal about humanity's tendency toward destruction, Fromm does not hold to Freud's pessimistic position that this destructive impulse cannot be overcome. As we have mentioned, the destructive impulse arises from the frustration of a deeper life-affirming im-

---

[63]Erich Fromm, *Psychoanalysis and Religion* (New York: Bantam, 1967) 84-85.
[64]Paul Tillich, "Erich Fromm's *The Sane Society*," in *The Meaning of Health*, ed. Perry LeFevre, 96-99.
[65]Tillich, "Erich Fromm's *The Sane Society*," 96.
[66]Tillich, "Erich Fromm's *The Sane Society*," 99.

pulse. Thus, Fromm does not necessarily see the death instinct, with all its accompanying aggression, as a permanent fixture within the human psyche. As Guy Hammond states, "The main tenor of his work seems to imply that the regressive impulse (or the 'death wish') is not an ineradicable instinct in human nature. It can be overcome, and perhaps eliminated, through the power of consciousness, through a social and historical process."[67] Fuller consciousness will bring less destructiveness. In fact, fuller consciousness is the key to all our ills. Fromm believes we can use the positive elements of reason, creativity, and love to minimize and perhaps eventually dissolve human destructiveness. Again, we must supply our own healing. This will be a gradual, evolutionary process.

For Tillich, because estrangement invades all dimensions of our being, we can never offer ourselves redemption or healing. Fromm's perspective, while insightful, does not take into consideration the primary reality of our alienation, namely, we are estranged from the Ground or Source of life. This separation from God spills over into the other dimensions of alienation, including alienation from ourselves as well as others. As finite creatures, we will never experience the kind of utopian full-consciousness Fromm describes. "Life in all periods is ambiguous, and there is no period in which the negative is absolutely predominant, nor will there be a period in which the positive is absolutely predominant."[68] This ambiguity will prevail and the ultimate healing of our estrangement will be a gift of grace.

The differences between Tillich and Fromm are profound. They emerged very clearly in the discussions of the New York Psychology Group. It is to this fascinating group of individuals who comprised the New York Psychology Group, and the particular tensions between Tillich and Fromm, that I now turn our attention.

---

[67]Hammond, *Man in Estrangement*, 63.
[68]Tillich, "Erich Fromm's *The Sane Society*," 98.

Chapter 4

The Psychology of Faith and Love: The New York Psychology Group, 1941–1943

> *Faith precedes all attempts to derive it from something else, because these attempts are themselves based on faith.* —Paul Tillich

Theology's dialogue with psychology, and particularly Tillich's involvement, probably found no better forum than the so-called "New York Psychology Group," which met from 1941 to 1945. This group, along with its intensely interesting discussions, has received very little attention. Even though group members included such figures as Erich Fromm, Rollo May, Ruth Benedict, Seward Hiltner, Carl Rogers, David Roberts, and Tillich himself, very little has been written about this group's meetings. The primary source for the group, as I mentioned in the preface, has been Allison Stokes, whose exemplary book, *Ministry after Freud*, contains a very informative chapter on the group.[1] As I stated in the acknowledgments, I am indebted to Allison for providing me with a copy of the New York Psychology Group materials, a copy she received directly from one of its founding members, Seward Hiltner. As I previously indicated, Hiltner, perhaps the most important figure in forming this group, had given her the entire notes of all the meetings. A stenographer had been present at all the group meetings and therefore all the discussions were accurately recorded. This is a treasure of mid-century dialogue.

The group met for almost four years and their topics included "The Psychology of Faith," "The Psychology of Love," "The Psychology of Conscience," and "The Psychology of Helping." The group met twenty-nine times on Friday evenings in various New York apartments. Members included theologians, psychiatrists, psychologists, philosophers, anthropologists, and others. There were representatives from both Freudian and Jungian perspectives.

What I attempt in this chapter, as well as the following one, is a brief, narrative summary of the key issues brought up in this group. Granted, like all hermeneutical investigations, my own interest and preunderstanding limit the possibility of a completely neutral summary of the group's

---

[1] Allison Stokes, *Ministry after Freud* (New York: Pilgrim Press, 1985).

discussion. The mere fact that I attend to some comments more than others indicates that I enter these discussions already looking for certain things. However, in my attempt to be a fly on the wall at these historic meetings, I have tried to allow the most pressing issues of the group to speak to me. What I attempt, then, is a summary of these discussions. While the group's comments are interspersed with my own attempts at clarification, I have worked hard to not put words in anyone's mouth. I reserve extended commentary until the end of the chapter.

Because of some overlapping concerns, I have lumped together the first two years in this chapter and the second two years in the following chapter. This is why this chapter bears the name "The Psychology of Faith and Love," and the following chapter is called, "Ethics and Psychotherapy."

Perhaps I should briefly mention the names of the individuals involved, but for an excellent overview and short biography of all the persons present, please see Allison Stokes's excellent chapter.[2] Other than Hiltner, Tillich, and Fromm, who were quite regular attendees, many other members were very loyal to these meetings. These included clinical psychologist Harry Bone; General Theological Seminary professor Thomas Bigham; psychiatrist Gotthard Booth; Union Seminary professor David Roberts; hospital chaplain Otis Rice; Freudian analyst Ernest Schachtel; Jungian analyst Elined Prys Kotschnig and husband, Walter Maria Kotschnig, professor of Comparative Education; Jungian analysts Violet de Laszlo, Frances Wickes, Martha Glickman, Elizabeth Rohrbach, and E. McClung Feming; artist Hannah Tillich; Freudian analyst Greta Frankley; anthropology professor Ruth Benedict; Kent fellow Helen Nichol; Union Seminary professor Harrison Elliott; humanistic psychologist Carl Rogers; and, of course, Rollo May who was very attentive to the group until he had to drop out for health reasons. At one point or another, other people participated briefly in the group, but I have named the central members.

First Year: Psychology of Faith

During the first year of the New York Psychology Group, 1941–1942, the topic was the psychology of faith. The general direction of this discussion leaned more toward the nature and dynamics of faith itself as a psychological process rather than a concern with the specific objects of faith. The

---

[2]Stokes, *Ministry after Freud*, chap. 6.

relationship between faith and healthy personality, faith and doubt, and faith and freedom were central concerns. However, the inevitable relationship between the *process* of faith and the *content* of faith soon emerged in discussion. Faith as a psychological attitude moved toward a discussion of belief in a particular content. In *what* should we have faith? For some of the group members it seemed clear that faith should be invested in human potential, a kind of this-worldly commitment which refused to acknowledge any legitimacy to a transcendent realm. Other group members spoke about the need for a dimension of the infinite, the unconditioned, or the ultimate in life—a dimension which clearly goes beyond human finitude. If nature and humanity represent the first two realms, this transcendent dimension represented the third. Whether or not this realm should be symbolized by the word "God" was an open question.

A careful reading of the presentations and discussions of the first year of meetings quickly reveals that Erich Fromm and Paul Tillich were the two most central representatives of an emergent division within the group. Throughout the entire first year, Fromm never missed a meeting, and provided more input in the discussion than anyone else. Fromm was fresh from having just published *Escape from Freedom* (*The Fear of Freedom* in Britain, 1941) and his comments often reflect the themes of that book: the hazards of authority, the nature of sadomasochistic religion, the idea that empowering God means disempowering humanity, and the deep Feuerbachian conviction that "God" is a symbol for the best in humanity.[3] Fromm was the primary spokesman for group members who believed that a theological dimension, or reference to a transcendent reality, was at best useless, and a distraction from faith in human aspirations. Simply stated, Fromm was the representative of a thoroughgoing secularism. All references to "God" were references to the potentialities of the human. Any faith which looks for God in a transcendent realm, independent from the human, is inevitably an irrational, authoritarian religion. And for Fromm, the word "authoritarian" is about the most despicable word in our vocabulary.

Tillich, on the other hand, was the primary spokesman for the other side of the group, a representation which is rather outstanding considering the fact that Tillich missed four out of the eight meetings during that first

---

[3]Erich Fromm, *Escape from Freedom* (New York: Holt, Rinehart, and Winston, 1941).

year. Some group members recognized the need for an ultimate, unconditioned realm which one could encounter in the depths of the human dimension, but which was *not identifiable with the human dimension*. This dimension of the infinite, "the holy," and the unconditioned, is clearly more than Fromm's human potential. Further, recognizing our dependence on this ultimate realm does not necessarily involve an insult to human aspirations, as Fromm believed. Instead, we "belong" to this other dimension even though we are currently separated or estranged from it. For Fromm, we are only estranged from ourselves and others. For Tillich, we are also estranged from our Ground and Source. This ultimate dimension is the dimension of Being-Itself or the Ground of Being. "God" is the symbol for this unconditioned realm. Because all language is finite, conditioned, and limited, we cannot possibly speak about that which is infinite, unconditioned, and unlimited. Therefore, the language of faith is the language of symbols.

An interesting issue during this first year of discussion is that Fromm does not believe that Tillich is being completely honest about theological language. Sounding almost Barthian, Fromm believes Tillich's abstract, ontological language about God as "Being-Itself" is inconsistent with what the biblical tradition (both Old and New Testaments) referred to by "God." By refusing to describe God as a Divine Being, Tillich, according to Fromm, is not being consistent with the clear meaning of the entire Judeo-Christian tradition. If Tillich wants to believe this, that's fine, but he should not pretend that this is what the history of both Jewish and Christian traditions have been saying about God. By "ontologizing" and "depersonalizing" God, Tillich does not represent the Western tradition.

Tillich was not present on December 5, 1941, the first meeting of the group. Fromm quickly asked whether the group would consider the issue of the psychology of doubt as a part of the psychology of faith. For Fromm, this was important since there is more clinical evidence on the issue of doubt than on faith. Fromm was particularly interested in the issue of compulsive doubt. The group agreed that this was an important topic as well, particularly since the focus would be primarily on faith as an attitude or psychological experience.

Early in this first session, the issue of "faith in goodness" and "faith in evil" came up. Seward Hiltner asked Fromm how he would distinguish "good" and "evil" faith. Fromm responded that the distinction would be based on whether or not the person is acting freely or spontaneously. Stated differently, "good" faith emerges from a "free character structure." In this comment, we see the strong optimism in Fromm: to act freely, to act unencumbered by the distorting influences of society, is to act ethically and with good faith. As long as our freedom is not impaired by contaminating external factors, we can completely trust our own ability to act in good faith. The similarity with Carl Rogers, Abraham Maslow, and other humanistic psychologists is obvious. As we saw in chapter 3, Fromm's view that the source of estrangement is strictly in the social order put him in conflict with Tillich, who believed this to be a minimization of the problem of alienation.

Elined Kotschnig then asked the interesting question of whether faith does not always include "some kind of belief in the fundamental goodness of the universe."[4] Fromm immediately responded that this question also raises the issue of whether faith differs among persons according to their personality types. For instance, using his categories of the symbiotic and sadomasochistic personalities, he suggested that these individuals are incapable of a "faith in the goodness of the universe."[5] Hiltner then suggested that this faith in the goodness of the universe should perhaps be called "basic faith" to distinguish it from our normal usage of faith.[6] Fromm added that the Hebrew word for faith refers to "firmness" rather than a "body of opinions."[7] Fromm then made the following observation about faith: "It is an expression of something attitudinal (whole personality), the term in itself not implying relationship to a 'special object.' "[8]

In Fromm's mind, then, this basic faith or "firmness of faith," does not necessarily need an object. One wonders exactly what Fromm meant by this. While faith may *seem* like a vague or general disposition toward life, if we press it, doesn't it eventually have a content, also? Surely, Fromm was speaking about a faith in *human possibilities* or a faith in *the rationality of life* or faith in *an ontological structure of meaning*. Even having "faith in faith" refers to a specific content, namely, that we believe the attitude of faith to be healing.

---

[4] The New York Psychology Group of the National Council on Religion in Higher Education, 1941–1945, 3. (Hereafter cited as NYPG 1941–1945.)
[5] NYPG 1941–1945, 3.
[6] NYPS 1941–1945, 3.
[7] NYPG 1941–1945, 3.
[8] NYPG 1941–1945, 3.

In looking at this first meeting, as well as the discussion for the entire first year of the New York Psychology Group, it is clear that Fromm was the key player. He provided the direction for many of the discussions. The topics dealt with major themes of Fromm's work: faith as "firmness," destructive or authoritarian faith, the radical importance of human freedom, the relationship between faith and personality structure, and sadomasochistic religion.

Tillich was present at the second meeting. The general theme dealt with the inner psychological experience of faith. Dr. Martha Glickman began with a very brief clinical description, written by one of her patients, of the emergence of faith during psychoanalysis. This patient moved from (a) faith in nothing, to (b) faith in the analyst, to (c) faith in the larger reality of life. Elined Kotschnig then described her own experience in analysis, a process she portrayed through several pictures she had drawn. Of particular note was a ship sailing into darkness, which she interpreted as a new attitude of confidence or a faith in exploring something which might be dangerous. She suggested that in the process of analysis she was "saved to" a sense of the newness of life. Her pictures, she said, all pointed toward the redemption of darkness in her own inward journey.

> Salvation comes from facing the perils with the discovery that there is something that can hold them in check. If they are faced, they turn out to be good things in disguise—sheep in wolves' clothing.[9]

True discovery must therefore involve both the darkness and the light. Mrs. Kotschnig went on to show other drawings which unconsciously symbolized this duality of darkness and light. The recognition of these dual principles, she suggested, indicates that we need not repress the darkness because there is a power which holds the two forces together. For Mrs. Kotschnig, then, "the first salvation is to have faith in somebody in whom one can confide, that there is in humanity help to be given."[10]

Frances Wickes opened the final clinical presentation before the general discussion. She described an extremely repressed woman who was mercilessly driven by a radical faith that her life should be a perfect, self-sacrificing imitation of Christ. Selfless service, under all conditions, pushed her constantly. Wilkes described her this way:

---

[9]NYPG 1941–1945, 5.
[10]NYPG 1941–1945, 5.

Her ideal was sacrifice, her guilt was her wicked rebellion against fulfilling all the petty demands which would make her husband happy and realize his ideal of feminine perfection. Tortured, guilty, and self-accusing, she entered analysis.[11]

After a great deal of struggle, this woman accepted the validity of her own inner world and decided, rather courageously, to "be herself." "This marked an act of faith in the individual self and in an indwelling light of conscience in which values could be appraised."[12]

After this clinical material was presented, a general discussion took place. Fromm opened the discussion by asking whether the material presented allowed for a generalized formulation about the psychological phenomenon of faith. Wickes responded that faith always has to do with the "emergence of self-discovery, spontaneity, and with truth."[13] Fromm then asked whether or not this type of faith is connected with religion, and specifically, with the idea of God. Kotschnig affirmed that for her it was, saying that "there is a staggering realization that comes from hindsight that there is mind and purpose directing one's growth just as the growth of the body is directed according to a pattern."[14] Bone followed this statement by referring everyone to Fromm's previous comment about a structure of life one can come to know, understand, and with which one can cooperate. In that sense, said Bone, there is "something" beyond the individual's consciousness.

Fromm then explicitly stated his conviction that this faith in the discovery of the self has no connection to a traditional religious belief in God. One can possess faith while denying the existence of God. This comment revealed an ongoing theme in Fromm: Faith does not have a transcendent reference; theology is actually psychology; and consequently, humanity needs to "take back" all the Divine attributes it has placed on God and realize that faith in an outside God is authoritarian, irrational faith.

Then Tillich stated that he didn't believe we are forced into the alternatives of faith in self-discovery or faith in God. However, if by God we mean the existence of "a being," then Fromm is right. Tillich thus dis-

---

[11]NYPG 1941–1945, 7.
[12]NYPG 1941–1945, 7.
[13]NYPG 1941–1945, 7.
[14]NYPG 1941–1945, 7.

engaged himself from traditional theism, yet suggested that God means something else. Tillich went on to say that we cannot adequately understand the human situation in purely internal, psychological terms. Something beyond the self is involved.

Fromm responded that he agreed "up to a point."[15] The self is related to the universe, to other people, and to itself. While self-awareness includes a recognition of this connectedness, it does *not* necessarily lead to a belief in a God-concept. It would have been very interesting to see this discussion continued, but the topic shifted.

Roberts, Tillich's colleague and in many ways a representative of Tillich's thought, eventually brought the God question back up by asking, "If faith is not faith in God (existentially) then what is it in?"[16] Bone then questioned whether or not faith in the structure of life is necessary in order to have faith in oneself. Fromm repeated what he had said before about faith being an attitude of "firmness." Fromm further commented that "the question is not in what one has faith—that is secondary. What is the state of mind surrounding faith."[17]

Tillich then added that it will *always* be necessary to symbolize our experience of faith. This may be, as Fromm says, a secondary step but it is an inevitable one. If we grant the necessity to symbolize our experience, said Tillich, then the next question is "What are the right symbols?"[18] The task becomes using symbols from everyday experience to express the ultimate. If these symbols do not express the unconditioned, then they are limited.

Bone concluded the second meeting by a summary of what the group had been attempting to do. He said the group had been trying to discover whether there is a "state of mind" or "psychological condition" which can, itself, be called "faith." Future meetings, it was agreed, would look at how this psychological description of faith is connected to philosophical, theological, anthropological, and historical material. This concluded the second meeting.

The exchanges between Tillich and Fromm during this meeting would largely "set the stage" for many future discussions between "secular" and

---

[15] NYPG 1941–1945, 8.
[16] NYPG 1941–1945, 9.
[17] NYPG 1941–1945, 9.
[18] NYPG 1941–1945, 9.

"nonsecular" faith. The fact that Fromm refused to acknowledge any meaningful referent to the notion of "God" except as a symbol for human potential did not indicate a lack of familiarity with the Judeo-Christian tradition. Fromm was particularly well trained in the Hebrew Bible. However, a major issue between Fromm and Tillich was not merely the God question. Instead, it concerned the relationship between human dignity and the Protestant understanding of human passivity in the reception of Divine grace.

The third meeting revolved around the interesting topic of authentic faith arising after the destruction of pseudofaith. Harry Bone started the meeting with a brief presentation of his own views about the nature of faith. He described a threefold process which happens in many individuals: they move from (a) pseudofaith, which is based on illusions, to (b) a nihilism which has faith in nothing, to (c) genuine faith. Genuine faith is an outgrowth of experiencing all dimensions of oneself. By contrast, "unfaith,' which involves pessimism, cynicism, and nihilism, results from a "thoroughly self-frustrated personality."[19] The end result of this "unfaith" is suicide. Then Bone adds a most interesting comment about faith as an expression of the entire self: "Thus faith in the structure of life, faith in the possibilities of human nature, faith in one's fellows, faith in oneself, faith in life, faith in the world—are all aspects of one indivisible life attitude."[20]

Pseudofaith always involves a mixture of faith and unfaith. It is a false affirmation of life based on the particular illusions one refuses to face. Such an individual affirms life, but only on terms peculiar to him or her. Illusions about oneself and the world are interconnected. Thus, reality is not faced honestly. While the person of unfaith is against all life period, the person with pseudofaith is against *real* life, a life free of illusions. This person is "against the life of a free-and-responsible human being in an open, growing, world-in-the-making which is in part insecure and unpredictable."[21] Pseudofaith gives persons a false sense of strength without which they believe they cannot live.

Fromm then provided a brief statement of his perspective. He discussed the issue of doubt as an attitude and listed three types of doubt: rational doubt, irrational doubt, and indifferent doubt. Rational doubt is progressive

---

[19]NYPG 1941–1945, 10.
[20]NYPG 1941–1945, 10.
[21]NYPG 1941–1945, 10.

and associated with a growing freedom within persons. Fromm stated that psychoanalysis can greatly aid this form of doubt.

> The process of analysis evokes growing emotional freedom from oppressing authority and growing doubt about everything it stands for and represents. We can say productive doubt results from profound faith, from "firmness," from some belief in one's own ability to think, to test, and to judge.[22]

Note that, for Fromm, this is essentially faith in ourselves.

Irrational doubt, on the other hand, is compulsive doubt. While this compulsive doubt may appear as a mental obsession, there is an underlying emotional conflict beneath it. While productive doubt reflects a growing sense of inner freedom, irrational doubt reflects an inward division and unacknowledged rebellion. An analysis of doubt will reveal two things: (a) an attitude toward authority, and (b) a relationship with others. In genuine faith, we'll find an attitude of love, solidarity, and most of all, freedom. In irrational doubt, we will not find these things. In a sweeping statement, Fromm puts it this way: "Any authority which hampers or blocks development is irrational. Rational authority acts for the optimum development of those believing therein."[23]

The third form of doubt involves an indifference, a relativism, a complete lack of concern with truth. It represents a bewildered person who is rather cynical and so completely taken over by skepticism that all forms of faith are seen as hopeless and meaningless. This is not to say, however, that nonneurotic people must have a conviction that life is "friendly."

The meeting concluded with Roberts, again sounding much like Tillich, saying that "faith as an attitude" must inevitably be symbolized or it will be left hanging in a vacuum. Tillich then pointed out that Fromm had left out the whole notion of "naïve faith," a kind of unbroken faith which has not been scrutinized by doubt. Tillich, who had said nothing throughout the meeting, ended the meeting with the comment that many people have this naïve or unbroken faith.

The fourth meeting was full of rich discussion, a conversation which would have greatly benefited from Tillich's input. However, Tillich was unable to be at both the fourth and fifth meetings. In the fourth meeting,

---

[22]NYPG 1941–1945, 12.
[23]NYPG 1941–1945, 13.

Fromm provided the presentation. He began reiterating points he had made during the previous session, but he added a more direct statement. Irrational faith is "faith or belief in something outside of oneself based on the relationship of the individual to an authority not of his own experience or his own activity."[24] The connection to this outside authority is an emotional one, a kind of master-slave bond. Fromm further stated that our intelligence will not protect us from the destructiveness of this relationship to authority once we have an emotional relationship to it.

> [T]he intellectual processes are greatly dependent on emotional processes in the sense that the submission to an authority not only creates belief in that person but also verifies everything which that person says. The stronger, the more intense this relationship is, the stronger is the verification. The most absurd thing becomes intelligent even for the most intelligent person.[25]

Fromm then described this surrender to an outside authority as a masochistic movement which functions "like a drug in its effect on the brain, a drug which people are not even aware of taking."[26] Freedom is abandoned in this master-slave relationship. Thinking, feeling, and acting spontaneously are sacrificed for this opiate-like relationship to an outside authority. Marx's influence on Fromm here is obvious. Fromm never found room in his thinking for the idea that one could find a nonauthoritarian relationship with a transcendent God. Of necessity, to Fromm, a belief in an "outside God" always meant a devaluation of the "inside person." He insisted that the symbol of God can only refer to two things: (a) the perfection for which human beings are striving, or (b) external authority. While the first faith in God, which is really faith in humanity, is healthy, the second is always a detriment to human fulfillment.

Fromm also affirmed that the future of rational faith will lie outside of traditional religion. Institutional religion is tied to a social structure and authority which blocks human freedom.

> There is a close connection between a social structure in which authority rules and hinders the full emancipation of man and the theological structure in which God rules over the world. In the concept of God at all

---

[24]NYPG 1941–1945, 15.
[25]NYPG 1941–1945, 15.
[26]NYPG 1941–1945, 15.

periods, the profoundest wishes of men were symbolized and expressed, but the symbol of God also became the symbol of authority, linked with the social structure.[27]

Sensitive to the constant threat of external oppression and violation of human freedom, Fromm operates within an ethical egoism in which he believes that human fulfillment through freedom is the supreme good. However, he does not believe that people can arrive at this freedom by themselves. Instead, we can only arrive at this experience of inner freedom, and therefore rational faith, *if we are in relationship with others*. This is not something we can achieve on our own in isolation.

Clearly, Fromm wants to divorce the concept of faith from any sort of theological content. Faith is "psychologized" as a quality of human experience. There is no transcendent "other." Thus, religious faith can be evaluated in purely psychological terms. Dependence on any sort of outside authority is destructive; spontaneity and freedom are the great healers. Submission to anything outside oneself is the beginning of a sadomasochistic faith.

Again, this was a crucial meeting and it was a loss to the group (and to us) that Tillich was not present. The issues Fromm brought up would have greatly interested him.

The fifth meeting was in many ways a continuation of the fourth. There were no theoretical or clinical presentations. Instead, the entire meeting was devoted to discussion. The initial conversation revolved around whether rational and irrational faith could really be separated. More particularly, Ernest Schachtel suggested that many brilliant thinkers such as Kierkegaard and Kafka would not have made their breakthroughs without a quality of obsessive doubt. Thomas Bigham added that while we often think that rational faith evolves out of irrational faith, it often does not. Schachtel then responded that the categories of rational and irrational faith are ideal types and that in real life we always find a mixture.

Roberts inserted that he did not believe cultural critics such as Kierkegaard were produced by a particular culture; instead, Kierkegaard would have rebelled and reacted in any culture because of his prophetic inclination.

---

[27]NYPG 1941–1945, 17.

People like Kierkegaard would be maladjusted in any period; there is no conceivable cultural pattern where they would find certainty. Their dilemma is that of the man of genius who confronts incurable spiritual suffering.[28]

Fromm followed this comment with the speculative question as to whether being well adjusted in an evil world is itself "sin."

Then conversation shifted due to another of Fromm's comments. Fromm stated that he didn't fully understand what the notion that "God is a symbol" means. Fromm saw only two possibilities. Either (a) God is a Being who created the world and determines the world's fate, or (b) there is no God at all. He added, "God as we find him in the Bible or history was not a symbol. We are not doing justice to the historic tradition of God, which is not a symbol."[29] This is a most interesting comment, particularly coming from Fromm. He clearly rejects the notion of God in the Judeo-Christian tradition, but he wants to treat this concept with integrity. He believes, with some obvious reference to Tillich here, that we are not being historically or theologically fair to call God a "symbol." This was not the intention of the ancient Hebrews or the early Christians.

Roberts then responded that an anthropomorphic use of words in reference to God is obviously inadequate. He went on to defend a Tillichian position:

> In speaking of God as a symbol, one must recognize that one can't mean it literally. There are no terms that can express a relationship between the eternal and the temporal. . . . It is more honest to recognize that when one is talking about God in history one's language is figurative, not literal. That does not suggest that because the concept has to be used symbolically, the symbol is a projection into a void and does not stand for anything.[30]

Fromm was not convinced. In fact, in this situation he would perhaps make strange bedfellows with more traditional Jewish and Christian theologians who believe that Tillich's concept of God is based far more on philosophical abstractions than on the God of the Abrahamic traditions. Certainly this conversation made the group ripe for the next meeting—a presentation by Tillich on the historic and biblical meaning of faith.

---

[28]NYPG 1941–1945, 23.
[29]NYPG 1941–1945, 27.
[30]NYPG 1941–1945, 27.

Tillich began the sixth meeting with a presentation divided into four parts: (a) faith in the Old Testament, (b) faith in the New Testament, (c) faith in Catholicism, and (d) faith in Protestantism, particularly the Reformers themselves. The Old Testament, argued Tillich, conveys a basic relationship between humanity and God based on fear and a sense of awe and the numinous. Tillich's similarities with Rudolph Otto are quite clear.[31] This fear also moves throughout Christianity but it does not involve a flight from God. There is an attraction to this awe. This is "the Holy," which is not a moral quality but a power which is at the center of life. At the same time, however, this holy power is the principle of morals. "Thus out of the feeling of transcendent power, the idea of morals arises. The fear of God is the basis for the absolute principle of justice."[32] Tillich continues with an important summary of faith in the Old Testament:

> Faith, in the Old Testament, is a nontheoretical attitude. It is paradoxical, contradicting that which seems to be on the basis of experience. This faith is based not on any elements in the situation, but on something transcendent which turns around all of the character of the finite possibilities."[33]

Tillich then moves on to New Testament faith, mentioning that Jesus never uses the word "faith" for himself. The struggle in Jesus' life is never with faith. Instead, it is with natural tendencies away from unity with God. But this is an issue of obedience, not faith. Tillich adds that because in Jesus we find no struggle with faith, "a real imitation of Jesus is not possible."[34]

Tillich goes on to describe the meaning of faith in Paul, which he also believes is highlighted in Augustine and the Reformers. Faith, for Paul, becomes the reception of a Divine act by which God declares us acceptable. This acceptance occurs in spite of our unrighteousness. It is fully an act of grace based on no human merit whatsoever.

> The faith implies the negation of every activity of our own except the mere openness which is the forgiveness. The justification by faith does not mean creating faith in ourselves but the simple acceptance that God is recon-

---

[31] See Rudolph Otto, *The Idea of the Holy* (New York: Oxford University Press, 1958).
[32] NYPG 1941–1945, 28.
[33] NYPG 1941–1945, 29.
[34] NYPG 1941–1945, 29.

ciled, that there is reconciliation in being, that we are reconciled with the meaning of our own life. The simple acceptance that this is done is decisive. Everything in the Christian life is done in faith. The main point is the acceptance of the paradoxical gift of God, on the basis of a turning around of the moralistic interpretation of life.[35]

Tillich further mentioned that this acceptance is not the acceptance of doctrine, but instead the acceptance of the reality in which one finds oneself.

Tillich said this New Testament understanding of faith largely went underground and that faith deteriorated into a form of knowledge. The acceptance of faith became the acceptance of a philosophic tradition and doctrine. This set of beliefs, rather than God, became the source of faith. Sin was overcome in baptism and holding correct doctrinal beliefs became the focus of salvation. "Believing" meant "thinking with assent."[36]

Protestantism, for Tillich, was driven by three central themes concerning faith: (a) the intellect cannot go far enough to reach faith, (b) the will, which drives the intellect, is disabled and unable to produce faith, and (c) the magic ceremonies in the Church do *not* impart salvation. Faith, in Protestantism, is merely receptive. The reception is of God and not a cluster of ideas *about* God.

> All this is a dynamic person-to-person relationship. This is not the psychological form, but the theological concept. The *only* sin, therefore, is *unbelief*. Unbelief does not mean that we do not believe doctrine; unbelief is the nonacceptance of God's paradoxical coming to us. This is sin and everything else follows from it.[37]

As the discussion followed after Tillich's presentation, he remarked that faith in classical Christianity is always something which cannot be derived from human experience, or even the totality of experience. Instead, it comes from a level of the unconditioned. In this sense, human beings are never self-sufficient. Or as Tillich liked to say, the conditioned realm is always dependent on the unconditioned.

Given the nature of this first year of discussions, the psychology of faith, Tillich was saying something most remarkable. He was moving

---

[35]NYPG 1941–1945, 30.
[36]NYPG 1941–1945, 31.
[37]NYPG 1941–1945, 31.

completely away from any idea which would reduce faith to individual biography, psychological experience, or even Fromm's character structure. Trying to explain faith from within human experience simply cannot be done. As Tillich said, "It is always the answer which comes to us from some other realm."[38] Stated still more boldly, *there is no naturalistic explanation of faith.* Tillich went on to say that biblical writers and theologians have always asked themselves why people resist faith in God. Distortion of truth, pride, and injustice have been suggested. However, said Tillich, "it would be an error to imagine that the analysis of the resistance of faith is able to lead us to the cause of faith itself."[39]

While other issues were bandied back and fourth during this session, Fromm suggested that the two divisions concerning faith within this group pivoted around the notion of "God." Fromm insisted that Tillich's idea of faith is inseparable from the concept of God, whereas his is concerned with human virtues outside of God. "Our discussion," argued Fromm, "shows that this difference in premise is relevant."[40] Tillich then protested that Fromm always seems to use the term "God" in a highly deteriorated form, as a kind of object human beings have formed. Again, it seems that Fromm thought Tillich was not fairly representing traditional God-language, and Tillich thought Fromm refused to examine carefully his understanding of God as the Ground of Being. This disagreement would never go away.

In many respects, the seventh meeting of the group seemed very much out of step with what the group had previously discussed. Ruth Benedict provided a brief, but comprehensive, look at primitive cultures. Because (a) Tillich was not present at this meeting, (b) the discussion does not really offer a continuity from the previous session, and (c) we have limited time, I will move on to the eighth and last session, a session which takes up again the issues discussed in earlier sessions.

The final meeting of first year of the New York Psychology Group of 1941–1942 again focused on the psychology of faith. Fromm reminded the group that the major viewpoint brought up during this first year of meetings was the *psychological* investigation of faith. The interest had not been in the object of belief, but in the dynamic process of faith. Fromm then began to lay out what became a familiar theme in his writing.

---

[38]NYPG 1941–1945, 34.
[39]NYPG 1941–1945, 34.
[40]NYPG 1941–1945, 34.

From the psychological viewpoint the object of one's belief cannot be entirely separated from his attitude because since it is rooted in a certain type of personality, necessarily certain objects of belief are excluded from faith.[41]

Thus, for Fromm, in contrast to Tillich's earlier statements, a particular psychological attitude and character structure produce a particular type of faith. Faith, as a human attitude, is always related to character structure. Fromm seems to completely disregard the idea that faith might have a transcendent Source. He goes on to describe rational faith:

Rational faith is a quality of certainty and unshakability of one's own experience based upon a character structure the syndrome of which includes independence, integrity, the ability to love, and courage. Any conscious belief must be scrutinized from this level. Certain conscious beliefs or contents of faith would prove to be valueless unless they were voiced by a person whose attitude was one of rational faith.[42]

So Fromm is saying that the determining factors in assessing the rationality or irrationality of faith are independence, integrity, ability to love, and courage. Any belief must be psychologically scrutinized to determine whether or not these characteristics are present. Thus, for Fromm, we have a normative criteria by which to determine the quality of faith. A Barthian, of course, would be appalled at the easy way in which faith is submitted to human tests for authenticity.

Making what seems like a direct attack on Tillich's previous presentation on faith in Protestantism, Fromm insists that rational faith is based on the *active involvement* of the individual, and not something merely receptive. He states it quite directly.

From the theological angle, rational faith is one where the weight is upon the active experience of the individual and not on his receiving the gift of grace from God or any authority; those formulations of faith in which the individual is comparatively passive and is overwhelmed by the gift would be nearer irrational faith.[43]

---

[41]NYPG 1941–1945, 44.
[42]NYPG 1941–1945, 44.
[43]NYPG 1941–1945, 44.

This comment is loaded. It is clearly Pelagian, and thus disagrees with Tillich's appropriation of Augustine and Luther. Fromm greatly resists any notion of grace as a passive reception. Passive reception always ends up insulting human dignity and results in submission to authority.

Tillich, not surprisingly, asked Fromm if his method was based on an a priori assumption that there could be no truth in the content of the Christian faith. In a very important response, Fromm said "that to him the statement of the experience has no reality in any sense except its being a symbolic expression of certain views and insights which are more adequately, more rationally, and more truthfully, expressed in terms in which God does not appear."[44] Fromm then went on to describe an evolutionary view of the concept of God.

> To him the religious formulation was an approach which was adequate to a certain stage of human development, but today we have an approach which would be truer. The concept of God has expressed the most profound longings of humanity, some of the most essential truths about the world and men and therefore cannot be taken lightly in the sense of being considered rationalization.[45]

Yet whatever respect Fromm may have had for previous longings for God, the notion of God is no longer necessary. We have outgrown it. It is no longer useful.

Schachtel then made a very interesting observation that the group seemed divided into two perspectives. One group, which clearly included Tillich, Roberts, and May, believed that love, freedom, and courage are grounded in a structure larger than humanity. This is the realm of the unconditioned, the transcendent. This realm is what the word "God" symbolizes. The other group believed that love, freedom, and courage need to be kept within the human sphere and not transferred to another level. This group believed that Divine qualities secretly belong to humans and have been projected onto the symbol of God. There is therefore no need to speak of "God" as a trancendent reality. In fact, to speak of such a God inevitably places humanity in a position of submission to an authority. Humanity can understand itself without reference to this "higher"

---

[44]NYPG 1941–1945, 44.
[45]NYPG 1941–1945, 45.

dimension. To put it differently, a well developed anthropology and psychology will eliminate a need for theology.

Fromm then restated his fear that God is connected to oppressive authority. He was quite blunt.

> Historically the idea of God was always linked up with a certain hierarchy in societies, with a certain assumption of authority to which man has to submit. In whatever form the idea of God is brought into the discussion, it implies some picture of man's submission or limitations of freedom.[46]

For Fromm, then, because the notion of God interferes with the sacred issue of human freedom, the idea of God has got to go!

Fromm continued by saying that he holds somewhat of a tragic view of life since he has no Divine consolation. Nothing guarantees justice and love except human effort. Tillich stated that he believed a worldview in which there is only finiteness is always a tragic one. He then asked Fromm how he maintains hope in human possibilities. Fromm replied that his view is not *essentially* tragic even though it contains a tragic element. The mere fact that humanity continues to love and strive for the truth reduces its sense of tragedy. Tillich then countered by saying that the moral imperative can be fulfilled only on the basis of a power which surpasses finite human possibility and is received by the foundation of our being.

Again, what clearly comes forth in this final meeting is a division which has been mounting in all the previous meetings, namely, a disagreement over whether or not any reference to the realm of the transcendent is necessary. This division clearly seems led by the voices of Fromm and Tillich. Fromm thinks the traditional idea of God as a being outside of humanity has outworn its usefulness. He further believes that Tillich is not being fair by introducing an abstract notion of "Being itself" and using traditional God-language. He has no interest in God as the "Ground of Being." He believes that this "God" is better described by simply referring to what it really is—a projection of human potential and perfection. While Tillich may use sophisticated philosophical language, his notion of God is merely a symbol of the self, and he, too, is an example of Feuerbachian projection. To make matters worse, Tillich advocates the passive view of grace as acceptance, a Reformation view which Fromm detests. It is a blow against human dignity and inevitably leads to further alienation by

---

[46]NYPG 1941–1945, 48.

describing God as a transcendent "other" who oppresses human freedom. In short, Tillich should drop his theology and simply be a psychologist. Human beings are only alienated from themselves and each other. There is no "God" from which to *be* alienated.

For Tillich, Fromm holds out an overly simplistic utopian ideal. I will not replicate the Tillichian critique of Fromm developed in chapter 3, but suffice it to say that Tillich argues passionately that all human efforts at self-redemption, including Fromm's, are doomed to fail.

Reflections on the First Year of Discussion

The group's first year of discussions brought up some basic differences which are very much still with us over sixty years later. Does transcendence refer to a reality beyond the self? Is Tillich's use of theological language so nontraditional that it does not describe the Abrahamic traditions? Should we have faith in God or faith in humanity? Further, does faith in God cancel out faith in humanity? How important is the destruction of pseudo-faith on the journey to faith? What role does doubt play in faith? Does faith in God inevitably turn into authoritarian religion? Are naturalistic explanations of faith really adequate? And finally, is faith a gift or does it necessitate the active involvement of the individual? All these questions emerged in the group's conversation.

As I have previously mentioned, it seems as if Fromm and Tillich became the two natural leaders in the group, leaders who held quite different perspectives. I would like to further reflect on some of their ongoing differences concerning transcendence, grace, authority, the Protestant Reformation, and a few other concerns. Again, many of these issues are still with us and divide a secular and nonsecular approach to the psychology of religion. I would then like to turn to Tillich's more systematic statement dealing with the psychology of faith in his well-known *Dynamics of Faith*.[47]

Having fled Nazi Germany in the early thirties, Fromm remained very leery the remainder of his life of anything which seemed even slightly authoritarian. His entire life's work until his death in 1980 seemed to be one long protest of the dangers of authoritarianism. For Fromm, religion inevitably becomes authoritarian insofar as it believes in a Divine being.

---

[47]Paul Tillich, *Dynamics of Faith* (New York: Harper & Row, 1957).

God's sovereignty always means humanity's depravity. The notion of grace, so central to Tillich, is seen as humanity's weakness, powerlessness, and defeatism. It reflects a sadomasochistic relationship toward God. Fromm detested notions of humanity's passive reception of Divine grace. This passive submission is in fact masochistic. Worse still, as humanity increasingly becomes masochistic toward God it then becomes sadistic toward others. The idea that human beings need a "savior" is a profound insult to human dignity and an illustration of deep self-hatred. The larger God becomes, the smaller humanity becomes.

As we saw in the chapter 1, Tillich has been deeply influenced by Luther's understanding of grace as "accepting our acceptance." Fromm could not be any further removed from this point of view. He believes that both Luther and Calvin were largely enemies of psychological health. His estimation of the Reformers is dismal. Here is his summation of Luther.

> But Luther did more than bring out the feeling of insignificance which already pervaded the social classes to whom he preached—he offered them a solution. By not only accepting his own insignificance but by humiliating himself to the utmost, by giving up every vestige of individual will, by renouncing his individual strength, the individual could hope to be acceptable to God. Luther's relationship to God was one of complete submission. In psychological terms his concept of faith means: if you completely submit, if you accept your individual insignificance, then the all-powerful God may be willing to love you and save you. If you get rid of your individual self with all its shortcomings and doubts by utmost self-effacement, you free yourself from the feeling of your own nothingness and can participate in God's glory. Thus, while Luther freed people from the authority of the Church, he made them submit to a much more tyrannical authority, that of a God who insisted on complete submission of man and annihilation of the individual self as the essential condition of salvation. *Luther's "faith" was the conviction of being loved upon the condition of surrender*, a solution which has much in common with the principle of complete submission of the individual to the state and the "leader."[48]

For Fromm, self-doubt and self-hatred in Luther pushed him toward a security in an all-powerful God, a God which seemed to Fromm frighteningly similar to an all-powerful dictator. Again, the submission is in reality a kind of *masochism*. Humanity shrinks so that God can become even

---

[48]Erich Fromm, *Escape from Freedom* (New York: Avon Books, 1941) 100.

bigger. Thus, Fromm attempts to unmask a very unhealthy psychological condition which underlies humanity's eager willingness to eliminate freedom for the purposes of security. This indictment is a most serious charge: the theology of Luther was driven by a pathological self-hatred, worship of authority, and willingness to reject a large percentage of the population.

Calvin does not fare much better in Fromm's estimation. In some ways, Calvin's explicit doctrine of predestination is even more dehumanizing than Luther's faith. Fromm states his disdain for Calvin and Calvinism most directly.

> Calvin's God, in spite of all attempts to preserve the idea of God's justice and love, has all the features of a tyrant without any quality of love or even justice.... The psychological significance of the doctrine of predestination is a twofold one. It expresses and enhances the feeling of individual powerlessness and insignificance. No doctrine could express more strongly than this the worthlessness of human will and effort. The decision over man's fate is taken completely out of his own hands and there is nothing man can do to change his decision. He is a powerless tool in God's hands. The other meaning of this doctrine, like that of Luther's, consists in its function to silence irrational doubt which was the same in Calvin and his followers as in Luther.... The Calvinists quite naively thought that they were the chosen ones and that all others were those whom God had condemned to damnation. It is obvious that this belief represented psychologically a deep contempt and hatred for other human beings—as a matter of fact, the same hatred with which they had endowed God.[49]

Thus, Fromm's estimation of the two leading figures of the Reformation is that they were two of the "greatest haters" in the history of the human race.[50] Their hostility toward both themselves and others served as the psychological context out of which they fashioned their demeaning understandings of God's grace. The vicious cycle is that humanity's dependence on an irrational authority produces more guilt feelings and the guilt feelings reinforce further dependence. Submission to authoritarian religion and self-hatred walk hand-in-hand.

It doesn't take long to realize how utterly rooted is Fromm's thought in a Feuerbachian projection theory of religion. Ludwig Feuerbach attempted to reduce theology to anthropology, or what we would now call psychol-

---

[49]Fromm, *Escape from Freedom*, 107-109.
[50]Fromm, *Escape from Freedom*, 115.

ogy.⁵¹ For Feurerbach, theology tells us only about our own needs, aspirations, and fears. Theology is an external picture of what is really in the human psyche. Religion reveals us not to God but to ourselves. It tells us nothing about the metaphysical realm. Human beings project what is their own best qualities onto this image of a Divine being. This projection process is often unconscious. The result is that humanity feels empty while it worships its own capacities in an imaginary God. Stated simply, we create God out of our own psyches.

The problem with this, for Feuerbach, is that it leads to enormous self-alienation. Again, all of the "good" aspects of ourselves are projected onto God and we are left with the "psychological leftovers." These "leftovers" are only what we condemn. In a way, God robs us of our goodness because we are too busy handing it over to the Almighty. We personify our own projected perfection as a deity independent of us and then miserably compare ourselves to this image. It is a teeter-totter relationship: for God to be up, humanity must be down. Metaphysically, religious beliefs tell us nothing. Psychologically, they tell us much about our own alienated potential.

Feuerbach thus inverts Hegel's understanding of the Divine-human relationship. For Hegel, God or "Absolute Spirit" alienated Godself by becoming human, and thus a part of nature and history. J. Stanley Glen describes Hegel's perspective.

> This meant that nature and history were really God but in an alienated form. It also meant that they retained a hidden tendency to be reunited (synthesis) with him and to recover their original deification. Since man is part of nature and history, the same applied to him. God as Absolute Spirit estranged himself from himself in becoming man. The differentiation by which man emanated from God and became objectified in the process signified his alienation from God. It meant that man was God in an alienated form and retained within himself a tendency to be reunited with him and to recover his original deification.⁵²

For Feuerbach and Fromm, all this gets reversed. Instead of God becoming human, God is generated out of human imagination. This pro-

---

⁵¹Ludwig Feuerbach, *The Essence of Christianity*, trans. George Eliot (Buffalo NY: Prometheus Books, 1989).

⁵²J. Stanley Glen, *Erich Fromm: A Protestant Critique* (Phiadelphia: Westminster Press, 1966) 116.

duces self-alienation and leads to self-contempt. In order for humanity to regain its rightful place in the universe, it must "take back" what it has given to God. By withdrawing this projection, humanity can once again affirm is own potential. As long as theism is in the picture, human self-affirmation will be enormously limited. To sum up then, contrary to Hegel, *we are not part of God, but God is part of us.*

Glen, in his defense of Reformation theology, argues that this Feuerbach/Fromm picture of the Divine-human relationship fundamentally misses the nature of the human condition. Rather than weak and feeble individuals turning all their powers over to God and then worshipping that indirectly, Glen suggests that humanity has a greater tendency to rely on its own resources, attempt to live independently from any need for its Divine ground and Source. As he puts it, "the picture of the frail, weak, timid and lonely little man quivering in fear of the big, booming world around him and the forces of nature that add to the threat of the world has been overdone in psychological criticisms of religion."[53] For Glen, the primary human reality is an attempt to escape from God, not to escape human freedom.

Tillich's response to the Feuerbach critique is fairly well known. He states it perhaps the most directly in volume 1 of his *Systematics*. In describing our images of God he says the following.

> They are images of human nature or subhuman powers raised to a superhuman realm. This fact, which theologians must face in all its implications, is the basis of all theories of "projection" which say that the gods are simply imaginary projections of elements of finitude, natural and human elements. What these theories disregard is that projection always is projection *on* something—a wall, a screen, another being, another realm. Obviously, it is absurd to class that on which the projection is realized with the projection itself. A screen is not projected; it receives the projection. The realm against which the divine images are projected is not itself a projection. It is the experienced ultimacy of being and meaning. It is the realm of the ultimate concern.[54]

---

[53]Glen, *Erich Fromm*, 134.

[54]Paul Tillich, *Systematic Theology*, vol. 1 (Chicago: University of Chicago Press, 1951) 212.

Thus, Tillich would say, "Of course there are going to be elements of the human psyche projected." However, this in no way dismisses the reality of that transcendent realm onto which these projections are made.

The disagreements between Tillich and Fromm on the issue of transcendence are profound. Further, while it is unnecessary to revisit chapter 1's exploration of the enthusiasm Tillich had for Luther as *both* theologian and depth psychologist, I will simply say that it is hard to imagine two brilliant minds (Fromm and Tillich) coming to such radically dissimilar views of the major themes of the Reformation.

To conclude these reflections on the first year of the NYPG, I'd like to turn briefly to Tillich's further-developed understanding of faith in his little classic, *The Dynamics of Faith*.[55] The very title of that book indicates a linkage to the New York Psychology Group discussions in that Tillich asserted the possibility of exploring the essential dynamics of faith without necessarily discussing faith's specific content. The content matters enormously to the person holding the faith, but faith's general dynamics can be described.

Faith, as ultimate concern, is a centered act which involves one's entire being. Thus, there are both conscious and unconscious elements in faith. Faith, in order to be genuine, must be born out of human freedom and not simply driven by the unconscious. This, for Tillich, would involve compulsion and not faith. Contrary to Freud, faith is not simply an obedience to the internalized image of the Father, because faith has the power to transform this image. Instead, faith is "ecstatic" which means that it "stands outside of" or transcends both the conscious reason and the unconscious. Again, while it includes both elements, it is not identical with either of them.

Tillich does not like William James's notion of a "will to believe." This is far too Pelagian in that it seems to assert an ability to step over all resistance and simply declare faith as an act of willpower. For Tillich, faith does not come that way. It is neither a creation of our will nor something we simply "decide" to do. Following Luther, Tillich argues that the human will can never be the *cause* of faith. And this means that there is not a psychological mechanism which can explain how faith comes about. Again, Tillich does not believe there is a naturalistic explanation of faith. He is against all psychologies of religion which claim an ability to reduce the

---

[55]Tillich, *Dynamics of Faith*.

phenomenon of faith to underlying psychological processes. As Tillich puts it, "Faith precedes all attempts to derive it from something else, because these attempts are themselves based on faith."[56]

So what, then, *is* the source of faith or ultimate concern? First, Tillich believes that while human beings belong to the temporal, finite realm, they nevertheless have a kind of intuitive sense of another realm, the realm of the "unconditioned." This eternal realm is not subject to space and time. It is beyond us and yet we feel that we belong to it. This can be intuited in a variety of situations—a walk on the beach, an observance of sunset, or the simple longing of our heart for ultimate meaning and purpose. As Tillich puts it, "Man is driven toward faith by his awareness of the infinite to which he belongs, but which he does not own like a possession."[57] This experience has to do with the depths of life, a yearning and a fascination with the mysteries of existence. So faith, which must live in the conditioned, finite world is concerned with the infinite and unconditioned world.

In order to talk about this unconditioned world, we must use symbols. The reason for this is that all language is conditional and finite, meaning historically, culturally, and socially situated. Language bears all the marks of finitude. We cannot "translate" the realm of the unconditioned into the vocabulary of the conditioned. Like it or not, we are stuck with symbols. Yet symbols have a capacity to open up a whole new realm of being. While they cannot be taken literally, they *do* participate in the reality to which they point. This point has been mentioned before, but it needs to be reiterated because it is such a central, and controversial, aspect of Tillich's thought: Because of temporality and human finitude, we can say *nothing* about the Divine which is *literally* true. Theology is saturated with the language of symbols. It cannot be otherwise. While it is certainly true that all faith has a content, that content, for Tillich, must be understood symbolically. Tillich makes the following claims about these symbols: (a) they must point beyond themselves to something else, (b) they participate in the reality to which they point, (c) they open up levels of reality which are not ordinarily available, (d) they cannot be produced intentionally, but instead grow out of the individual and collective unconscious, and (e) they cannot be invented.[58]

---

[56]Tillich, *Dynamics of Faith*, 8.
[57]Tillich, *Dynamics of Faith*, 9.
[58]Tillich, *Dynamics of Faith*, 41-54.

Unlike Bultmann, Tillich is not in favor of dismissing myths and replacing them with an existentialist vocabulary. It *is* important to understand myths *as* myths. This recognition is what Tillich means by "broken myth." For Tillich, the radical prohibition against idolatry thus asserts that there can be no unbroken myths. An unbroken myth, once again, would involve an expression of an infinite concern in finite language, a set up for idolatry. Tillich states this emphatically.

> [T]he presupposition of such literalism is that God is a being, acting in time and space, dwelling in a special place, affecting the cause of events and being affected by them like any other being in the universe. Literalism deprives God of his ultimacy and, religiously speaking, of his majesty. It draws him down to the level which is not ultimate, the finite and conditioned.[59]

Tillich goes on, however, to distinguish natural and reactive literalism. Natural literalism is simply the act of taking the contents of one's religious beliefs at face value. It is a condition prior to doubt, a sort of innocent or naïve position. Interestingly, Tillich believes that one should not disturb such a faith until the person becomes doubtful. In other words, allow another the pilgrimage of coming to his or her own questions and do not engage in a "myth busting" exercise, which may indeed be more sadistic than helpful. A reactive literalism, on the other hand, is what is usually meant by fundamentalism. It attempts to quiet its own doubt with authoritarian statements.

What is crucial for Tillich is the notion that *we can only attack one faith from the standpoint of another faith.* For Tillich, Fromm's perspective is grounded in as much "faith" as is his own position. Fromm's faith is in the capabilities of humanity.

> For humanism the divine is manifest in the human; the ultimate concern of man is man. All this, of course, refers to man in his essence: the true man, the man of the idea, not the actual man, nor the man in estrangement from his true nature. If, in this sense, the humanist says that his ultimate concern is man, he sees man as the ultimate in a piece of reality or as mystical faith finds in the depth of man the place of the infinite. The difference is that the sacramental and mystical types transcend the limits of humanity and try to reach the ultimate itself beyond man and his world, while the humanist

---

[59]Tillich, *Dynamics of Faith*, 52.

remains within these limits. For this reason the humanist faith is called "secular," in contrast to the two types of faith which are called "religious." Secular means belonging to the ordinary process of events, not going beside it or beyond it into a sanctuary.[60]

This emphasis that all perspectives, even ones that seem clearly scientific, are ultimately rooted in a world of presuppositions and "faith" is particularly important in postmodern discussions. Clearly, Tillich's objections to all forms of foundationalism, perspectives which believed they could reach final answers to life's mysteries as a result of a detached, Enlightenment understanding of reason, are helpful today. As we have seen before, Tillich is a master at seeing the ontological assumptions that dangle beneath so-called "purely" scientific perspectives. This is especially true in his encounter with psychology. The inescapability of ontological assumptions is something he tirelessly, and to some, annoyingly, drives home.

But how does one "evaluate" an ultimate concern? For Tillich, the key criterion for evaluating an ultimate concern is fairly simple: Does it indeed point toward that which is truly ultimate? Conversely, an ultimate concern which has a finite object becomes idolatry, or worse still, demonic. An ultimate concern can be just as destructive as it can be healing.

But the natural question most of us may want to ask is this: How does one "get" ultimately concerned? The answer, again, is relatively simple: We are grasped by an ultimate concern. We don't conjure it up, create it, or go searching for it. It "finds" us. Ultimate concerns cannot be tracked down or trapped. Nor can faith emerge from accumulating enough evidence. While faith presupposes reason, reason cannot "serve up" faith. Again, nothing finite, and this includes human reason, can produce faith.

> Man is finite, man's reason lives in preliminary concerns; but man is also aware of his potential infinity, and this awareness appears as his ultimate concern, as faith. If reason is grasped by an ultimate concern, it is driven beyond itself; but it does not cease to be reason, finite reason.[61]

While faith had better not contradict reason, it always goes beyond reason. Faith is a gift.

For Tillich, of course, this is the central meaning of grace. We are accepted into an ability to accept ourselves. And for Tillich, our guilt is

---

[60]Tillich, *Dynamics of Faith*, 63.
[61]Tillich, *Dynamics of Faith*, 76.

very real. The reality of our experience is that we are broken, estranged, separated from our essential self and from our grounding in God. We cannot "fix" our problem with finite tools. The infinite must instead come to us. As we are grasped by faith it drives us beyond the limitations of our finitude. This is not about making God seem great while we seem small. There is nothing masochistic about it. It is instead, the acceptance of a gift of reunion with our essential self and our Source. Under the conditions of finitude, of course, estrangement will always prevail. This is the meaning of Luther's notion that we are simultaneously saints and sinners. But for Tillich, as we saw in chapter 1, this experience of grace is similar to the experience of acceptance in psychotherapy. It is not about self-hatred and the need to submit to an authoritarian God who grants us relief from our neurotic guilt. Instead, it is the experience of liberation which accompanies unconditional acceptance. Rather than sacrificing oneself at the altar of an authoritarian dictator, this experience involves a kind of coming home to one's essential self. It enables us to affirm our lives in spite of the self-contradictions we feel.

Also, as Guy Hammond has suggested, Tillich's *Dynamics of Faith* and *The Courage to Be* offer a balance between faith as reception and faith as affirmation. Clearly, *The Dynamics of Faith* emphasizes the more receptive process of being grasped by an ultimate concern, whereas *The Courage to Be* accents the active ingredient of faith, namely, the courage to affirm commitments in the face of uncertainty and risk.[62]

Second Year: The Psychology of Love

The second year of the New York Psychology Group's meetings, 1942–1943, focused on the issue of love. The concerns spread over self-love, love of others, and love of God. Seward Hiltner set the stage for the year's discussions by outlining several issues worthy of focus. Hiltner began with the issue of whether love could be approached psychologically, as faith had been approached psychologically during the previous year. He stated that he was interested in love as an expression of the entire personality rather than as a feeling, instinct, or idea. Hiltner mentioned that approaching the

---

[62]Guy Hammond made this valuable point to me in a conversation at the annual North American Paul Tillich Society Meeting in San Antonio, Texas, November 2004.

topic of love psychologically did *not* mean that philosophical, theological, biological, and sociological elements could not also be included.

Hiltner's layout of potential topics was very impressive. Again, they paralleled many of the psychology of faith concerns. One issue to be discussed was the relationship between genuine love and pseudolove, and its impact on the developing person. Another issue was the relationship between self-love and object love. Hiltner specifically mentioned that the group might want to consider Fromm's position that self-love is a necessary first step toward love of others. Fromm's distinction between selfishness and self-love would be food for thought. Also, the relationship between eros and agape would be an important topic. He clarified this by saying, "The Eros-Agape issue in common parlance is understood to mean the distinction between love as an attitude of desire and love as an attitude of giving."[63] Hiltner also raised the issue of what constitutes the opposite of love. He further distinguished hate and hostility by saying that hate is a "character-ingrained readiness to be hostile," while hostility, itself, is often simply reactionary.[64]

> The real opposite of the attitude of love is unreadiness to love. This is not absence of love. Hate may be produced by it but not necessarily; it is therefore more nearly anxiety than anything else. Ingrained fear is therefore closer to being love's opposite than anything else.[65]

This issue of the relationship between love and hate, particularly self-love and self-hate, would prove to be one of the most discussed items of the entire year. Hiltner then went on to mention the issue of whether love is more of a gift or a developmental achievement, whether it is "natural" to love, and whether or not the love of our enemies is possible. Again, his questions, comments, and suggestions for discussion were very provocative.

The second meeting of the psychology of love group was led by Fromm. Not surprisingly, Fromm attempted to relate aspects of love to different character structures and attitudes. He described an attitude as "a characteristic mode of relatedness to others and to oneself."[66] He went on

---

[63]NYPG 1941–1945, 51.
[64]NYPG 1941–1945, 52.
[65]NYPG 1941–1945, 52.
[66]NYPG 1941–1945, 56.

to describe three types of attitude. The first is passive receptivity in which persons assume that everything they need comes from outside themselves and that the world is friendly enough to provide it. From this perspective, love is a gift they have a right to expect. The second attitude is one of robbing and exploiting. Like the passive reception attitude, this view believes that everything one needs is outside oneself, but it is necessary to aggressively take it, and thereby deprive others of it. In fact, this attitude often involves a desire for something *only if one can take it from another*. The last attitude is one of hoarding or holding something back and not using it. This is a withdrawn and detached stance.

Fromm went on to say that each of these attitudes is conveyed in the symbolism of Freud's oral stage of development. While Fromm wants to deliteralize Freud's belief that the actual body parts are the centers of our attitudes, he believes that the mouth illustrates each position. With a passive receptive position, the mouth remains open, ready to receive or be fed from an outside source. It is a dependency in which love rests on the notion of being fed. In the next attitude, the more aggressive one, the mouth is biting, as if the person is "biting the hand who feeds him or her." In the final attitude, the hoarding, detached, and uninvolved attitude, the mouth is completely closed as the person remains "tight lipped" and nonself-disclosing.

Note that these three attitudes are very similar to Karen Horney's three movements in the face of anxiety.[67] Horney describes the "moving toward" position as one of accommodation and attachment to another as the source of one's own identity; the "moving against" position as the combative and aggressive tendency to dominate and conquer another; and the "moving away" position as the detached, aloof position of emotional avoidance.

Fromm believes that the common thread in all three attitudes is a lack of productiveness, which later becomes his primary criterion for healthy living. By "productive love," Fromm means active, responsible relatedness born out of freedom, reason, and faith in human potential. As we saw in the first year of discussions, Fromm's emphasis on the active, participatory character of all love left him with little respect for the Protestant Reformer's understanding of grace as passive receptivity, or what Tillich called "accepting our acceptance." For Fromm, there are "hooks underneath

---

[67]Karen Horney, *Our Inner Conflicts* (New York: W. W. Norton, 1945).

this lure," even with Divine grace. It leaves human beings far too feeble and incapable of resolving their own condition.

Fromm, who frequently expands Freudian notions to give them a larger social significance, then recalled that Freud believed love starts with incest because the child wants to possess the mother. Enlarging this notion, Fromm argued that "incestuous" love, on a larger scale, is the ability to love only that which is familiar. Like a child who is incapable of reaching out to anyone except the incestuous fixation on mother, the individual is incapable of reaching out to the stranger and therefore becomes stuck in an incestuous relationship with that which is familiar. This is what occurs in ethnocentrism—a kind of mother fixation on one's own familiar world. Feeding on the milk of one's own group, one is incapable of reaching out to others.

The group continued to reflect on the appropriateness of the word "productivity" in describing love and Fromm concluded the session by acknowledging that there are different approaches to the problem of love and his own approach represented only an attempt to relate love as an attitude to different character structures. He concluded by saying "Productiveness is related to a particular kind of character structure, and the quality of productiveness is one significant criterion in differentiating the phenomenon of love."[68]

In the third meeting of the psychology of love discussions, Frances G. Wickes made a presentation on love in Jungian psychology, and more particularly, on the concept of eros. The group seemed intrigued, even if somewhat unfamiliar, with Jung's contribution. Wickes's presentation was far too broad in scope to fully address, so I will focus on those elements which most pertain to the theology/psychology relationship. Central issues seemed to be (a) the relationship between eros and logos, (b) the acceptance of the "shadow," (c) the significance of projecting our own self-hatred onto others when we have not accepted this shadow, (d) the relationship between unconscious and conscious processes in love, and (e) the three directions of love: toward oneself, toward others, and toward God.

Wickes emphasized what has become one of the most popular aspects of Jungian thought: When we fail to accept the dark region of ourselves which *seems* quite unlovely (our shadow), we are in danger of then pro-

---

[68]NYPG 1941–1945, 60.

jecting and hating those elements in others. A failure of deep self-acceptance leads to excessive judgment of others. Surely Dr. Wickes was one of the most eloquent members of the group as she stated the following:

> Nothing is more destructive of love than the weapons of so-called righteous indignation or of hate which projection places in our hands. Instead of removing temptation, we serve the tempter, and the sorcerer within sinks back in the unconscious where he awaits another victim, a victim who is always in the last analysis the self, the destroyer and the destroyed. Projection cannot lead to real conscious love."[69]

Wickes went on to describe the emergence of love from an unconscious to a conscious process. An early unconscious manifestation of love is what Wickes called the "participation mystique," a kind of merging of ourselves with another or the collective. Here, there is a sense of oneness which seems to preclude the possibility of separation or individuality. It is submergence or fusion. "It is a phenomenon of the collective soul, a primitive state of unconsciousness in which persons are at one with each other not through true relatedness but through identification."[70]

As we develop, we become more differentiated. We separate ourselves. Our love becomes more conscious. We share, cooperate, and relate. Again, Wickes describes this beautifully.

> We come again to participation, but we come voluntarily; we are related, not submerged. Every step in individual consciousness carries one further from the security furnished by infantile dependence and obedience. One is cast out from Eden and the labor and pain of individual life is begun."[71]

This describes also the movement from "falling in love," which is a way of falling into the stream of the unconscious, to a more conscious, separate sense of loving a partner as someone different than ourselves.

Wickes then offered a very interesting definition of self-love. She described it as "charity, understanding, nurturing responsibility directed toward the self."[72] She went on to say that she believed this self-love is necessary for love of neighbor and love of God. As she put it, "True self-love leads to the type of love which neither violates others not permits itself

---

[69]NYPG 1941–1945, 62.
[70]NYPG 1941–1945, 62.
[71]NYPG 1941–1945, 62.
[72]NYPG 1941–1945, 63.

to be violated; it is self-respecting and self-responsible and self-loving and therefore able to give respect, responsibility, and love in relation to another."[73] Wickes further added that we cannot have a positive relation with ourselves unless we have an accepting relationship of our past.

Wickes concluded her discussion by saying that the true inner experience which can make us whole is reached by a threefold love. A love of self enables us to move out into life in a creative way, fighting our own demons, and being generous to the world. A love of others moves from an unconscious biological love to conscious personal relationships and commitment to others. A love of God, whether we believe God to be an outer or inner reality, involves complete commitment to that loving Source of all relatedness.

The discussion which followed Wickes's presentation involved a keen interest in learning more about Jung. Wickes suggested some important readings. Kotschnig brought up the issue of male and female being representatives of the logos and eros concepts. Abstract, conceptual thinking is more tied to logos, which is typical of men. Conversely, thinking in more personal terms is connected to eros, which seems more typical of women. Kotschnig quickly added that these two modes of thought are important compliments to each other. Wickes then responded that it is difficult for men to give up their abstractions and engage in a more personal discussion. Nevertheless, eros and logos should not be in opposition to each other. They are two sides of life, which together, offer a sense of completion.

The fourth meeting of the 1942–1943 discussions was led by Gotthard Booth and dealt with the physiology of sex. A great deal of this presentation involved a biological discussion which seems outside the parameters of my review of the New York Psychology Group materials. Because of the issue of time and relevance, I will skip this meeting and move on to the next. However, because the issue of self-love became such a lively debated issue during the second year, one of Gotthard's comments about the nature of self-love is worthy of quoting.

> To love one's neighbor as one loves oneself usually is demanded with the emphasis on the neighbor. In the light of biology and psychology this is an unnecessary, because impossible, demand. It appears that we cannot love others to any greater extent than to the extent to which we have accepted

---

[73]NYPG 1941–1945, 63.

ourselves. The rational meaning of the demand is that we should develop our love and understand it as the completion of ourselves. If it is misunderstood as a challenge to give more to others and less to ourselves, it happens that the ego drives take the center of the stage and destroy the partner in spite of all moral intentions.[74]

For Booth, love necessitates an equal regard for the dignity of ourselves as well as another. While it may not be true that each person has equal *power* in the relationship, it should always be remembered that he or she has equal *dignity*.

In the fifth meeting, Ruth Benedict led the group with a presentation about love in "primitive" cultures. The discussion which followed her presentation seemed, quite frankly, more interesting than her presentation. Fromm asked her four straight questions about issues of sexuality and family structure in undeveloped societies. His first question was whether or not it is possible to make any general statements about men being more sexually aggressive than women. Benedict responded that there are probably more societies which regard men as the aggressor, but that number would be barely over one-half. In fact, she said, "In some societies the extent to which men are regarded as timid and unaggressive, needing to be chaperoned, etc., seems fantastic from our point of view."[75]

Fromm also asked whether some societies give rewards for having children. Benedict said that in some societies, children represent both prestige and insurance. Large families pool their resources and provide greater security for everyone. There is especially more security for the parents as they get older. Fathering one's first child is in many ways the equivalent in our culture of getting one's first job—it represents a transition from boyhood to manhood.

Yet it is also true in some societies that spacing in-between children could add to children's self-esteem. It is as if a child can boast, "Look how much my parents loved and devoted themselves to me. They abstained from intercourse so they could concentrate on me." Benedict went on to say, however, that this didn't produce "spoiled children."

Benedict also pointed out that in these extended family communities, the idea of morality and family obligation is deeply associated. This association is deeper than morals and sexuality, which seems to be connected in

---

[74]NYPG 1941–1945, 68.
[75]NYPG 1941–1945, 76.

many Western societies. In China, for instance, to be moral means to fulfill one's obligations to the group. Tillich then spoke up and said that these cultures would not distinguish morality as social norms from moral principles which stand apart from these social expectations. Benedict agreed.

The sixth meeting consisted of three parts: two brief presentations and a discussion. Ernest and Anna Hartoch Schachtel were the presenters. Both used Rorschach test results as a major part of their presentation. Ernest Schachtel's presentation dealt with the relationship between love, knowledge, and perception. This presentation, which dealt with some technical aspects of the process of perception, did not provoke as much discussion as Anna Schachtel's presentation on the manner in which children develop love. Her case studies and use of Rorschach tests were quite captivating.

More specifically, Mrs. Schachtel dealt with the conditions under which children do or do not develop the capacity to love. She discussed three possibilities: (a) parents who love their children and their children know it, (b) parents who do *not* love their children and their children know it, and (c) parents who pretend to love their children, but who, in fact, do not. This last position is called pseudolove, and according to Mrs. Schachtel, contains the potential for the greatest danger to the child. False love is the most hazardous psychological atmosphere in which to live.

> I think that not being loved is better than the experience of pseudolove for a child. A child who feels that he is not loved may of course in many cases experience a permanent loss of love in his life, but he may also, more often than most people think, develop on his own . . . and become a person more sincere and more capable of love than a child who has lived in an atmosphere of pseudolove.[76]

Pseudolove leaves a child suspended in insecurity, self-preoccupied about his or her own lovability. It also keeps a child going back to an emotional empty-well because parents give the false hope that they will provide for the child's emotional needs.

There is, of course, a possibility that a complete absence of love will push the child toward detachment and a refusal to bond with anyone. This could lead to psychopathic behavior. Yet many factors other than the parents help determined this, not the least of which are teachers and friends.

---

[76]NYPG 1941–1945, 86.

The seventh meeting of the psychology of love discussions turned quite theological. Infrequent attendee, Cyril Richardson, produced a paper called "Love: Greek and Christian." This was to appear in an edition of the Journal of Religion and reprints were sent to the group members prior to the meeting. Thus, there was no official presentation at the meeting, but the discussion was very lively and loaded with theological significance.

A major issue throughout the discussion was the extent to which a relationship with God parallels a good human relationship. How does God's love compare to humanity's love for each other? How does our love for God reflect a similar dynamic of our love for our neighbor? Behind these questions was a deep concern which has always surrounded Paul Tillich: to what extent can we talk about God in personal terms? There were many disagreements, exchanges, and interesting challenges during this session.

The discussion began with Ernest Schachtel's disagreement with Richardson's statement that a relationship with God is of a completely different nature than a relationship between human beings. Richardson replied that religion has gotten itself into trouble whenever it thinks of God as a "Self." He added, "The great theologians always have to deny that what is true of human relationship can be true of relationship to God."[77] Roberts then added that in the biblical idea that "if you do not love your brother whom you have seen, how can you love God whom you have not seen," there is an indication of a parallel relationship. Roberts went on to say that this did not mean, however, that the love is the same. Mr. Schachtel came back with the comment that as he thought about the actual relations of humanity to God in prayers and daily life, he could not imagine this difference. Thomas Bigham then raised the question of whether we should view the relationship from person-to-person as the relationship of brother-to-brother, whereas the relationship between humanity and God could be viewed as a human-to-Father. The human-to-Father relationship expresses more dependence, though it is not completely different than the brother-to-brother relationship.

Tillich entered the discussion with his familiar reminder that all talk of God is by necessity symbolic. We are trying to describe the infinite but we must use finite words. Mr. Schachtel then made the interesting comment that he could understand the vast difference between humanity and God if

---

[77]NYPG 1941–1945, 89.

we were trying to *describe* God, but instead we are asking whether the relations between human to human, and human to God, are similar. Elliott then commented that the assumption that the relationship to God is an entirely different kind of relationship than we have to each other is precisely what causes so many problems in religion. He went on to say, "This asks of us a kind of abandonment in our relationship to God which is different from the kind you have with human beings. This causes our difficulties."[78]

Richardson repeated his belief that it is very problematic to think of God as a "Self" with whom humans have a relationship. Then Elliott, with an obvious reference to Tillich, said that the notion of the "Ground of Being" is not an adequate and illuminating understanding of what Jesus meant by "Father." Richardson then responded that the term "Ground of Being" is philosophical language while the term "Father" is religious language. One is symbolic and the other is not. Schachtel then disagreed by saying that he didn't believe it is possible to have one type of relationship with other men and a completely different type of relationship with God. He put it sharply: "If the relation of man to God is so very important, it is hard to conceive that it can be expressed in terms other than those which express the best relation man has with man."[79]

Roberts remarked that historically, theology has often assumed that humanity owes a kind of relationship to God which would not be appropriate from person-to-person.

> A kind of capitulation to God is appropriate when a similar one to man would be destructive. The unnecessary authoritarian ideas about God which theology has annexed make us shy away from this relationship. But if we conceive of God as one who wills our complete freedom because it is in harmony with Him, then to capitulate is a self-realizing experience, one genuinely confirmed by the individual in his own life. We have a right to rebel against slavishness to God. But if God wills freedom and justice among men, it is not wrong to submit to that authority.[80]

Yet Mr. Schachtel said that the difference in the relationship with God is one of *degree* but not one of *kind*. Elliott then agreed with Schachtel.

---

[78]NYPG 1941–1945, 90.
[79]NYPG 1941–1945, 90.
[80]NYPG 1941–1945, 91.

Richardson disagreed with them both as he argued that there were no human parallels to our dependence on "the Ultimate."

Fromm mentioned that in human relationships an individual is sometimes "deified." If this is not appropriate from person-to-person, is it a healthy attitude toward God? In other words, he questioned whether *any* relationship deserved this type of devotion. Ever aware of the possibility of human inclinations toward masochistic submission as an escape from freedom, Fromm did not like any relationship which involved "surrender."

The discussion then shifted to the issue of self-love and self-hate. Tillich asked Richardson if there is any clear tradition about self-hate in Greek or Christian writing. Richardson said that he believed self-hate had two qualities: (a) a belief that one is inferior and rejected, and (b) defiant and aggressive attitude because of this feeling of rejection. Tillich responded that he saw this as more a matter of bitterness than self-hate. Fromm immediately disagreed with Tillich and offered a very powerful portrait of a self-hating person.

> Very rarely is it conscious because it is so completely contrary to all socially acceptable ideas, it is against all conventions. Nevertheless that it is real hate can be seen in the judgments and actions of the person toward himself. He speaks of himself exactly as he would of his enemy. If he does something slightly wrong or inferior, he despises himself, punishes himself. He has very real hate of himself. From this wrong self-love, egocentricity springs, especially where self-hate is not conscious and has not reached a basis where it hinders egocentricity from developing. It can lead to an amount of self-destruction which will not even show this compensating egocentricity. Where there is egocentricity you can find hate.[81]

This is a rather fascinating comment: where there is egocentricity, there is in reality self-hate. Egocentricity involves a kind of self-preoccupation which is born far more out of self-doubt and self-disdain than of self-flattery.

In the eighth session of the psychology of love meetings, Tillich made a presentation on the ontology of love. He began by stressing the necessity of ontology in all thought. Philosophy, even when it denies it, involves a rational explanation of the structure of Being. Even if it does not directly

---

[81] NYPG 1941–1945, 93.

deal with ontological issues, it nevertheless assumes an ontological framework.

Tillich went on to address issues about God which were relevant to the last meeting. God is not *a* being, but Being itself. Atheism, said Tillich, is an important tool for the theologian because it regularly reminds us that God as a "being' does not exist. Tillich then commented that the ontology of love is classically stated in the simple expression, "God is love." Further, one cannot be connected to this Ground of Being without love.

> Loving God, therefore, can only mean loving love as the ultimate, as Being itself. Therefore, it is a "lie," that is, an essential impossibility, to be connected with the ground of Being without loving.[82]

Love, justice, and power are inseparable in Being itself, but they are separable in finite existence. For Tillich, every self-realization is partially limited and even unjust because it conflicts with other powers of being.

A central theme emphasized by Tillich, an issue which will be brought up a great deal in the following discussion, is his conviction that love is always, in every one of its forms, "ecstatic." In other words, it is self-transcending. Even the most pathetic expressions of deteriorated love are attempts to reach beyond oneself. This is the most important criteria of love: it transcends itself.

This is why Tillich argued that the notion of self-love is inappropriate unless it is used analogously. He believed we must be quite cautious with this terminology. For Tillich, many have confused self-love with the excitement they feel as they become conscious of their self-actualization. Yet this is not self-love. Again, love necessitates self-transcendence and *self*-love does not qualify.

> Selfishness or evil self-love or egocentrism or egoism are altogether words for the infinite self-realization which is lacking the ecstatic self-transcendence. There the use of the word self-love is not admissible at all, because the uniting, self-transcending character of love is lacking and just the opposite, separation, seclusion takes place.[83]

Again, love always contains this element of rising above oneself in the thought of union with another.

---

[82]NYPG 1941–1945, 95.
[83]NYPG 1941–1945, 99.

The discussion after Tillich's presentation revolved primarily around the issues of self-love and self-hate. Roberts began the conversation by saying that he was not clear on Tillich's distinction between the "analogous" and "proper" uses of the terms "self-love" and "self-hate." He believed that it is possible to observe self-love. Fromm then questioned Tillich's notion that since love, by its very essence, is relatedness to something outside of ourselves, the notion of self-love is therefore a contradiction. Fromm suggested that as we reunite with "the other" within ourselves, the estranged part of ourselves, it is right to call this love.

> In other words, the experience of loving oneself is really not contradictory to the idea of love as being related to the stranger since we are strangers to ourselves. In that sense we forgive ourselves—an act of love in the agape sense. If we cannot forgive ourselves, our forgiving of others is not quite true.[84]

Harry Bone wanted to relate the concept of self-love to valuation. When we value something, including ourselves, we love it. Tillich, however, said that he could not accept the concept of valuation as a part of love. The conversation moved on before Tillich explained his difficulty with the concept of valuation. Bigham suggested that the note of self-transcendence is a major part of "ecstacy," to which Tillich responded that self-transcendence is a part of *all* forms of love. "Every kind of love," Tillich said, "every going beyond the closed self, is an ecstatic act because in reality we are always closed into ourselves."[85]

In the ninth and final meeting of the 1942–1943 year dealing with the psychology of love, Martha Glickman provided an overview of the topics which had been discussed during the second year of these meetings. Then Glickman returned to the issue of self-love, saying that perhaps the reason we are so afraid of it is that we have confused the notion of the "Self" with the "ego." Her comment, though lengthy, is worthy of quoting directly.

> Does not our fear of the implications of self-love come from the character of Western culture? Here we find that the greatest values have been accorded by our society to power, prestige, and possession, and to the "rugged individualist" who can acquire them. Thus individuation has stopped short of individuality. True integration and relatedness have been

---

[84]NYPG 1941–1945, 101.
[85]NYPG 1941–1945, 102.

sacrificed at the altar of power and superiority. The rational ego has been enthroned upon a toppling dais. Psychology has developed from the concern for the wreckage caused by these attitudes. The blatant, power-ridden, selfish ego has become the feared and despised object. Hatred is the only tenable ethical attitude for such a monster. Self-hatred is really ego hatred because ego and self are confused.[86]

Following Jung's perspective, we must get beyond the possessive ego to the "Self." The ego, particularly as it developed in Western culture, is not particularly "lovable." But the "Self," which transcends the possessive ego, *is* lovable.

Glickman than said that the true inner experience which can create wholeness can be reached through a threefold love: (a) love of self which "makes us go out into life in generous creativeness,"[87] (b) love of others which "progresses from unconscious biological love to conscious personal relationship with our fellow men in a true responsible commitment,"[88] and (c) suprapersonal love, which "breaking down barriers of caste or race or privilege, is at the service of life itself."[89]

Fromm suggested that the reason many people are not able to love themselves is that they rarely experience themselves as human beings. Instead, they experience themselves as commodities. This "commodity mentality" clearly stands in the way of a more wholistic understanding of ourselves which makes the experience of love possible. This concluded the second year of the New York Psychology Group's discussions.

The Psychology of Love: Reflections on the Second Year

While many interesting issues were brought up during the second year, the two most abiding concerns seemed to be (a) the appropriateness and meaning of self-love, and (b) the extent to which human love parallels Divine love. As we saw at the end of the first year, the group was divided on the issue of a transcendent realm beyond human finitude. Similarly, the end of the second year reveals a division on the question of self-love. Once again, Tillich and Fromm were key players on both sides of this argument. Tillich argued against the notion of self-love while Fromm argued in its favor.

---

[86]NYPG 1941–1945, 105.
[87]NYPG 1941–1945, 106.
[88]NYPG 1941–1945, 106.
[89]NYPG 1941–1945, 106.

Fromm is well known for his argument that self-love is a necessary precondition for loving others.[90] He believes that much of the problem with the notion of self-love is a confusion between self-love and selfishness. Selfishness is *not* self-love. In fact, it is the opposite of self-love.[91] This confusion runs from Calvin to Freud. The misunderstanding revolves around the idea that if one loves oneself, there will be no love left for anyone else. In other words, Freud reduced self-love to narcissism, the turning of the libido back onto itself. For Freud, our love is either directed toward others or ourselves; it cannot be dually directed. Fromm disagrees:

> If it is a virtue to love my neighbor as a human being, it must be a virtue—and not a vice—to love myself, since I am a human being too. There is no concept of man in which I myself am not included. A doctrine which proclaims such an exclusion proves itself to be intrinsically contradictory. The idea expressed in the biblical "thy neighbor as thyself!" implies that respect and love and understanding of one's own self, cannot be separated from respect and love and understanding for another individual. The love for my own self is inseparably connected with the love for any other being.[92]

Fromm further contends that selfishness is in reality a form of self-hate. While a person may *appear* to be excessively self-involved, the reality behind this self-absorption is a deep sense of inferiority or inadequacy. Out of an inner fear, selfish persons become very greedy. They are insatiable. They can never seem to get enough attention, love, wealth, or security.

Fromm's thinking on this issue of self-love and self-hate is very similar to that of Karen Horney.[93] Horney rather masterfully portrays how individuals fall into what she calls "neurotic pride," a condition which looks like excessive self-love, but is in reality based on self-contempt. These persons, out of a disdain for the actual self, construct an imaginary, "idealized self" with which they identify. Their actual self is not good enough, so they must retreat into the laboratory of their own imagination to create a fiction of who they really are. They may appear very arrogant, conceited, and self-

---

[90]While this is a theme in much of his writing, perhaps it is most explicitly stated in his widely read book, *The Art of Loving* (New York: Harper and Row, 1956).

[91]Fromm, *The Art of Loving*, 51.

[92]Fromm, *The Art of Loving*, 49.

[93]See, esp. *Neurosis and Human Growth* (New York: W. W. Norton, 1950).

aggrandizing. Nevertheless, when we strip away all the fictional characteristics they have given themselves, we often find individuals who do not appreciate and care for themselves at all. Thus, Horney points toward a theme that clearly reflects her life's work, namely, the insight that narcissistic pride and self-hate are really two sides of the same coin.

This is particularly interesting in light of recent feminist debates with traditional Augustinian-bound theologians such as Reinhold Niebuhr, and to some extent Tillich. In his famous *Nature and Destiny of Man*, Niebuhr rather brilliantly offers a new rendition of the older Augustinian notion that pride is primary in the human condition.[94] While he also mentions the problem of an undeveloped self or the refusal to become a self, the major focus of Niebuhr is on how pride or exaggerated self-concern is the primary factor in sin. Feminist theologians, such as Valerie Saiving, Daphne Hampson, Susan Nelson Dunfee, and especially, Judith Plaskow, challenged the Niebuhrian pride thesis and argued that "women's experience" indicated that self-loss, more than pride, is perhaps the central concern for women.[95] While this highly interesting conflict between Niebuhr and some feminists scholars is beyond the scope of the present book, I have attempted to extensively deal with it in my book, *Sin, Pride, and Self-Acceptance*.[96] I essentially argue that Karen Horney's insight into the reciprocal relationship between pride and self-depreciation can greatly aid in this conflict.

Most of the members of the New York Psychology Group seemed to favor the notion of self-love. As we saw in the discussion, Martha Glickman, from a Jungian standpoint, wanted to make sure that "self love"

---

[94]Reinhold Niebuhr, *The Nature and Destiny of Man*, vol. 1 (New York: Scribner's, 1964).

[95]Valarie Saiving, "The Human Situation: A Feminine View," in *Womanspirit Rising: A Feminist Reader in Religion*, ed. Carol P. Christ and Judith Plaskow (San Francisco: Harper & Row, 1979); Daphne Hampson, "Reinhold Niebuhr on Sin: A Critique," in *Reinhold Niebhur and the Issues of Our Time*, ed. R. Harries (Grand Rapids MI: Eerdmans, 1986); Susan Nelson Dunfee, "The Sin of Hiding: A Femininist Critique of Reinhold Niebuhr's Account of Sin of Pride," *Soundings* 65/3 (1982): 316-26; Judith Plaskow, *Sex, Sin, and Grace: Women's Experience and the Theologies of Reinhold Niebuhr and Paul Tillich* (Lanham Md.: University Press of America, 1980).

[96]Terry D. Cooper, *Sin, Pride, and Self-Acceptance: The Problem of Identity in Theology and Psychology* (Downers Grove IL: Intervarsity Press, 2003).

did not refer to "ego love," which, in her mind, was a different issue. Yet nevertheless, most members affirmed the importance of self-love.

But Tillich, as we saw, had some deep reservations about the notion of self-love. From his early writings until his final public appearance with Carl Rogers, which I reviewed in chapter 1, Tillich believed that the term self-love, while it often points toward something valuable, is misguided. His view is not Freudian in the sense that if we love ourselves we will drain our love reserve. Instead, he believes that self-love is not literally possible. While the term "self-love" can be used in a metaphorical way, we would be better off dropping it altogether and speaking of self-acceptance, self-affirmation, or in some cases, selfishness.

As the discussion revealed, Tillich had a couple of reasons for his reservations about the notion of self-love. The first reason for opposing the concept of self-love, as I have already pointed out, is because he believed that the character of all love is "ecstatic." "Ecstatic" always means self-transcending. Self-love, taken literally, involves no self-transcendence. The second reason is similar to the first. Love always presupposes the separation of the loving subject from the loved object.[97] Love, for Tillich, is the drive toward union of that which is separated. Within our own consciousness, there is simply not the kind of separation that exists between ourselves and others. Connecting with unconscious elements within ourselves is not the same as connecting with another human being.

Again, Fromm very much disagreed with this notion. He insisted that the concept of self-love is appropriate because we frequently encounter parts of ourselves which have been separated from the primary consciousness. As we encounter these "new regions" and get to know the unconscious elements, the word "love" is appropriate. It is a sort of internal homecoming with parts of ourselves which have been split off and alienated. In short, it *is* a union of that which is separated. Tillich and Fromm remained in disagreement on this issue.

Another key issue in this year's discussion was the extent to which we can make parallels between Divine love and human love. In other words, can we describe the love of God in personal terms? Or, to state it differently, to what extent is there a similarity between a love from human-to-

---

[97]Paul Tillich, *Love, Power, and Justice* (New York: Oxford University Press, 1954) 6.

human and a love from God-to-human? Can human experience help us understand the nature of our experience with the Divine? The group was divided on this issue, and Tillich's perspective aroused the same concern we observed in chapter 1 as I explored his connection between Divine and human acceptance. The underlying Tillichan thesis, here, as I explored earlier, is that we can say nothing about God which is nonsymbolic. God does not *literally* love, for to do so would indicate, once again, that God is a "Being" rather than the Ground of Being. What is interesting in the discussion, once again, is that some of the so-called "secular" psychologists or psychiatrists echoed a theme of some of Tillich's theological critics, namely, that his concept of Being Itself is not adequate for the highly personal encounters with God. John Sanders addresses this issue.

> Interestingly, Tillich's understanding of God as fully immanent in the cosmos arrives at a conclusion held by many classical theists who emphasized divine transcendence: God can have no external relations with creatures. To think of having personal relations with God or being his partner in action is impossible if God is Being-Itself, since to have such a relationship is to posit two beings existing alongside each other.[98]

The question, then, as Stanley Grenz and Roger Olson point out, is whether one can have a personal encounter with this "ontological ground of all things personal."[99] Tillich claimed that the idea of a "personal God" is a confusing symbol.[100] While God is not a person, God is not less than the personal. But atheism is correct to rebel against any notion of God as a Divine person or being. Again, we can say nothing about God other than God is being itself. Thus, even the notion of God "loving" humanity is not literally true. As we saw in chapter 1, the insistence upon using symbolic, nonpersonal language in reference to God makes parallels with psychotherapy most difficult and may, in fact, eliminate keen insights into the Divine life. And then, of course, the ongoing question remains whether this "God beyond God" is the God of personal religion. It appears to many as the

---

[98]John Sanders, *The God Who Risks: A Theology of Providence* (Downers Grove IL: Intervarsity Press, 1998) 159.

[99]Stanley J. Grenz and Roger E. Olson, *Twentieth Century Theology: God and the World in a Transitional Age* (Downers Grove IL: Intervarsity Press, 1992) 127.

[100]Paul Tillich, *Systematic Theology*, vol. 1 (Chicago: University of Chicago Press, 1951) 245.

product of ontological speculation and not the God of the Judeo-Christian tradition. Obviously, that question remains with us and is beyond the purposes of my investigation. Indeed, it may still be *the* most hotly debated issue in Tillich's system.

Perhaps the most interesting aspect of this debate can be stated this way: Just as some theologians decry an anthropomorphic God and want to make sure that the symbol of God is beyond all human categories, some psychologists question the entire purpose of trying to have a "relationship" with a God who does not manifest the personal traits so deeply prized by humans. This God does not literally "accept us," "love us," or "forgive us." These are human categories, we are told, which cannot possibly be descriptive of the Divine life. God is quite above and beyond these finite experiences and they cannot be used to describe God's nature. Again, all we can say is that God is the ground of Being. Yet, once again, one then wonders how the highly personal language of psychotherapy, which Tillich chooses to use, can possibility be revelatory concerning this picture of the Divine. Stated more bluntly, I cannot help asking if Tillich's ontology does not bulldoze over his deeply insightful use of psychotherapeutic analogies. And this seems no where more apparent than in the issue of love.

Chapter 5

Ethics and Psychotherapy: The New York Psychology Group, 1943–1945

The deepest guilt feeling always comes from the message of grace, not from the proclamation of the law.   —Paul Tillich

The third year of the New York Psychology Group dealt with psychology and ethics or, as it was labeled, "the psychology of conscience." This year of conversation contained many discussions which continue to have relevance for today's issues. Some of these exchanges are most interesting when seen in light of postmodern thought, philosophical hermeneutics, and the current discussion of psychology's relationship to ethics. It is important to move through these materials with an eye toward their present relevance. Again, I will attempt a fair narrative of the central issues, realizing that others might find other items in the discussion of greater importance.

Third Year: Psychology of Conscience

Fromm offered the first presentation of this year's discussions and it was packed with interesting material. In fact, it set the stage for future discussions to such a degree that many later presentations were all but ignored in an effort to get back to Fromm's comments.

The third year indicates what we have already seen: Erich Fromm was the most important figure in the New York Psychology Group. There was more discussion surrounding his thought, more input from him, and more questions asked by him than any other group member. As in the first year, a division emerged in the group, a division led, to a large extent, by Fromm on one side and Tillich on the other. Fromm represented an emphatic insistence that faith must be faith in humanity and not faith in any transcendent realm beyond the human. For Fromm, transcendence referred only to a human capacity to rise above our own actions and reflect rationally on our behavior. It did *not* refer to the realm of the unconditioned as Tillich argued. Similarly, in this year's discussions, Fromm made a strong case for what he called "anthropocentric ethics," which essentially means that humanity, not some transcendent God, is the source and norm of all ethical thinking. Thus, the issue of whether or not there is any region of human experience beyond the mere human once again became a primary contention within the group.

Fromm began the first meeting with a two-part presentation. The first part examined Freud's development of the notion of conscience and the second part set forth some of Fromm's propositions concerning the nature of anthropocentric ethics. Let's first turn our attention to Fromm's summation of Freud.

As usual, Fromm was quite clear in his overview of Freudian theory. He admitted that one's first impression of Freud would probably be that Freud was a complete ethical relativist. Freud certainly reduced the function of conscience to a purely psychological and nontranscendent source. Conscience, for Freud, referred to the voice of the Superego, the internalization of the father's prohibitions and rules. After a rivalry with the father over the sexual object of the mother, the boy identifies with the father's commands and prohibitions. Fear of castration prompts this accommodation to the father. After a while it becomes easier to fear one's own internal demands than to fear the father. This is the point at which conscience develops. Stated differently, the development of conscience indicates the resolution of the Oedipal conflict.

For Freud, it does not matter if the voice of the superego is "valid" or not. The point is that it represents the internalized fear. By introjecting the father's superego, culture is transmitted from one generation to the next. Fromm believes that Freud stated something very crucial here, namely, that for most individuals conscience equals fear. Fear of what? Fear of an external authority.

Fromm continued his presentation by mentioning that for Freud behind every ethical norm or sense of "good" is in reality something "bad." A master of suspicion, Freud looks beneath the surface and wants to know what "the good" is compensating for or denying. Freud holds that the original ethical norm is a reaction against the original sin of wanting to kill the father so the child can possess the mother. In Freud's view, the issue of envy always underlies our sense of justice. Envy is the dark element behind justice. We do not want anyone to have more than we have, so we develop a sense of justice which says that no one should have any more than anyone else. Thus, the emphasis on fairness and justice grows out of this rationalization of envy. And the taboo against killing is a reaction-formation of our primitive desire to kill our father. Ethical standards are thus seen from a strictly psychological standpoint. For Freud, there clearly is no transcendent validity to any moral value.

Fromm further pointed out that Freud's concept of "sin" has interesting religious parallels. For Freud, once again, the first wish, the incest wish, becomes forbidden because it challenges the father's right and might. Thus, the original sin is linked to disobedience just as the first couple in the Genesis account understands the first sin to be disobedience. Fromm notes that God gave no reason for not eating the forbidden fruit other than He simply forbade it. God was, in fact, jealous of humanity's desire to be like Him. From the human standpoint, eating the forbidden fruit was the beginning of choice and reason; but, from the Divine standpoint, it was rebellion.

Fromm further noted how often in clinical settings what patients call "sin" is usually their fear of having been disobedient. Virtue becomes a matter of pleasing those we fear. Conversely, sin is displeasing them.

Again, Fromm admitted that from this angle Freud's system seems very relativistic. Yet he also believed there is another way to look at Freud in which he is not a complete relativist. Freud always holds onto one key virtue—truth. When Freud speaks of the virtue of truth, he does not speak of something beneath or behind truth which is "bad." Truth is not a "compensation" for a darker process. In fact, truth is the ultimate aim of human life. It may be unpleasant and difficult, but it always remains virtuous.

Fromm then moved into the second half of his presentation. This involved an elaboration of the central tenets of his anthropocentric ethics. First, he said, anthropocentric ethics is a system of ethics which does *not* need any transcendent authority as its source. Second, the concern of ethics should always revolve around what is good or bad *for human beings*. Third, we can arrive at a rational decision of what is "good" or "bad" for humanity, *as a result of a deep understanding of human nature* and the laws which guide its development. As Fromm put it, "In other words, anthropology or psychology is the basis for such an anthropocentric and rationally valid system of ethics."[1] And finally, anthropocentric ethics holds one very significant premise: growth is better than decay. Thus, Fromm believes it is possible to have a system of ethics which is completely human-centered, rational, and even objective because it would be based on knowledge of human nature. Modern dynamic psychology could greatly aid this understanding of human nature. As Fromm states it, "From this standpoint the concept of ethics would be the full realization of man's growth in terms of

---

[1] Tillich, *Systematic Theology* 1:112.

his empirical nature."[2] Interestingly, Fromm goes on to say that because of this radically human focus, the concept of guilt is no longer disobedience, but instead, self-mutilation. The backbone of immorality is that it hurts persons, not that it disobeys some transcendent rule or authority.

During the discussion, Roberts stated that Fromm's notions of "growth" and "decay" already contain ethical presuppositions and a value orientation. Fromm agreed, but then stated that his was a "rationally valid statement based on the basis of our knowledge of man."[3] Thus, he claimed to have arrived at his ethical convictions on the basis of an objective observation of the history of human nature. Roberts seems to have been suggesting that Fromm's perspective made implicit claims about the ultimate context of our lives. Fromm did not appear to be aware of the metaphysical assumptions he was making about the natural order, nor did he seem to appreciate how his image of human fulfillment was founded on a vision of human possibilities as much as a survey of previous human behavior.

What is of keen interest is that apparently Tillich said nothing during this discussion. Had he heard Fromm say all this before? Was he anticipating his own presentation during the following meeting next month? We are left with a question about Tillich's silence during this initial meeting in which anthropocentric ethics were laid out.

In the second meeting of the third year, Tillich offered a presentation entitled, "Conscience—Historical and Typographical Remarks." This somewhat informal presentation became the basis for Tillich's important article, "Conscience in Western Thought and the Idea of a Transmoral Conscience," in 1945, an article which revealed once again Tillich's mastery of intellectual history and his ability to trace a key concept's development.[4]

Tillich began his presentation by saying that the concept of conscience emerged in the Greek and Roman cultures. It emerged more as a popular, rather than as a philosophical, idea. The idea was based on the Greek word which means "know with" or "being guilty with" oneself. In popular terms,

---

[2]Tillich, *Systematic Theology* 1:112.

[3]Tillich, *Systematic Theology* 1:113.

[4]Paul Tillich, "Conscience in Western Thought and the Idea of a Transmoral Conscience," *Crozer Quarterly* 22/4 (October 1945). This article is reprinted by permission under the title, "A Conscience above Moralism," in *Conscience: Theological and Psychological Perspectives*, ed. Nelson Carl Ellis (New York: Newman Press, 1973).

this meant looking at oneself as a witness. Philosophy referred to this as self-consciousness. Philo, said Tillich, followed the Old Testament understanding of self-observation as "self-consciousness." Yet Tillich makes an important distinction: "The philosophers are interested in the objective ethical norms, not in the subjective reception of them. This is left to popular experience, as expressed, for instance, in popular proverbs."[5] Human beings are thus divided into subjects which act and subjects which observe this action. The judgment, of course, is accusing. This is why the notion of conscience quickly became "bad conscience" and was related to self-condemnation. A good conscience is not discussed. It refers simply to the absence of a bad conscience. Stated differently, *when conscience speaks, there is always something wrong*.

Also, the emergence of conscience indicates a movement from "we-consciousness" to "I-consciousness." Tillich appears fond of the old comment, "the self is discovered through sin." Animals do not accuse themselves. This appears to be unique to human beings. Further, Tillich believes that Paul mediated this Graeco-Roman understanding of conscience to the Western world. Tillich is quick to point out that conscience is an ethical concept, not a religious one. Paul assumes that *everyone* has a conscience and that it is not merely the possession of Christians. "The conscience is the judging, not the law-giving organ; therefore it can be erroneous in its judgment. . . . There is no 'religion of conscience' in the New Testament."[6]

Again, conscience is strictly accusatory. It does not give laws, but instead, accuses those who do not fulfill the law.

Scholasticism raised the question concerning what norms the conscience uses to judge and how these particular norms are recognized. The answer, for the scholastics, was "synteresis," which meant the perfection of reason which would then be able to recognize "the good." Stated differently, conscience was understood as human reason acting in accord with natural law. This intuitive reason acts immediately and infallibly. Yet while the natural law is infallible, the application of it to the specific situations of our lives through conscience could be erroneous. In order to prevent these errors, the authorities gave more and more advice to the

---

[5]NYPG 1941–1945, 115.
[6]NYPG 1941–1945, 116.

Christian. Trust in individual conscience, apart from the authority of the Church, became very suspect. The immediate knowledge of "the good" was out of the reach of the layperson. Ultimately, the voice of individual conscience had to match the collective tradition of the Church.

Tillich argues that in both religious and autonomous ethics there is often an appeal to move beyond the moral level into a transmoral sphere. The conscience, in this sense, transcends itself.

> A conscience may be called transmoral which does not judge in obedience to a moral law but according to the participation in a reality which transcends the sphere of moral commands. A transmoral conscience does not deny the moral realm, but is driven beyond it by the unbearable tensions of the sphere of law.[7]

This does not, however, abolish the conscience; instead, it transforms it. Luther, according to Tillich, was clearly the best example of the transmoral conscience. Luther, as we saw in chapter 1, experienced attacks of Divine wrath which closed him in on himself and filled him with angst. He was driven toward both despair and a hatred of God. In Luther's experience, the "bad conscience" could not be conquered no matter what he did. Yet for Luther, God subjects Himself to the consequences of his own wrath. Paradoxically, we stand only before our own accusations and God defends us against ourselves. Notice that this is *not* a "good conscience." Our lightness of heart does not come because we are morally perfect. Instead, our hearts are light because we stand justified and accepted in spite of our sin. Luther knew that a "good conscience" was not possible because of sin. A joyful conscience, however, recognizes that we are forgiven in spite of sin.

Tillich strongly emphasized that the privatization of conscience came from the sects which followed the Reformation, and not from Luther, himself. The conscience, for Luther, was *not* a divine illumination or source of revelation. Tillich, in a later article, stated this very straightforwardly:

> Luther's refusal to recant his doctrine of justification is an expression of his conscientiousness as a doctor of theology. He declares that he would recant if he were refuted by arguments taken from Scripture or reason, the positive source and the negative criterion of theology. But he does *not* say—as often has been stated by liberal Protestants—that his conscience

---

[7]NYPG 1941–1945, 57.

is the *source* of his doctrine. There is no "religion of conscience" either in the New Testament or in classical Christianity before the sectarian movements of the Reformation period.[8]

There was a growing belief that one could find a mystical contact with God. Conscience came to be interpreted by some individuals as the authority of individual experience.

> The sects created a new concept of conscience; the place where the spirit speaks to us out of our own depths (if through suffering we have reached these depths). Not *we* in us, but "the God in us." The "inner light" refers to the concrete decisions, i.e., it is conscience.[9]

Tillich continued by saying that with George Fox this inner light produces the truth itself. Note the change: Up until now, conscience represented the voice of judgment; it did *not* provide the content of what to do. Now, in Fox, we see a dramatic shift. The conscience, itself, produces revelation, insights, and ethical guidance. The conscience *is* the inner light of God.

Thomas Muentzer and his followers taught that the Divine Spirit speaks to us out of the depths of our souls. This is *God* talking to us and not our talking to ourselves. Suffering opens up the door to this Divine, internal revelation. All of the enthusiasts understood this Divine Word in a very concrete sense and identified it with conscience. Thus, conscience became a source of religious insight and not just a morality alarm.

From these and related movments, the "freedom of conscience" notion emerged. Again, Tillich points out that this understanding of conscience was quite different than Paul. While Paul advocated paying attention to conscience in ethical decision-making, he did not believe that conscience was a source of revelation and new religious principles.

> The quest for the "freedom of conscience" does not refer to the concrete ethical decision, but it refers to the religious authority of the "inner light," which expresses itself through the individual conscience. And since the inner light could hardly be distinguished from practical reason, freedom of conscience meant actually the freedom to follow one's autonomous reason, not only in ethics, but also in religion. The "religion of con-

---

[8]Tillich, "A Conscience above Moralism," in *Conscience: Theological and Psychological Perspectives*, ed. Nelson, 50-51.
[9]NYPG 1941–1945, 117.

science" and the consequent idea of tolerance are not the result of the Reformation but of sectarian spiritualism and mysticism.[10]

Tillich understands that the issue of a transmoral conscience is a very delicate issue which is easily misunderstood. Nazi Germany made such a claim and ended up turning a supposed "transmoral ethic" into an antimoral practice.

The issue of a transmoral conscience proved to be a central focus of discussion throughout the remainder of the year. At the end of this section, I will include a later statement Tillich later made concerning the nature of this important topic.

In the third meeting of the psychology and ethics sessions, there were three short presentations and a discussion. Violet de Laszlo, the first presenter, spoke about Jung's understanding of conscience. Jung, she said, refuses to use the concept of "conscience" because he believes it is too deeply associated with conventional morality. Instead, Jung talks about establishing a balance between the dynamic of opposites in the personality. Jung holds that we are constantly tempted to think that what was once good always remains good eternally. Unlike Freud, Jung also holds that consciousness and the unconscious are always complimentary and that *morality resides in the unconscious as well as in consciousness.* The unconscious, for Jung, is much wiser and friendlier than Freud's rather ugly picture of unconscious processes. As de Laszlo put it, "In Jung's opinion, morality is not misconception, conceived by an ambitious Moses upon Sinai, but something inherent in the laws of life and fashioned like a house or a ship or any other cultural instrument in the normal processes of life."[11] In other words, there is a natural law of human nature and this law is the highest moral principle. This law clearly rises above the concerns of individual egoism. De Laszlo states this well.

> [W]rongdoing could consist in the deviation from the inner law which itself is not a static principle but a corrective for whatever onesidedness of attitude may be prevailing in regard to any given situation. It is a kind of living, self-regulating principle, which assumes meaning only if the inter-

---

[10]Tillich, "A Conscience Above Moralism," 53.
[11]NYPG 1941–1945, 124.

action between the conscious and the unconscious is experienced as vital and creative.[12]

Jung much prefers the notion of obedience to this inner life over the word "conscience." This "transcendent function" contains both a conscious and unconscious element and is similar to Tillich's transmoral conscience.

This is also a part of the process of individuation, whose goal is the maximization of these inherent possibilities. This process does not lead to greater isolation but to greater solidarity with the human race. Further, when conscience is associated with fear, this is because morality is perceived as an external prohibition rather than an inherent part of one's own nature. As long as conscience is preoccupied with external prohibition, it will remain uncreative, and will long for liberation.

Harry Bone provided the next, very brief, presentation. His main focus revolved around whether an individual accepts the responsibility of self-determination. In evaluating the ethical character of persons, we must look at the direction of their entire lives and not just their immediate traits. There are two important characteristics of self-determination. The first is a repudiation of external authority as the determiner or judge of one's actions. This may involve a transitional hatred of the formative years of one's life. The second characteristic is "self-activity," meaning the freedom to feel, think, and act from within oneself. Responsibility will follow from this inner freedom.

Then Bone continued by asking and reflecting on a question which clearly anticipated concerns of our own time.

> How is psychotherapy related to ethics? Psychotherapy as a process is not a school of ethics (much less a school of morals), but is concerned with the indispensable precondition of ethics, viz., with the achievement of self-determination. Full ethical maturity is achieved by the independent person in direct relation to life, independent of the psychotherapeutic relationship. The relation of the therapist (as therapist), to the person concerned ends when the forces of independent growth are released and well started on their way. The continuation of the specialized relationship beyond that point negates the essence of ethical living, viz., that claims no special assistance, dependency, immunities, etc.[13]

---

[12]NYPG 1941–1945, 125.
[13]NYPG 1941–1945, 127.

And then . . .

> Can psychotherapy experience give the joyous experience of the transmoral realization? In the sense of the full realization of one's potentialities for freedom, no. In the sense of the achievement of the crucial beginning of genuine self-determination yes. Furthermore this is a prototype of the later realization which it makes possible and probable; they will not be categorically different from it.

Thus, psychotherapy provides a kind of clearing away of inner conflict or neuroses which then allows an ethical life to be possible. I will say much more about this issue in the reflections on the group. For now, however, I will continue with the narrative.

The final presentation of this meeting was given by Thomas J. Bigham. He discussed the place in Catholic religion of what Tillich had called the "transmoral conscience." He acknowledged that the ongoing difficulty with morality is that it tends to become moralism. As he put it, "Freedom and fullness of finite being are narrowed to the satisfaction of code and category. Men rebel against this because it insults their being (angst)."[14] He went on to say that in Catholic thought moral law is seen not as a code but as a "divinely planted pattern of being."[15] Natural law is similar to scientific law. In other words, it refers to the observation of moral law in the same way that we refer to the observation of life processes in science.

As he reflected on the relationship between conscience and authority, Bigham made the following, rather interesting, observation.

> Catholicism allows for authority both in the sense of authoritarian and in the sense of authoritative, i.e., in regard to obedience to compelling forces and also in regard to obedient right reason. It seems that there is an authority of compelling force both individual and social; and this should not be dismissed as merely biological and merely cultural, for both affect man as a biological and cultural being. There is also the authoritative reason, clarifying the structure of things for us (the rational ego). Yet this reason becomes individualistic unless it takes biological and cultural unity of men into account; by this sense of unity it transcends individual isolation.[16]

---

[14]NYPG 1941–1945, 128.
[15]NYPG 1941–1945, 128.
[16]NYPG 1941–1945, 128-29.

Bigham stated that he did not understand Fromm's reluctance to recognize the need for this outside compelling authority. Clearly for Bigham, this authority did not threaten the development of an internal rational authority.

In the discussion which followed these presentations, I find it interesting that the entire dialogue focused again on Fromm's anthropocentric ethics. Bigham's last comment must have set the stage for the remainder of the evening. As a consequence, de Laszlo's discussion of Jung was not even mentioned. The beginning comment of the discussion was a request for clarification of Fromm's naturalistic ethics, and the group's attention, once again, focused on Fromm's thought.

Fromm pointed out that "rational authority" refers to a competency which proves itself valid for the purpose of guiding us. Conversely, irrational authority refers to any authority accepted on the grounds of anything except competence, such as fear. In both ethics and science there are *degrees* of competency which serve a guiding function. Human progress requires such authorities. They continue to be valid only if they are justified by their competency as they are ongoingly critically appraised by their followers.

Fromm then went on to contrast two views of the word "transcendent." One view of transcendent is that it refers to an objective meaning to life based on something beyond humanity, such as God. Thus, human life, in this view, derives its significance from God. Life is meaningful because of God, not because of humanity. Meaning comes from this "additional" source.

By contrast, another view asserts that there is nothing beyond humanity. We must rely on what humanity sets for itself by the aid of its own reason. Meaning or purpose cannot be deducted from God; instead, it is up to us. As Fromm put it, this view states that "there is only life, and the purpose of life is only what men can recognize as such in the history of species."[17]

Fromm further added that in anthropocentric ethics, norms are not transcendent because they do not refer to authority or phenomenon above the human. The norms are instead developed on the basis of the power of human reason. Yet for Fromm, this rationality is not divorced from the total

---

[17]NYPG 1941–1945, 129.

life of the individual. It also includes emotion and is not therefore exclusively cerebral.

> Our reason, applied to observation of human nature as evidenced in history, leads us to recognize what is good and bad for men on the assumption that good and bad refers to the process of growth in terms of peculiarity of human nature. Often an awareness of what we should do appears with great force and power and perhaps in the form of an intuition. What we call intuition is one of the forms of rational knowledge. We have very powerful rational experiences about what is right which are not necessarily ones to which the process of thinking is applied, and they are authoritative only in the sense of being true, i.e., that they have competency.[18]

Tillich responded that the idea of transcendence could be traced back to Greek philosophy where it does *not* have a definite religious meaning, but is in fact merely a reference to the realm above sense impression. "The logos beyond the immediate experience is valid and should be called in some way transcendent."[19] However, another quality of transcendence, argued Tillich, involves the realm of the unconditioned. Tillich described this realm of the unconditioned as follows:

> The experience of something inescapable, something which we must fulfill, is something in our consciousness. It is the element of the numinous—the freeing from and being attracted by the numinous. If one denies it, one can only deny it in the name of something which has the same character although it is expressed in scientific terms.[20]

Tillich continued this line of thought by saying that he believed that Harry Bone's notion of self-determination could only be achieved "under the auspices of some symbol of religious experience as he has described it, in which the unconditioned character is involved in such a way that there is a paradox, namely, we always know that we are not always in the situation of self-determination and are therefore never entirely in the ideal ethical situation."[21] In other words, Pelagian self-determination is not really possible. The realm of the unconditioned or ultimate must break into our finite lives and enable us to accept ourselves in spite of our unacceptability.

---

[18]NYPG 1941–1945, 130.
[19]NYPG 1941–1945, 130.
[20]NYPG 1941–1945, 130.
[21]NYPG 1941–1945, 131.

We are then able to affirm ourselves because of this unconditioned affirmation. Put simply, grace allows for self-acceptance.

Bone then responded that certainly there is no such thing as "perfect" self-determination, but that it is instead a progressive process. He further expressed some question about Tillich's notion of the necessity of symbols, saying that there are so many available, and that the individual must "supply" his or her own. Not surprisingly, Tillich disagreed with this latter notion and stated his familiar perspective that we are "grasped" by symbols which provoke us to take our lives with utmost seriousness. We do *not* invent them or conjure them up for our own purposes.

Fromm then added that he had great sympathy for this notion of "seriousness" about which Tillich so often speaks. For Fromm, this term refers to a particular state of mind of an individual who has a genuine experience of his own life, which means that he/she also has connection with the lives of others. Fromm, as we have seen before, does not think it possible to have "deep experience" all on one's own. Fromm went on to say that if we identify this seriousness about our lives and those of other beings as *religious*, then surely the atheist and the theist are both religious persons. But, Fromm objected, the word "serious" refers only to a certain type of human attitude, and does not mean that we are suddenly above or beyond the fact that the serious nonreligious person would question the content of the religious person's beliefs. In fact, he or she would find the beliefs of the religious person to be quite irrational. "If the religious person contended that seriousness was identical with belief in the transcendent element, this would be begging the question."[22]

In other words, being serious about one's life does not mean being religious. Fromm believes Tillich is changing words around in an unfair way. Earlier we saw that Fromm did not like Tillich's equation of the God of Abraham, Isaac, and Jacob with the "Ground of Being." Nor did he agree that the Father of Jesus was the same as "Being itself." He did not believe this ontological notion represented both the Old and New Testament understanding of God. Similarly, here, Fromm believes Tillich is further confusing things by equating the human attitude of seriousness with religion.

Again, the interesting element of this discussion is that Fromm, as a quite secular psychoanalyst, is setting forth what has become a central theo-

---

[22]NYPG 1941–1945, 131.

logical critique of Tillich, namely, that the specific contents of religious faith are minimized in his attempt to identify faith as an attitude of ultimate concern. God becomes synonymous with "depth" and faith becomes synonymous with a serious concern about life. The world of *content* or *belief* becomes rather unimportant and the attitude one brings to life becomes all important. Like Fromm, many theologians have objected that the content of one's beliefs have a great deal to do with being religious.

In the next meeting, David Roberts provided the presentation. His focus was, once again, on Fromm's anthropocentric ethics. Yet Roberts wanted to discuss the metaphysical and theological questions connected to Fromm's radically humanistic ethical framework. Roberts began by agreeing with Fromm that ethics could and should be anthropocentric in that it grows out of individual commitments. Also, we can say, in a sense, that everything falls under the category of "human experience." Thus, problems having to do with ethical norms and motives are indeed *human*.

In certain other aspects, however, Roberts questioned anthropocentric ethics. He certainly didn't think we should simply survey the diversities of human nature, put a stamp of approval on it, and then say that our ethics must always flow out this pattern of human nature. Instead, argued Roberts, any conceivable ethic should be based on a normative consideration which transcends the position of specific people and cultures. Certainly, ethical development involves what human beings contribute, but this also occurs within an atmosphere of interaction with something which transcends humanity. When we envision what we want to become, for instance, we appeal to norms and structures which are beyond what is individual and social. Mere adjustment to a social pattern may be good *or* bad. We appeal to something which lies beyond individual and social conditioning.

> In that sense, man's own ethical achievements and judgments are set within a framework which is not completely at his own disposal, so that wisdom, mental health, inner peace for every individual are partly dependent upon his own initiative and partly upon his coming to terms cooperatively with structures and truths that he did not create and does not sustain by any effort of his will and that he discovers in reality rather than leads into reality.[23]

---

[23]NYPG 1941–1945, 133.

Roberts further declared that religion refers to this as a saving power which is able to break through human resistance.

Roberts also claimed that the law or conscientiousness has played a twofold role in Christian thought since Paul. On the one hand, it has pointed toward humanity's responsibility and capacity to abuse the freedom with which it has been given. We have the ability to either fulfill or violate certain definite principles of our individual and collective lives. This moral structure of the law can be seen as evidence that the universe is concerned with moral values, and that there are cosmic foundations to human ethical concerns.

At the same time, however, it has frequently been recognized that the law or conscientiousness is a stage which includes much inner conflict and that persons do not arrive at inner peace until they move beyond this intrapsychic battle. Thus, this is perceived as a "stage" of development.

> Guilt feelings, conflicts between duty and impulse, spirit and flesh, etc., must be passed through in the process of reaching maturity, but the final stage of goodness is seen as lying beyond this conflict. This insight of Christianity (grace and God) has been lost sight of or imperfectly expressed in subsequent theology. Unless it is possible to pass beyond moralism, then the Christian life is still an imperfect one.[24]

Roberts goes on to say that for Catholics the sacraments relieve this relentless moral tension, and for Protestants, the notion of justification by faith frees us from the bondage of moral effort and frustration. However, this sense of grace was largely lost and Christianity unwittingly contributed to an internal fear about moral failure. It became preoccupied with moral codes and behavior which it thought would insure the stability of culture.

Roberts concluded his presentation with an important Tillich-sounding comment. He said that while Christianity asserted that the individual may contribute something to this resolution of inner conflict, the healing reality of this resolution is grounded in a Source larger than the individual or society. Old barriers are broken down and new possibilities are awakened.

In the discussion which followed, Bone asked Roberts whether he understood conscience as simply keeping the law, and Roberts replied that for him, conscience refers to something we must pass beyond as we move toward a more adequate outlook concerning our relations with each other

---

[24]NYPG 1941–1945, 134.

and God. Roberts said that the word conscience suggests that "the flesh is still an enemy and has not yet been made an ally."[25] Consequently, it still reflects a *divided self*. For Roberts, the concept of "oughtness" invariably leads to a resistance, even if we impose this "oughtness" on ourselves.

Elliott questioned Roberts's reference to this moral or ethical standard beyond or above the social standards. Roberts then responded that our ethical ideas are indeed grounded in individual and social patterns, but it is impossible to discuss what is "good" for us without looking at ourselves from a cosmic framework. As he put it, "One cannot avoid questions as to whether the purpose and values which man finds himself wanting to promote are or are not in some kind of alignment with the nature of things."[26] In other words, we feel driven to ask whether our deepest sense of ethics, values, and justice match the nature of Reality itself. Do we microcosmically reflect a macrocosmic perspective?

At this point in the discussion Fromm reviewed his principles of anthropocentric ethics. He began with reason, which includes the emotions, and is the *only power* whereby humanity can recognize ethical standards. Fromm clearly implied that if the unassisted human reason cannot locate ethical standards, it will certainly get no help from any transcendent source. Further, the concept of how we ought to live is part of evolutionary wisdom. Ethics only goes beyond the individual person by moving away from individual isolation and connecting to other people. We are all related to each other. Second, anthropocentric ethics are beyond the particular social and historical location of a person's life because they can envision how life could and should be lived. While the norms of society are designed primarily for survival, there is a prophetic side to human ethics which looks beyond particular societies to arrive at a higher standard of goodness. These so-called transmoral standards are transcendent only in the sense that they rise above the here-and-now and envision what life might be like. But this is a *fully human act of imagination and does not involve some transcendent power*. It does not point toward some region of ultimate reality which is beneath or above the human.

> The one who cries in the wilderness is a prophet: his object is man and his vision is how man should be regardless of what the particular need of any

---

[25]NYPG 1941–1945, 134.
[26]NYPG 1941–1945, 135.

given society is. In terms of man's destiny, in how man should act, this transcends any social apparatus, but it refers to what human reason can recognize as good and bad for man over the thousands of years in which man and reason have not changed very much. No anthropocentric ethics can say the last word because man changes in his ability to recognize what is good and bad for man.[27]

Fromm's ongoing concern, as we have seen before, is the issue of what we mean by "transcendent." Stated differently, when we talk about something being "outside" of us, he wants to ask, "Outside what?" He believes that to talk about "outside" means to talk about what is outside the conscience or the will. Intuition comes from "outside" these intellectual efforts, yet this never means "outside" of the self or the human condition. Fromm believes that his understanding of "outside," which is still "inside" the human sphere, is the only adequate meaning for the word, "transcendent." It certainly does *not* refer to an extra-human force or power. Stated differently, for Fromm, *the transcendent realm is still the realm of the psychological and not the theological.* Thus, Fromm regularly states that he refuses any reason which is "outside of man."[28]

Roberts directly challenged Fromm by questioning whether or not anyone could possibly have enough evidence to affirm or deny whether there is reason outside of man. Fromm responded that it is much harder to affirm than to deny. Havice interrupted them by saying that this is an epistemological difficulty because one cannot define ideals and norms except empirically. Roberts disagreed by saying that these norms are more than strictly empirical because they can envision a life which has not yet been lived. Fromm said that prophetic ideals, however, must conform to the possibilities of human nature. Roberts agreed, but then said something most interesting. He said that we carry our norms with us even as we observe these possibilities of human nature. Thus, our norms influence what conditions we find. This statement seems to reflect a philosophical hermeneutic in which our preunderstanding and implicit norms shape what we find in the "evidence" of human nature. In other words, we do not investigate human nature from the standpoint of a neutral or blank-slate perspective. Our assumptions will influence and color what we find. Thus, Roberts seems to be acknowledging the important role of preunderstanding in our

---

[27]NYPG 1941–1945, 135.
[28]NYPG 1941–1945, 136.

investigations. Our consciousness has already been shaped by inherited cultural assumptions. We may be able to distance ourselves, as Ricoeur frequently states, from these assumptions, but we will hardly be able to come up with an objective description of human nature.[29]

As the conversation shifted, Fromm pointed out how psychoanalysis greatly contributes to our understanding of conscience. He pointed out that when persons say they *ought* to do something, they are usually not referring to themselves, but to some outside authority which they have identified with themselves.

> There is not so much the struggle between the flesh and the spirit as the struggle between the self and the authorities which want to manipulate one. The fight of conscience is not a fight within the individual but between the self and something transcending it which is conceived subjectively as if it were going on within. Pychoanalysis shows that the experience of guilt and sin results mostly from displacing those of whom one is afraid and is not a moral phenomenon.[30]

Tillich, who had been silent during the discussion, spoke up at the end and questioned why there had been no reference to the contents of "this self out of which all good things come."[31] This comment seemed directed at Fromm, who then responded that the center of the self is "the center of the organized, structuralized productive activity of the total personality."[32] Thus, this meeting ended with a sense of vagueness, and in my view, a somewhat frustrating sense of incompletion. It would have been interesting if Tillich would have entered the discussion earlier with his question. As it stands, neither the question, and certainly not Fromm's response, seems clear.

The next meeting of the New York Psychology Group involved a presentation by Gotthard Booth entitled, "Disease and Guilt." Tillich was not present at this meeting. Given this, along with the fact that this presentation was at times medically tedious and outside the flow of the year's discussion, I will move on to the group's final meeting during the 1943-44 year.

---

[29]See Paul Ricoeur, *Hermeneutics and the Human Sciences*, ed. and trans. John B. Thompson (Cambridge: Cambridge University Press, 1981) esp. chap. 4.
[30]NYPG 1941–1945, 137.
[31]NYPG 1941–1945, 139.
[32]NYPG 1941–1945, 139.

In the final presentation of the year, Seward Hiltner began with a helpful summary of the year's discussions before moving into some of his own thoughts. He said that the group had agreed, for the most part, that the primary reference to conscience meant the internalization of cultural demands as the individual interprets them. Thus, the central characteristic of conscience is to prohibit, and therefore has a negative connotation. It is not creative and it arises out of fear. Further, it is normally authoritarian.

Hiltner went on to survey the year's discussion by referring to the meaning of transmoral or "free conscience." From a psychotherapy standpoint, it means that the inward, integrated "self" is in charge. Inner conflict can be faced because of the integrity of the "self." This implies freedom, rationality, and relatedness. From a theological standpoint, this process of a transmoral conscience can be found in Tillich's description of Luther. Hiltner went on to say that for Tillich this transformation does not happen automatically whenever one hits the bottom of desperation. There has to be a moment of receptivity.

Hiltner then raised the question of the relationship between the "law conscience" and the transmoral or free conscience. Is the conscience under the law, the conscience of internalized cultural norms, a step along the way to a free conscience or is it possible that it can be skipped altogether? Hiltner said that he believed there is an inherent connection between the two. In fact, he called it a "stage" toward transmoral conscience. This does not mean, however, that a law conscience automatically leads to the transmoral conscience.

It is interesting to note in this last statement how Hiltner anticipated the moral development theory of Lawrence Kohlberg. The cognitive-developmental approach would emerge later to offer a fuller explanation of Hiltner's moral "stages." This marked the end of Hiltner's comments and the end of the third year of discussion.

Tillich later wrote an article which deals with many of the themes of this year's discussion. The article was called, "The Nature of a Liberating Conscience," which appeared in *Ministry and Medicine in Human Relations*[33] before reappearing in C. Ellis Nelson's *Conscience: Theological and Psychological Perspectives*, a book to which I have already referred.

---

[33] Paul Tillich, "The Nature of a Liberating Conscience," in *Ministry and Medicine in Human Relations*, ed. Iago Galdstone (New York: International Universities Press, 1955) 127-40.

Because Tillich dealt with issues such as the difference between moralism and morality and further reflected on the notion of transmoral conscience, I believe it is important to briefly examine this article as a conclusion to the third year of the New York Psychology Group meetings.

Following Kant, Tillich argues that what lies beyond all moralisms is a moral imperative.

> What Immanuel Kant has called the "categorical imperative" is nothing more than the unconditioned character of the ought-to-be, the moral commandment. Whatever its content may be, its form is unconditional. One can rightly criticize Kant because he establishes a system of ethical forms without ethical contents. But just this limitation is his greatness. It makes as sharp as possible the distinction between morality which is unconditional, and moralisms, which are valid only conditionally and within limits.[34]

Tillich further adds that if we understand this we will be able to acknowledge that all concrete ethics, which he calls moralisms, are relative. Therefore, the findings of sociologists and anthropologists which point toward the wide variety of ethical standards, need not intimidate our belief that the moral imperative is both universal and unconditioned. We must, however, always make this distinction between the moral imperative and the particular, concrete moral content. "If we disregard this distinction, we either fall into an absolute skepticism which, in the long run, undermines morality as such, or we fall into an absolutism which attributes unconditional validity to one of the many possible moralisms."[35]

Also, the unconditioned character of this moral imperative is not some imposition from an external authority, but in fact, calls us back to our *essential* being. It is *not* an outside law which invades our consciousness (as Fromm suggested), but instead, the law of our own essential nature. Again, Tillich does *not* believe that the imperative is authoritarian and therefore a threat to our being. In fact, this imperative invites us toward our essential being.

---

[34]Tillich, "The Nature of a Liberating Conscience," in *Conscience: Theological and Psychological Perspectives*, ed. Nelson, 63.

[35]Tillich, "The Nature of a Liberating Conscience," 63.

The moral command is unconditional because it is we ourselves commanding ourselves. Morality is the self-affirmation of our essential being. This makes it unconditional, whatever its contents may be.[36]

Tillich is quick to point out that this self-affirmation of our essential being is *not* simply the affirmation of our desires and fears. Those are always conditioned.

While Tillich clearly sees that specific ethics are relative in the sense of being context-dependent and shaped by psychological factors, he does *not* like the term relativism when it refers to the notion that one standard is just as good as another. For Tillich, this is philosophically self-defeating. While relativism as a dependence on historical time and place makes sense, Tillich rejects the notion that all perspectives are therefore of equal validity.

Tillich acknowledges that against the notion of ethical relativity, Catholics have a concept of "natural law." This Roman Catholic interpretation of natural law holds that natural law has *specific contents* which are unchanging and upheld by the authority of the Church.

For Protestants, on the other hand, natural law refers to humanity's essential nature which has been lost, or at least distorted and estranged, by the Fall. Protestantism, unlike Catholicism, interprets the contents of natural law largely by ethical traditions in a more dynamic way without the final authority of the Church. Yet Protestantism has fallen back into a moralistic framework, a mentality which denies the Reformation principle and fosters legalism.

Tillich believes that conscience is formed through the imposition of ethical rules through various authorities—Roman Church, quasi-religious authorities, totalitarian governments, and secular authorities. But simply imposing these laws is not enough. They must also be successfully internalized.

Conscience is not the infallible voice of God, nor is it the voice of an unerring natural law. It is, as Heidegger frequently said, the call back to ourselves. Yet it is at this point that Tillich differs with Heidegger. While Heidegger sees conscience as the call back to the authentic, existential self, Tillich sees it as a call back to the essential self. For Tillich, conscience does not call us back to estranged existence, but instead, to our essential

---

[36]Tillich, "The Nature of a Liberating Conscience," 64.

nature. Nevertheless, conscience cannot tell us *who* we essentially are even though it serves the important function of calling us back. In fact, conscience can judge us erroneously. The problem seems to be that the conscience is not always unified. It may be split, and hence, ambiguous. Which voice, then, do we follow?

The result, for Tillich, is that *all moral acts involve risk, and therefore require courage.* Again, while the ethical imperative is absolute, there are no absolute ethical authorities: Not reason, the Church, scripture, or human experience. They are all ambiguous.

> In order to become human, man must trespass the "state of innocence"; but when he has trespassed it he finds himself in a state of self-contradiction. This situation, which is a permanent one, is symbolized in the story of paradise. Man must always trespass the safety regions which are circumscribed by ethical authorities. He must enter the spheres of unsafety and uncertainty. A morality which plays safe, by subjecting itself to an unconditioned authority, is suspect. It has not the courage to take guilt and tragedy upon itself. True morality is a morality of risk. It is a morality which is based on "the courage to be," the dynamic self-affirmation of man as man.[37]

For some, Tillich leaves us with the same frustration we find in Kant. While we have a generic ethical imperative, we have no specific guidelines. Instead, Tillich only invites us toward a life of moral courage in the face of life's ambiguities. The only certainty we seem to have is that risk is inevitable.

As I have indicated, the discussions of the fourth year met only for several months and had a definite continuity with the third year's focus on the relationship between psychotherapy and ethics. For this reason, I will explore the fourth year of dialogue before making comments on the overall theme of ethics and psychotherapy in both the third and fourth years.

Fourth Year: The Psychology of Helping

The final year of the New York Psychology Group dealt with the issue of what constitutes effective psychological help to persons in need. Erich Fromm began these discussions by suggesting some theoretical issues and questions on which the group could focus. Referring to this helping

---

[37]Tillich, "The Nature of a Liberating Conscience," 67.

function as one of the most basic functions that exist, Fromm mentioned that there are sometimes two extreme attitudes individuals take toward being helped. The first is the attitude of complete reliance on outside help. This mentality assumes that all goodness exists *outside* of the individual and that the primary orientation to life is one of receiving. This is Freud's oral character with the mouth wide open ready to be passively fed from outside sources. While the ability to receive is an important psychological function, this attitude is excessive.

The second attitude is to view any need for help as humiliating and self-demeaning. This entails a refusal to ask for any outside help. Fromm believes that there are two roots to this attitude. One root involves an overcompensation for any need to be helped whatsoever. The person denies what he or she secretly wants and needs. The other root is a sense of remoteness and detachment from the world. Security is connected to an aloof, detached, disconnection from others.

Similarly, there are different character structures which motivate the helper, also. One, unfortunately, is the need to dominate and have power. These individuals enjoy the position of being in control of another's life. Yet other individuals desire to help because they have a sense of solidarity and love with other human beings. Given the emphasis on self-sufficiency in Western culture, Fromm believes that this attitude is rare.

Fromm then turned toward the type of needs people bring to the counseling office. Interestingly, the first need he mentioned had to do with individuals trying to make sense of their own existence. Fromm said that this is particularly true now in ways that it was not true in the middle ages or even through the nineteenth century. Today there is enormous bewilderment over questions of purpose, meaning, values, and identity. Often when individuals come for psychotherapeutic help, argued Fromm, they are really looking for a philosophical orientation. Thus, Fromm suggested the following to the group.

> One of the questions we might discuss, then, is to what extent the psychic helper has the function in our culture of helping people to find some philosophical orientation. Today it seems as if psychiatrists have taken up the tasks of priests and other helpers. The philosophy they stand for, as a rule, is not metaphysical or religious as any theologian could have.[38]

---

[38]Tillich, "The Nature of a Liberating Conscience," 158.

Thus, in Fromm's mind, the issues in therapy clearly move beyond a practical clinical focus of adjustment. Instead, they often involve an entire horizon of meaning and the need to interpret one's life in a much larger context.

The next need individuals bring to psychotherapy, according to Fromm, is a need for authority. By this, Fromm means an irrational authority and a dependence on something or someone outside oneself. In other words, some individuals come to psychotherapy with a hope that their lives will be "taken over" by the psychotherapist and that a final security will be provided. This may also be tempting for the psychotherapist, as he or she might feel flattered by the expectation. The patient may not even be aware of this unconscious expectation. Nevertheless, an authority figure is unconsciously sought.

Other needs which bring people to see a psychotherapist are the need for advice, the need for dependable human contact, and the need for someone to help untangle psychological disturbance. It is very important for the therapist to know what is being sought by the patient. These needs seem to appear in all cultures. Someone has always occupied the role of "helper."

Fromm then turned toward specific questions he thought would be helpful for discussion. The first question concerned whether there are religious, philosophical, or political differences which limit psychological help? For instance, does it make any difference whether or not a person believes in God? The second question revolved around the implicit and explicit philosophical differences in various theories of helping. The third question asked about the aim of therapy. In other words, do we simply work toward the satisfaction of the patient or is there a more objective standard? Should patients always get what they want? Another question had to do with the use of irrational authority in psychotherapy. And the final question had to do with the significance of uncovering unconscious processes and therapy. Thus, Fromm set the course for the final year of dialogue.

The discussion which followed Fromm's presentation seemed to affirm the basic direction he had laid out. It was interesting that Hiltner's beginning comment for the discussion suggested that the group should have more of a social focus, also. While we normally think of psychotherapy as individual help, we should also consider the influence of groups.

Hiltner also thought it would be interesting to examine the significance of the actual personality differences among therapists. Further, to what extent do therapists consider success or failure to be due to their own philosophical similarities or differences with patients? It was also suggested that there are often antagonisms between the person who needs help and the helper. Hiltner concluded the discussion by saying that he thought that uncovering unconscious factors would be a very important issue.

The next meeting was led by Harry Bone. He related his own perspective to the questions and issues brought up by Fromm during the first session. Bone told the group that his particular type of therapy deals with people with developmental problems. By this he meant psychological problems which block the development of a person's full potential. These sorts of individuals, said Bone, often feel inferior because they have not been able to adapt successfully to social standards. Yet for Bone, these individuals are often *superior rather than inferior*. They are often unfortunate victims of unhealthy cultural pressures. They are emotionally punished for their failure to conform, but in reality many of the standards to which they are expected to conform are neurotic patterns.

For Bone, the purpose of the therapy setting is to provide a place where their unfulfilled potentialities will have a chance to be realized. The therapist is in no way "superior" to the patient. "The helper must, of course, have certain competence, must have solved his own essential problems, but in terms of his various abilities and capacities, he does not have to be superior."[39] Bone added that many persons cannot receive help until they become reassured that the relationship between the patient and therapist involves equality.

Bone then proceeded with several explicit assumptions which govern his work. These included the following: (a) life is uncertain and insecure and there is no absolute security for human values in theory or practice, (b) the security we are able to find in human values depends on identifying the conditions of emotional health and the regularities of life, conditions which are indeed *knowable* and not simply mysterious, (c) the discovery of these conditions of mental and emotional health may be basic to everyone but they must be discovered through an individual journey.

Bone went on to raise the question of a theistic versus a nontheistic outlook. He wanted to know if a person can help another who has very different religious or philosophical beliefs. Bone suggested that if by "God" we mean the sum total of the conditions of well-being or that God is the name

---

[39]Tillich, "The Nature of a Liberating Conscience," 162.

for healthy relationships among people or that God is simply love, that would be fine. However, that is *not* traditional theism.

> In the Christian concept of the drama of the human soul there is profound insight and wisdom; conviction of sin, confession, repentance, faith, grace, forgiveness, conversion, atonement, justification, salvation, sanctification, etc., may refer to real and valid experiences. Christianity frequently does not distinguish between the valid from the invalid experiences that are described in these terms. Conformity is too often the test of validity. Actually, the experience is valid if it consists in a genuine personal fulfillment of the individual. If he merely gains "peace" or adjustment to his surroundings by successfully submerging important aspects of his potentially creative vitality, the experience is spurious.[40]

It is worth noting here that Bone is placing the issue of "individual fulfillment" as the criteria for "valid experience." While one may applaud Bone's concern about excessive conformity, one also wonders about the equation of individual fulfillment with truth.

Bone goes on to say that there is a central "defect" in Christian theism. In the process of conversion, argues Bone, individuals convict themselves for sin and try to correct this through obedience. A more therapeutic approach would acknowledge the "sinfulness" while maintaining that the prevailing conditions have determined the behavior. Given the particular cluster of factors in their lives, individuals had no real control. Some of the factors may have been internally determinant, but the actions were still determined. These persons have also been on the receiving end of so-called "sinful" actions, actions which also require forgiveness. Thus they are victims as well as offenders. As Bone puts it, "The genuine resolution of character conflicts is neither a question of submitting nor of asserting, but one in which these are elements of both. An individual has to discover that there is nothing to be forgiven on either side but something to be understood."[41]

One cannot help wondering what Tillich's nonverbal facial features looked like as Bone set forth this notion which was utterly at odds with his own perspective. The sense of the individual not being responsible, and hence not in need of forgiveness, is completely antithetical to Tillich's

---

[40]Tillich, "The Nature of a Liberating Conscience," 163.

[41]Tillich, "The Nature of a Liberating Conscience," 163.

framework. In Bone's system, understanding seems to push away any need for grace. The "in-spite-of" element of acceptance, which is due to our recognition of our own estrangement or sin, is lost as we have nothing for which we need forgiveness.

Bone went on to say that *both* freedom and "unfreedom" are determined.

> The deterministic viewpoint says that the client is right; his attitudes are right, that is, inevitable, for him at the time; they will change or be changed when some of the factors in this pattern of life are altered. The significant changes in an individual take place as a result of insight, a shift from one kind of determinism to another.[42]

This statement is loaded with implications. All behavior is determined by character structure. Note that the words "right" and "inevitable" are used interchangeably. Insight into character will produce a change in perception which will in turn lead to a change in behavior. Given the individual's character structure, he or she could not have done otherwise. This seems to be more than a nonpunitive stance. In fact, it seems to be a removal of all moral considerations from the person's life.

One can almost draw a parallel here between the therapeutic assumption that the patient always does what he or she thinks is right and the old Platonic notion that destructive or evil behavior is born out of ignorance and therefore never deliberate. To really *know* what is right is to do it. Similarly, once a person understands him/herself, the behavior will automatically become more constructive. This is why Bone can argue that there is no guilt, only a lack of understanding. There is only a perceptual problem, and not an ethical one. Calling it an ethical problem would presuppose the freedom of self-transcendence, a genuine possibility of not being completely determined by one's character structure.

In response to Fromm's questions during the last meeting, Bone said that he thought the process of uncovering unconscious processes is a major part of psychotherapy. He also added that he believed a therapist should minimize the use of rational authority because it tends to prevent the patient from achieving his or her own goals. Irrational authority, of course, should be completely eliminated.

---

[42]Tillich, "The Nature of a Liberating Conscience," 163.

In the discussion following Bone's presentation, Havice began with an objection to Bone's statement that the patient or client is always right. He said that all methods employed to provide insight are based on the assumption that the patient is not currently "right" but has the capacity to become "more right." Further, the assumption that there is *not* a complete determinism at work is what makes it possible to even work with the patient in the first place. Bone immediately responded as follows.

> [I]f you know the facts afterwards you see that the very expression of freedom was as deterministic as the unfreedom; change is possible because some of the factors shift. . . . Freedom is not in the transcending of the situation but a greater awareness of how one is related to the situation, and that gives a wider sphere of choice of conscious desires. The individual has become conscious of a larger number of determinisms.[43]

Thus, what appears as freedom is in reality determined by character structure. The idea of freedom as rising above the situation and making choices which are ultimately not controlled by one's personality structure, is simply not possible. This idea proved to be a very controversial topic in the remainder of the discussion. Because behavior is an inevitable manifestation of character structure, blame is useless.

While Fromm agreed with Bone that psychotherapy has no need whatsoever for irrational authority, he thought the issue of rational authority is different. For him, the rational authority, or competence, of the therapist is crucial in helping the patient feel more secure and hopeful about the future. Interestingly, Fromm pointed out that when the therapist has a "stake" in getting the person well, this is already an indication of irrational authority. As the therapist attempts to "prove" his or her ability to help, the patient may feel that the way to "win" or defeat the therapist is to not get well. The therapist must avoid the need to demonstrate effectiveness, and instead, have the patient's own interest in mind. Fromm further stated that the analyst "should not give a damn" about the patient's religious, political, or philosophical views. "If the divergence of views is made important, it turns the situation into one in which the therapist has something at stake."[44]

Tillich questioned the use of Bone's terms "deterministic" and "indeterministic." He further added that any notion of deterministic

---

[43]Tillich, "The Nature of a Liberating Conscience," 165.
[44]Tillich, "The Nature of a Liberating Conscience," 166.

freedom is like "wooden iron," a self-contradiction. He also said that Bone's view would lead a person to think that everything he or she had ever done was done out of necessity and could not have been otherwise. The person would never review his or her life and say, "I could have done better," or "I should have done something differently." Again, with this mentality there is no need for forgiveness—ever!

Bone responded to Tillich by saying that if it would help, he could use the term "universal causation" rather than determinism. He described how a nonpunitive perspective makes religion and morality obsolete.

> There is a sense in which he could have done differently if certain other factors which were not under his control at the time had been different. Depite the traditional point of view, the removing of the stimulus of the sense of guilt and sin leads to more effective results. Many moral and religious concepts are made obsolete by this viewpoint because the punitive viewpoint is part of the authoritarian structure in which the Christian conception of the drama of the soul's salvation has its setting, and this reflects the authoritarianism inherent in the patriarchal form of family organization and in the class-structured form of social organization generally.[45]

Note the full force of this comment. Essentially, Bone is saying that issues of morality are irrelevant, and even harmful, to the process of therapy. Personal responsibility is removed because one simply does what one's personality structure tells one to do. This intrapsychic determinism may differ from the external control emphasized in radical behaviorism, but the determinism is just as strong. Behavior is controlled by the structure of the personality and this structure is outside an individual's choice. It is senseless to feel guilty because we only do what we are pushed to do by our own personality structure. Ethical "choice" is therefore an illusion. Ethics are a by-product of character formation, which again, is outside the range of individual choice. Thus, therapy would be far better off without the unnecessary burden of guilt and the baggage of a moral vocabulary.

Tillich responded that it is important to analyze the voices of conscience. Notice the word "voices" in the plural. As we have seen, Tillich did not believe conscience always provides a unified front. Its message is sometimes ambiguous. Yet we cannot eliminate being a "witness to ourselves" or an evaluator of our own behavior.

---

[45]Tillich, "The Nature of a Liberating Conscience," 166-67.

Bone responded that what we normally experience as conscience is simply fear. Guilt, said Bone, is often perceived as more "respectable" than fear, but it is nevertheless fear which drives guilt. Therefore, guilt needs to be unmasked in therapy, and the underlying fear must be faced. Elliott concluded the session by agreeing with Bone that conscience is often more about fear than about guilt.

The next meeting of the NYPG focused on the role of the parish priest in the helping process. This presentation was led by Otis Rice. Because much of this presentation and discussion focused on the specific role of the parish priest, I will only highlight briefly some of the key themes. Rice provided an overview of the types of issues with which a priest must be prepared to deal. He emphasized the importance of being able to make an intelligent appraisal of a person's needs. Rice was clear that this was not a psychological diagnosis, but instead, an evaluation of what would be helpful for the person. The main factor, said Rice, is to be a caring listener. And he also talked about how this is grounded in his faith.

> The "counseling situation" as such appears to me as "two facing a third." I assume that whatever I can learn from psychology, theology, or other disciplines that will make me more effective will be part of God's truth and that no amount of prayerful intention will take the place of hard-headed knowledge of my tools. At the same time prayer is important in the procedure—not that I often pray with a parishioner—but it is a necessity for me personally in order to make possible the right attitude toward my parishioner and as a corrective to the manifold ways in which my own emotional drives and needs become involved in the counseling.[46]

Rice went on to say that through prayer and the practice of his religion that he is able to be more accepting and receptive toward people. He said that his faith that God loves this other person helps prevent him, as a counselor, from being shocked or judgmental about what the other person says. Yet he went on to say that the personal religious or philosophical views of the pastor come up far less frequently than he would have imagined. Then Rice made a most interesting admission:

> A personal assumption which I must make in all counseling is that there is an urgency of life toward completion or maturity, that the forces of life, when understood in proper perspective, can be trusted. The drives and

---

[46]Tillich, "The Nature of a Liberating Conscience," 170.

urgencies discovered in and by my parishioners constantly amaze me by their power and potential creativeness. If I parallel the psychiatric approach at any point, it is my belief that a fundamental function of the pastor is to help the parishioner discover his own resistance to growth and the conditions which force him to cling to the resistances.[47]

Rice continued by saying, however, that as a minister of the gospel he *does* have a sense of his life being bound up with this fellowship or community (church). This doesn't mean that he starts proselytizing, but this is always the frame or reference with which he approaches his work. He quickly added, however, that one of the minister's greatest temptations is to feel as if he or she must answer every question.

In the discussion, Rice stated that some people do indeed go see a minister for counseling with a masochistic expectation of being punished or judged. Yet if the counseling goes past the first session, argued Rice, this will normally disappear. Carl Rogers quickly added his conviction that once the counseling gets started, the social role of the counselor becomes unimportant. Whatever the setting, the key is for the counselor not to evaluate. Fromm immediately disagreed with Rogers. He argued that the social role of the therapist does indeed matter and often contains a great deal of authority.

With reference to the role of a priest, Fromm went on to say that the clergy person also has the blessing or burden of carrying a set of philosophical or theological convictions. The psychiatrist, says Fromm, handicaps himself on metaphysical issues by simply saying that he does not know. The priest, on the other hand, by his very position, has metaphysical input.

Rogers reiterated his belief that if the priest remains nonevaluative in the helping process, then his social role would not matter. Fromm was not going to change his mind on this one. Tillich then made the interesting observation that if he asked any of his secular friends whom they would see if they needed therapy, they would certainly *not* say a minister because they believed a minister works with a specific code of morality which he or she inevitably transmits. Elliott then quickly added that he believed that if a minister introduced his own theology into the therapy process, it would immediately shut the therapy down. It is important, said Elliott, that the patient or client find his own view and orientation toward life.

---

[47]Tillich, "The Nature of a Liberating Conscience," 171.

At this point Bone added that the more psychotherapy is completely free of value judgments, the better the therapy will be. Roberts quickly challenged the notion of value-free therapy and suggested that the underlying view of the human condition which guides the therapy process is *hardly without values*. Wickes then paralleled the therapy process with the growth of a child. In the earliest stages of life, children cannot live without a certain authority, but as they become older they take that authority upon themselves. At first, suggested Wickes, there is something between therapist/patient which is akin to parent/child.

Tillich, much like Roberts, objected to the notion that therapy can ever be value-free, and Rogers ended the meeting by saying that he did not mean to imply that counselors never make value judgments. It is just that they self-consciously restrain themselves for the purposes of promoting the client's growth. This is not, said Rogers, a total philosophy of life which is nonevaluative. It is instead a bracketing or suspending of the evaluation of the client.

The next meeting of the NYPG involved what may have been, in my view, the group's most interesting and lively discussion of psychology's relationship to theology. David Roberts provided a very stimulating presentation which clearly provoked much thought. Because many of his comments were, in my mind, so eloquently stated, I will take greater liberties to let him speak directly for himself rather than simply summarize his comments. The beauty, balance, and depth of his comments contribute to a deep sense of loss that Roberts died at such a young age—in 1955 at age forty-four. One wonders what sort of contribution he would have continued to make to the psychology/theology discussion if he had been permitted to live another thirty years. Roberts was only in his early thirties when he made such an outstanding contribution to the New York Psychology Group.

Roberts began with a sketch of what he called the assets and liabilities of the minister's position in mental health care before going on to speak directly about theological concerns.

> He is supposed to be kindly, interested in people, generous and sympathetic; he is available, without payment of special fees, to almost anyone who seeks his help. For people who are not alienated in advance by the very fact that he is a minister, he is sometimes the only person in the community to whom they can confide their troubles, and their dealings with him may be surcharged with the peculiar intensity and expulsive power which accompany religious faith and hope. The minister is expected

to believe in the possibility of salvaging shattered human lives; he represents the converting power of religion. Hence his office puts him in a position to provide considerable help or do considerable harm.[48]

In many communities, Roberts said, the minister is the only person who can offer professional assistance to persons who simply cannot afford help from psychiatrists or others in the mental health field. Then he described what he considered to be the major mistake ministers can easily make.

> They tend to provide "help" as a sort of prefabricated, finished product, instead of assisting the individual to develop capacities for self-help through maturing emotionally. Instead of passing a judgment of condemnation at this point, let us try to understand why this mistake occurs. In the first place, the minister is likely to have built up a fixed scheme of theological and moral assumptions which more or less satisfy him and his congregation. These are his set of "answers." They consist largely of generalizations about sin, salvation, God, Christ, the Bible, the Church, immortality, social progress, sex mores, and the omnipotence of faith, hope, and love. All too often these "answers" do not contain much of the minister's own spontaneous feelings, reactions and reflections. They are built up largely in terms of what his denominational standards demand and what is appealing to his congregation.[49]

Roberts added that many people approach a minister with the expectation that he or she will speak with the voice of authority. The minister can easily "buy into" this expectation and not want to disappoint the person seeking help. He or she is ever-conscious of the responsibility to promote a stronger faith. In addition, the minister may be perceived as the guardian of morality. Many clergy, said Roberts, operate with a conflicting desire: they want people to open up and freely talk about their behavior but they also notice behavior and attitudes they consider sinful.

But rather than simply criticize ministers for possible judgmentalism, Roberts explores why it is difficult for a clergyperson to take a permissive attitude. The minister has a responsibility to entire families, and actually, to the whole parish. The community's attitude toward the minister, Roberts says, can make or break him. The therapist, on the other hand, is responsible only to the client. The therapist can afford the luxury of being

---

[48]Tillich, "The Nature of a Liberating Conscience," 175.
[49]Tillich, "The Nature of a Liberating Conscience," 175.

indifferent toward social expectations or the larger community as he/she explores the client's psyche.

This is not to say that the minister's role is completely determined by the congregational setting or the denomination at large. Ministers can learn some things from therapists about how many patients come to counseling expecting magic. Analysis can help the minister realize that changes results from painstaking work, a procedure that does not move as fast as most would like. Perhaps the minister should use this as a model. Religion should not be seen as a shortcut which provides automatic transformation. Again, it is easy for the minister to get hooked by this expectation. Individuals do not usually know what to expect when they visit a therapist. However, when they see a minister, they often bring with them a whole baggage of assumptions.

Roberts then turned to a more fundamental question. He asked, "Is it 'really helpful' to encourage an individual to seek support, forgiveness, personal transformation, and improved relations with his fellows through right relationships with God?"[50] He said that one of the reasons that belief in God is important for religious people is that even though it may be difficult for individuals to find their own potential, the notion of God assures them that these principles have a secure foundation. In other words, one's own individual direction reflects the direction of ultimate reality.

> From a Christian standpoint, man has powerful motives for trying to run away from fellowship with God, since it involves an acceptance of suffering love; but so long a he continues to run away, he continues in self-defeat, since what he is running away from is his own beatitude. Thus belief in God, on one side of it, springs from a recognition that human beings find themselves continually in a state of conflict between their apparent good and their real good. Moreover, a resolution of this conflict, with resulting serenity, ethical empowerment and hope, frequently comes only when a tightly organized defensive structure of egotism, self-aggrandizement and distrust has been broken through. It is for this reason that Christianity speaks of salvation as coming, in the first instance, from outside or beyond the self. Something captures the believer against his will; before he is able to affirm it spontaneously as the expression of his own transformed desires and aspirations.[51]

---

[50]Tillich, "The Nature of a Liberating Conscience," 176.
[51]Tillich, "The Nature of a Liberating Conscience," 176-77.

Roberts recognized that this view of salvation can certainly be abused. It can expect God to pull us out of our self-created difficulties rather than work to deal with them ourselves. But belief in God does not *have* to have this neurotic quality of escaping ourselves. Instead, it can be liberating. Religion does not *have* to be an authoritarian imposition. But how does a person help another to understand the validity of this experience? How can one help another see that faith is not a childish regression toward total dependency? At this point, Roberts drew a very interesting parallel between this faith experience and experience in psychotherapy. With an aim toward helping the secular analysts in the room come to a better understanding of the nature of religious faith, Roberts mentioned the following.

> Once again I should like to draw a parallel between religious experience and psychotherapy. A person who feels that he has benefited greatly from having been analyzed may be willing to describe his experience and indicate his criteria; but if someone who has not been analyzed refuses to agree with him, he does not regard that as a threat to the validity of therapy. He feels fairly confident that if the other person could understand similar experience, the disagreement would largely disappear, and that otherwise the person just "can't understand." Similarly, for many religious people their talk about what God has done for them, all their talking about getting rid of an old self which was mired in misery and being granted a new self which comes to them as a mysterious and emancipating gift, is not put forward because of a desire to defend a rigid dogmatic system; it is not put forward because of a fear of God's authority and the penalties resulting from disobedience to Him. It is put forward because any other language would be false to what has actually happened in their lives. And they are not surprised that others, to whom it has not happened, are unable to understand.[52]

Roberts then stated that it is not at all possible to demonstrate that a dependence on God is itself neurotic. Instead, it is the manner in which a person holds and expresses the belief which determines its healthiness. And this is as true for atheism as for theism. This same statement would be made later by pastoral counseling leader Howard Clinebell when he wrote, "[R]eligion can be a constructive, healing, life-affirming force or a dark, re-

---

[52]Tillich, "The Nature of a Liberating Conscience," 177.

pressive, life-crippling force, depending on the way it is understood and used."[53]

Roberts reminded the group that their "doctrine of man" is the determining factor in their view of what constitutes effective psychological health. Like Tillich, Roberts had a keen ability to bring the group back to the realm of implicit assumptions in psychotherapeutic practice. Beneath even the most practical attempt to help another dangles assumptions about human need, human fulfillment, an ethical vision, and the ultimate context of our lives. Roberts states, "You may even refrain from ever exerting persuasive pressure, but surely your own worldview will operate consciously or unconsciously as a guiding criterion in estimating the extent to which the other person is facing reality or evading it."[54]

Interestingly, Roberts pointed out that while some nonreligious individuals believe that Christians are attempting to escape reality, some Christians believe that it is naturalistic psychotherapy which in fact attempts to escape the human dilemma. The very effort to achieve a kind of autonomy or self-sufficiency—a self-sufficiency which ultimately denies our finitude and dependence on the Unconditioned—may itself be an attempt to avoid our true state as we deny our need for God. While one group asserts that religious faith inevitably distorts reality by offering a delusion, the other group could say that the championing of human autonomy as the ultimate and final authority is itself a reality-denying mechanism.

Roberts said that he is not trying to be critical of psychotherapy's refusal to allow metaphysical questions to invade therapy and thereby turn it into a philosophical debate. However, what a therapist does with a client is completely related to a larger picture of the human condition, and therefore, metaphysical questions are unavoidable.

> There are times when it seems to me that therapy can preserve almost everything valuable in Christianity and help us to eradicate the rubbish. But there are other times when I feel that therapists have a lot to learn from Christianity in developing an adequate doctrine of man. In a praiseworthy effort to avoid fruitless speculation and abstract theorizing and with the praiseworthy motive of substituting openness for dogmatism,

---

[53]Howard Clinebell, *The Mental Health Ministry of the Local Church* (Nashville: Abingdon, 1965) 28.

[54]NYPG 1941–1945, 177.

therapy has often been represented as more presuppositionless than it actually is. We need to recognize the functional interrelationship between human welfare and the ultimate nature of the extra-human environment. This must not be circumvented by isolating psychological considerations from philosophical and theological ones. Moreover, I do not think that such phrases as "promoting growth," "developing fullest potentialities," etc., provide adequate criteria. . . . In the end, what constitutes good growth or good potentialities cannot be seen except by placing human life against the background of its cosmic setting, physical and spiritual. There are some forces of anxiety which cannot be dealt with adequately so long as religious issues are circumvented; and there is one kind of a sense of direction which religion alone can supply.[55]

Roberts's presentation generated much discussion. Not surprisingly, much of this focused on the issue of an anthropocentric vs. a theocentric worldview. Stated differently, what constitutes ultimate reality? As we saw in the first year of the NYPG discussions, the group seemed divided on the question of whether or not the human reality represents the final one. Fromm wasted no time in asking Roberts if he believed that religion is the only thing which could provide genuine goals for humanity. Roberts responded that a sense of direction in a person's life is greatly reinforced if he or she believes it to be the will of God. This individual may believe passionately that what he or she is doing does not result from internal inclinations alone, the pressures of the society, or any other external push. Instead, it is a conformity to the will of God. Granted, these feelings can take unhealthy, as well as healthy forms, but this conviction greatly motivates the person.

Havice wondered if this conviction about which Roberts was speaking would be different if one simply said it was "the will of man" rather than "the will of God." Roberts thought there would indeed be a difference because most persons do not worship the will of man. "This phrase constitutes something which is an ideal entity rather than an empirical generalization."[56] But Fromm immediately responded that it is much easier to understand the nature of man than the Divine will. Fromm also denied that there would be any difference in motivation or conviction between a

---

[55]NYPG 1941–1945, 178-79.
[56]NYPG 1941–1945, 180.

theistic or atheistic perspective before he said that he wished theologians would make a stronger case for theology.

Fromm also said that the word "security" is completely overplayed in current psychological thinking. He raised the question of how anyone could feel secure when they look at the historical forces which appear to govern life. For Fromm, the point is to learn to live in the world with a manageable amount of insecurity, not eliminate the insecurity. Besides, a certain amount of insecurity is productive. Therapy needs to help individuals become more productive in the face of insecurity.

Roberts then made the interesting observation that he would like to know more about this criteria by which a completely naturalistic therapist understands that the fundamental task in therapy is to help a person "come to terms with himself and other human beings in an environment that is basically indifferent to value."[57]

Fromm suggested what he had previously said, namely, that this "good" should be provided on the basis of what is good or bad for humanity. Yet Roberts responded that if one assumes human beings are immortal, this makes a big difference in what is "good" for them. In other words, the empirical reality of this world is not necessarily the only consideration. Fromm simply responded that we do not need a set of values which transcend humanity. Thus, the issue seemed deadlocked again.

Bigham suggested that it is the therapist's job to remove the psychological obstacles necessary for growth and the theologian's job to deal with the symbols of productivity. If a person is struggling with the meaning of life and it is not related to the psychological dynamics of character structure, then the minister should proceed with a "spiritual" orientation. Yet Havice stated that unless the notion of God is synonymous with what is good for humanity, people will then look for help outside themselves, which he said is not healthy. Roberts countered that he believes we are always dependent on things outside of ourselves as well as inside of ourselves. He then concluded the session by saying that from a theistic standpoint there are definitely resources beyond the human and that it is unwise not to rely on them.

The next meeting was led by Grace Elliott and dealt with her involvement with the YWCA and other ecumenical agencies. Elliott directed much

---

[57]NYPG 1941–1945, 180.

of her comments, at least initially, according to the agenda which had been laid out by Fromm during the first session. Fromm had suggested that the functions of the helper involve a focus on philosophical orientation, advice and wisdom, and guidance. To that list, Elliott wanted to add the importance of helping persons achieve healthy community relations. All of these functions, she believed, were interrelated. Then she made a very provocative observation.

> [S]o great is the individual's need in today's culture for help at the point of achieving solidarity with his fellows that the infantile solidarity of totalitarianism is inescapable if man cannot be helped to a more mature solidarity. Without specific provision for this need much of the individually oriented help given to individuals becomes ineffectual.[58]

For Elliott, the basic work of the minister, YWCA worker, parent or teacher is to make the job of the psychoanalyst less and less necessary. This is done, in large part, by helping individuals feel a sense of belonging in a larger community.

In response to Fromm's first question about the role that basic philosophical, religious, and political differences have on the helping relationship, Elliott provided an interesting answer. She said that one major concern is to help people with a frame of reference which provides for organizing the complex elements of human nature.

> Every man has done wrong, whether willfully or unwittingly, and feels guilty. Because of the capacities of human nature, there is always a gap between man's ideals and his actions and this produces a feeling of guilt. This failure to live up to one's standards of action threatens self-respect and so causes anxiety and fear. The pain from this conscious and unconscious guilt often seems unbearable. If it is to be removed, man must find for himself a faith which makes great enough demands upon him to guarantee the complete satisfaction of his nature, a faith which does not excuse his sin but removes his guilt so that he can meet the demands of life with confidence instead of fear.[59]

Elliott went on to say that while all persons have to arrive at their own orientation, they should take into consideration the collective wisdom of religious traditions.

---

[58]NYPG 1941–1945, 183.
[59]NYPG 1941–1945, 184.

In response to Fromm's question about whether the helper and helpee would have to share the same philosophical or religious viewpoint, Elliott believed that the main thing is that the helper has worked through his or her own philosophical conflicts as well as their emotional ones.

Elliott concluded her presentation by pointing out that the word "satisfaction" in helping did not necessarily mean tranquility. Security, she said, cannot rest on magic or a final, absolute authority. She asserted that the question of meaning and value is far more urgent today than before. But one cannot simply be "gifted" with a sense of meaning. Instead, it is necessary to work it out oneself. Her final words are colorful and insightful.

> My quarrel with the theologians is that too often they have paid too little attention to the *process*, that they have thought that they could preach or exhort or argue or persuade men and women into the Kingdom of Heaven. On the other hand my quarrel with the psychiatrists is that too often they won't admit that man cannot be whole without finding for himself those values, those goals, and that sense of direction which give meaning to life and security for its risks. Those helped by them may be all dressed up with no place to go, while the minister's clients know where to go but haven't any idea of how to get there. We must work together on goals and on understanding eh conditions for their achievement.[60]

This notion of psychology "getting us all dressed up with no place to go," and theology giving us a place to go without any notion of how to get there is, in my view, a wonderfully succinct way of summarizing the group's discussion.

In the discussion, Everett said that in his experience, introducing any sort of religious orientation to a group ends up defeating what the group might do because of the lack of meaning in the Christian symbols. He went on to say that the YWCA often presents religion as a kind of "happy feeling about life,"[61] rather than facing the tough theological task of reinterpreting those symbols. Bone then responded that this reinterpretation of the Christian symbols is secondary to a more general interpretation of life.

Everett then mentioned that his concern is the possibility that *all* religion is authoritarian. He pointed out that it is certainly important to say

---

[60]NYPG 1941–1945, 187.
[61]NYPG 1941–1945, 188.

that a statement is true because it is really true and not merely because it is Christian.

Tillich believed that Bone's perspective ends up dissolving all values into personal experience, and that this experience ends up becoming an absolute. Making one's own personal experience an absolute, for Tillich, is a dangerous thing to do. Bone responded that his experience is the most absolute matrix he has. The meeting ended before this disagreement could be further developed.

The final presentation of the NYPG was given by Carl Rogers. Unfortunately neither Tillich nor Fromm was available for this final meeting. Rogers's presentation was brief. He essentially laid out the core ingredients of his newly developed client-centered therapy. The central belief had to do with the conviction that the client has the capacity to resolve his or her own problems when provided with an atmosphere of acceptance and unconditional positive regard. The client must feel that all his or her feelings and attitudes are acceptable for expression. Questions are not advised because they tend to provoke defensiveness. Negative evaluation is completely unhelpful. And even positive evaluations are not wise because they unwittingly say to a client that the opposite feeling or attitude might be forbidden. The goal is to promote an accepting, empathic mirror for the client.

In the discussion, the question was raised as to whether these techniques would work with a psychotic person and Rogers asserted that his method presupposed the client's capacity to be responsible. It would not be effective with some psychotics.

The question also emerged concerning the appropriateness of Rogers's recordings of actual therapy sessions. Rogers believed that too many therapists are afraid to allow their therapy hour to be opened for evaluation. There is an element of mystique and the therapist can "claim" anything he or she wants. Rogers wanted to open up therapy for research so that identifiable patterns of helpfulness may be recognized.

As one might guess, the more psychoanalytically oriented members doubted that Rogers's approach could really resolve deep neuroses. Perhaps no one at the time knew that this small group's tensions between Freudian and Rogerian leanings would set the stage for the next several decades. Carl Rogers would go one to become one of the most influential psychotherapists in America's history. Thus marks the end of the New York Psychology Group's twenty-nine sessions of dialogue.

Ethics and Psychotherapy:
Reflections on the Third and Fourth Years

The third and fourth years of discussion brought up many issues about the relationship between psychotherapy and ethics, concerns which are still very much with us. Fromm's initial presentation of his "anthropocentric ethics" raised a crucial issue: Is it really possible to base ethical norms on a comprehensive investigation of human nature? In other words, can the social sciences deliver a portrait of how human beings should live their lives? Fromm, it will be recalled, claimed that a thorough and well-grounded understanding of human nature will provide us with a prescriptive understanding of ethical conduct. His argued that this could be done in a scientific way, a neutral and objective process which anyone interested could clearly observe. Roberts, however, contested Fromm's position as he argued that terms such as "growth" or decay" were already loaded with normative meanings. These understandings are *brought to* an investigation of human nature, and not *derived from* this investigation. In ways that seem very similar to a postmodern understanding of how our presuppositions color the data we investigate, Roberts pulled Fromm back to the assumptive world out of which he operated. As I have previously mentioned, Roberts's approach seemed to be a philosophically hermeneutical one—our own preunderstanding has a great deal to do with what we "find." While we may be able to distance ourselves somewhat from that preunderstanding, Fromm's call to a neutral, objective evaluation of the human condition was, for Roberts, philosophically naïve. Using contemporary language, it seems clear that Roberts was employing a post-Enlightenment understanding of scientific investigation.

A second major issue raised during the discussions dealt with Harry Bone's contention that once psychological conflicts have been largely cleared in persons' lives, and they have become "self-determined," then ethical living will flow naturally. The elimination of neuroses will automatically produce a moral lifestyle. This is a natural unfolding. This is why it is unnecessary for psychotherapy to be concerned with ethical matters; once individuals are adequately "therapized," solid ethical commitments will come naturally. This notion, of course, would later become a cornerstone of humanistic psychology. As individuals become self-actualized, they will naturally do what is in both their own best interest as well as the best interest of society. This view assumes a preestablished harmony in which everyone can simultaneously self-actualize without conflict.[62] It doesn't deal very well with the dilemma of one person's actualization interfering with that of another. Given the ethical egoism which drives many of the humanistic psychologies, it is hard to imagine a more difficult situation than two people's self-fulfillment bumping into each other.

In the past twenty-five years, there has been much discussion about the individualism, narcissism, and self-absorption connected with psychotherapy.[63] A great deal of this criticism has involved a strong belief that the individual concerns of psychotherapy need to be related to a larger ethical vision which involves families, communities, and society as a whole. Much of this discussion has blamed psychotherapy for operating in an ethical vacuum in which self-fulfillment automatically takes over. These conversations were anticipated by Don Browning in 1976 with his important work, *The Moral Context of Pastoral Care*. Many of Browning's earlier themes were picked up by William Doherty's extremely influential book in 1995, *Soul Searching: Why Psychotherapy Must Promote Moral Responsibility*. These two books greatly aid an understanding of the issues brought up by the New York Psychology Group.[64]

Browning's perspective offers a great deal of balance as it appreciates the personal and intimate issues of psychotherapy, and yet also wants to examine the larger ethical context out of which psychotherapeutic healing occurs. Personal problems and larger social and ethical problems cannot be

---

[62]See Don S. Browning and Terry D. Cooper, *Religious Thought and the Modern Psychologies*, 2nd ed. (Minneapolis: Fortress Press, 2004).

[63]See, e.g., Edwin Schur, *The Awareness Trap: Self-Absorption Instead of Social Change* (New York: McGraw Hill, 1976); Martin Gross, *The Psychological Society* (New York: Simon and Schuster, 1978); Christopher Lasch, *The Culture of Narcissism* (New York: W. W. Norton, 1979); Michael A. Wallach and Lise Wallach, *Psychology's Sanction of Selfishness: The Error of Egoism in Theory and Therapy* (San Francisco: W. H. Freeman, 1983); Robert N. Bellah et al., *Habits of the Heart* (Berkeley CA: University of California Press, 1985); Michael Lerner, *Surplus Powerlessness* (Oakland CA: Institute for Labor and Mental Health, 1986); Wendy Kaminer, *I'm Dysfunctional, You're Dysfunctional: The Recovery Movement and Other Self-Help Fashions* (New York: Vintage Books, 1992).

[64]Don S. Browning, *The Moral Context of Pastoral Care* (Philadelphia: Westminster Press, 1976); William J. Doherty, *Soul Searching: Why Psychotherapy Must Promote Moral Responsibility* (New York: Basic Books, 1995).

severed. Much of pastoral care in the earlier parts of the twentieth century became preoccupied with individual concerns at the expense of seeing the community, social, and ethical concerns. The courtship with a very individualized psychology has been excessive. However, Browning is in no way denouncing the importance of personal psychotherapy. We simply need to recognize the significance of both the individual and his/her social and ethical context.

Browning's balance on the importance of *both* individual and social considerations seems especially important as we now face the possibility that the pendulum could swing so far back toward socioeconomic issues that personal and intrapsychic issues become eclipsed. For instance, some in the field of pastoral counseling and theology have become so disenchanted with their previous love affair with psychology that pastoral theology could be in danger of losing a concern for the inner world of those it helps. While issues of race, gender, economic difference, male privilege, public policy, and social justice are all very important new emphases, it is also important to retain some aspects of psychotherapeutic attentiveness as well. If the field's earlier indulgence was psychology, perhaps today's indulgence is sociology.

An illustration from two important social critics may be useful here. In the mid-seventies, Edwin Schur provided a rather scathing indictment of the psychotherapeutic industry.[65] He argued that psychotherapy led to self-absorption and a conviction that the solution to all of our problems is within each of us. The inner world holds all the answers so we need not be concerned with "outer world" things such as public policy, social injustice, and so on. By convincing their patients that the secret to all their troubles is within them, said Schur, therapists are helping maintain the status quo. For instance, the potential anger over social injustice is instead turned into an intrapsychic problem we can resolve in the therapist's office. Psychotherapy, for Schur, does the same thing that religion did for Marx—it turns individuals away from the real social causes of their problems and thus dissolves the possibility for social change.

Three years after Schur's book, Christopher Lasch, well-known cultural historian, wrote his acclaimed *The Culture of Narcissism*. While his book is known primarily for his blowing the whistle on self-absorbed psychother-

---

[65]Schur, *The Awareness Trap*.

apy, Lasch, like Browning, maintained a balance in never suggesting that psychotherapy is not important. In fact, while he likes many of Schur's ideas, he chastises him for an excessive condemnation of psychotherapy. For Lasch, it is indeed true that individuals can run away from ethical and social responsibilities by a retreat to the inner world. Yet it is also true, argues Lasch, that persons can run away from their frightening inner world as they escape into social issues.

Much of Browning's understanding of psychotherapy's relationship to ethics can be seen in the following comment.

> When pastoral care relinquishes the attempt to reestablish at the level of the individual, a sense for normative values that might be shared by a general public, it is furthering the process of privatism and pietism. An ethos which suggests that moral values are to be bracketed and relegated to the private tastes of individuals involved makes one more contribution to the general idea that there is no shared or public moral universe. In that case, secular individualism becomes the dominant style of the day.[66]

In fact, it is only when there is a solid backdrop of ethical commitment that the counselor can bracket moral issues and explore psychological dynamics. Exploration of internal conflicts presupposes a nonjudgmental, accepting climate. This is perfectly appropriate because the person comes out of a normative set of values and ethical commitments. Yet what if the counselee has no sense of moral context? What if the person is not guided by a sense of ethical obligation? If that is the case, then acceptance, grace, and forgiveness will mean very little. Put another way, the temporary suspension of ethical judgment will not be helpful to someone who largely *lives* with a suspension of all judgments. Without this fund of moral meanings, argues Browning, there will be no point in temporarily bracketing them to work on psychological dynamics. The counselee would not have anything to "return to" after the therapeutic suspension. And this, according to Browning, is a weakness in both Freudian and Rogerian psychotherapy. The assumption is that the psychologically "healed" individuals will simply know, by intuition, what to do. There is little emphasis on posttherapeutic guidance on moral issues.

Browning is in no way suggesting that all psychological problems stem from unresolved ethical issues. He has no need for a moral police and he

---

[66]Browning, *The Moral Context of Pastoral Care*, 27.

certainly sees the benefit to therapy. Yet he does suggest that at least some psychological problems may be related to value conflicts. As nearly any therapist can attest, value confusion brings on psychological distress.

Also, Browning would differ with Harry Bone's contention that once the psychological debris has been cleared away, persons will automatically move toward "self-determination," as Bone called it, and act in ethical ways. For Browning, healthy, nonneurotic action simply means we are able to do something without internal conflict. This hardly guarantees that what we are doing is the right thing to do. Moral action takes on the additional consideration of how our actions impact family, friends, our community, and the larger society.

To repeat, the bracketing of ethical considerations for the purposes of psychological exploration is only meaningful when one *already has* a background of ethical commitments. The therapist can no longer assume that the client is most likely oppressed by a severe conscience, carrying a heavy load of guilt, or condemned by a strong Superego. The therapies and theologies of grace work very well for individuals who have been beaten down by their own self-recriminations. However, changing cultural patterns may well produce clients who feel more of a sense of entitlement than guilt; who are concerned more with self-interests than pleasing others; and who are not oppressed by perfectionistic standards as much as having virtually no standards at all.

> We cannot understand the meaning of forgiveness unless we first throw ourselves into a radical concern about the nature of right moral action. We cannot be delivered from the curse of the law unless first of all we know, contemplate, and strive to keep the law.[67]

For Browning, pastoral care should swing back and forth between practical moral thinking about normative patterns and the forgiveness, grace, and freedom which makes a moral life possible. In our attempts to avoid moralism, we need not eliminate a concern for morality.

Almost twenty years after Browning's book, William Doherty wrote his more general invitation for psychotherapists to consider the ethical horizons out of which they work. Similar in tone to Browning, Doherty is quite clear about the direction of his book:

---

[67]Browning, *The Moral Context of Pastoral Care*, 125.

> This book argues that therapists since the time of Freud have overemphasized individual self-interest, giving short shrift to family and community responsibilities. It calls for the inclusion of moral discourse in the practice of psychotherapy and the cultivation in therapists of the virtues and skills needed to be moral consultants to their clients in a pluralistic and morally opaque world. I argue that issues of moral responsibility and community well-being are always present in therapy, and that carefully balanced attention to these issues can greatly expand the contributions of psychotherapy to the alleviation of human problems.[68]

The loss of a moral vocabulary in the world of psychotherapy occurred because many therapists believed that psychological explanations eliminated any need for ethical discussion. Science could replace moral language and show that individuals only engage in destructive behavior because they have psychological conflicts. Once the conflicts are cleared up, ethical behavior will flow automatically. The assumption, which can certainly be seen in the New York Psychology Group discussions, is called into question by Doherty.

Doherty, too, makes Browning's earlier point about how a change in cultural patterns can produce far less guilt-ridden individuals in need of psychotherapeutic acceptance. Doherty points out that in Freud's day, and largely throughout the first 60 or so years of psychotherapy in the twentieth century, therapists could rather safely assume that clients coming to them were probably inhibited, guilt-ridden, and self-condemning. They had more than likely digested ethical norms to such a degree that they felt like failures. These individuals were oppressed and in need of psychotherapeutic liberation. And Doherty does not doubt that some such individuals still come for counseling. Some indeed need to discover their right to selfhood. Yet cultural patterns have shifted so radically that many individuals do not present these oppressive symptoms at all.

> By the 1990s, however, whatever has served as the moral center of mainstream culture seems not to be holding. Massive cheating in the business world and in military academics, unprecedented levels of crime and violence, shocking reports of physical and sexual abuse in families, widespread abandonment of children by divorced as well as never-married fathers followed by justifications based on personal entitlement, doing

---

[68]Doherty, *Soul Searching*, 7-8.

one's own thing, or victimization—these are examples of trends that undermine any concern that contemporary Americans have overlearned a rigidly conventional morality that they must be liberated from by an army of psychotherapists.[69]

Stated simply, changing times can bring different clientele. To assume that the previous therapy models—which were designed primarily for an overly moralized rather than under-moralized population—will continue to be effective with today's clients may be a mistake. What heals one generation may not heal the next.

---

[69]Doherty, *Soul Searching*, 11-12.

Chapter 6

Theology and Psychology: Tillich's Ongoing Relevance

Tillich listened to and still speaks to every questioning human being.
—David Tracy

In this final chapter, I will focus on Tillich's ongoing significance in theology's dialogue with psychology. To accomplish this, I will (a) examine the manner in which the Tillich vs. Barth conflict has evolved into the contemporary differences in revisionist and postliberal theology, (b) explore David Tracy's revision of Tillich's correlational method and its relevance for a dialogue with psychotherapy, (c) investigate the question of whether a critical hermeneutical approach offers the best of the revisionist and postliberal models, (d) consider the way in which Don Browning incorporates the work of Tracy and Ricoeur in his theological dialogue with psychotherapy, (e) examine the shifting paradigm in pastoral counseling and theology which insists that we must move from an individual to a more social and communal perspective, and, finally, (f) provide an overview of the continual contribution Tillich offers the theology and psychology dialogue. I will conclude that Tillich's influence is far from over. Tillich is much more than the greatest twentieth-century theological representative of the psychology and theology dialogue; his insights and contributions remain most helpful as this dialogue moves into the twenty-first century.

Apologetic and Unapologetic Theology

In Tillich's own period, a polarity frequently existed between what was called "apologetic" and "kerygmatic" theologians. This polarity has been with Christianity since early Christians encountered Greek philosophy. It essentially deals with the relationship between faith and reason and, more particularly, the theologian's responsibility to an unbelieving world. In other words, how much attention should be devoted to making the Christian message understandable and relevant to its contemporary audience? Apologetic theologians, of course, have always claimed that theology must speak to the questions and issues of its own day as it translates the Christian message to today's world. It needs to find points of contact with culture. Kerygmatic theologians, on the other hand, have been very alarmed about this process. Their concern is that the Christian message becomes something other than the traditional Gospel when one tries to find points of contact with secularity. Further, the Gospel carries with it a self-authenticating quality. The theologian need not convince on rational grounds one who questions and doubts the Christian message. In fact, there is no point of contact with unbelief.

As every student of twentieth-century theology knows, these two perspectives were largely represented by Tillich and Karl Barth. For Tillich, we need to carefully consider the situation in which we find ourselves and allow that situation to raise its own ultimate questions. Hence, a *theology of culture* is necessary. For Barth, on the other hand, we should simply announce the Good News and not become preoccupied with justifying the Gospel to contemporary objectors. For Barth, Tillich's approach assumes that human beings know the right questions to ask, an assumption Barth is not willing to make. Because of the effects of sin, human beings do not always ask the right questions. Further, according to Barth, the Gospel message becomes dependent on human questions and theology is then held captive by human concerns. Instead, argues Barth, theology needs the freedom to be loyal to Divine revelation without being tied down with the culture's latest preoccupations. For Barth, apologetic theology overvalues human reason and humanity's ability to diagnose itself. For Tillich, Barth's kerygmatic approach is irrelevant to the particular needs of the contemporary situation. The theologian must take the risk of being a citizen of culture.

These two poles of kerygmatic and apologetic theology have to a large extent evolved into two perspectives which occupy American theology. While these two perspectives may not perfectly reflect the positions of Barth and Tillich, the resemblance is obvious. On the Barthian side has been the development of postliberal theology. While there are variations within this group, the overall themes of Barth are quite present. On the other side of the table, Tillich's ongoing significance can be seen in the revisionist school. At the risk of generalization, one could say that for the revisionist group, Tillich is in the background and David Tracy is the contemporary representative. Similarly, in the postliberal group, Barth is in the background and George Lindbeck is perhaps the best representative. It is not an exaggeration to say that much of Christian theology in the past three decades has revolved around the differences between these two groups. One can even go further and say that American Christian theology has been dominated by the "Chicago school" (revisionist) and the "Yale school" (postliberal). Although Tillich spent only the last few years of his life at the University of Chicago, the work of Langdon Gilkey and David Tracy carried his influence forward. At Yale, Hans Frei and Lindbeck have carried forward Barth's perspective. These two schools have groomed many theologians who have advanced the causes of revisionist and postliberal theologies.

Again, I am aware that revisionist and postliberal theologies do not unambiguously reflect Tillich and Barth. Yet the similarities can easily be detected.

To understand the ongoing dialogue between theology and psychology, it is important to take a closer look at these conflicting theological perspectives. Should psychology be trusted to *bring forth* the questions that theology then feels obligated to answer? Should theology, instead, ask its own questions? Does psychology offer its own answers to the ultimate questions of life, answers which should then be compared with those of theology? To deal with these questions, I will pay particular attention to David Tracy's *Analogical Imagination* and George Lindbeck's *Nature of Doctrine*. Also, of particular help will be the work of William Placher, especially his *Unapologetic Theology*.[1]

From Tillich and Barth to Revisionists and Postliberals

Ten years after Tillich's death, David Tracy suggested that Tillich's well-known correlational method in theology should be appreciated but expanded.[2] Whereas Tillich wanted to bring the questions of the cultural situation into dialogue with the revelatory answers of Christian theology, Tracy pointed out that "the situation," to use Tillich's language, brings not only questions but answers derived from its own analysis.[3] For Tillich,

---

[1] David Tracy, *The Analogical Imagination: Christian Theology and the Culture of Pluralism* (New York: Crossroad, 1981); George A. Lindbeck, *The Nature of Doctrine: Religion and Theology in a Postliberal Age* (Louisville: Westminster/John Knox Press, 1984); and William Placher, *Unapologetic Theology: A Christian Voice in a Pluralistic Conversation* (Louisville: Westminster/John Knox Press, 1989).

[2] David Tracy, *Blessed Rage for Order: The New Pluralism in Theology* (Chicago: University of Chicago Press, repr. 1996; orig., 1975).

[3] Actually, Tracy's "revised correlational method" had been used a decade earlier in Guy Hammond's work, *Man in Estrangement.* Hammond correlated *both*

apologetic theology is an "answering theology" which presupposes a common ground with the person asking the question. A philosophical analysis of the culture will invariably lead to central questions the theologian must embrace. If the theologian addresses questions which have not been raised by his or her situation, then his or her answers will fall on deaf ears. As we have seen, for Tillich, this was the perennial danger of Barthian neo-orthodoxy. While he appreciated Barth's concern to maintain the purity of the Christian message, he believed that kerygmatic theology often did not take the important first step of cultural analysis. Consequently, its answers did not match the questions being asked. Again, Tillich trusted humanity to ask the right questions; Barth did not.

Tracy's point, however, is that the theologian can no longer afford the luxury of simply having questions served to him/her. Instead, culture offers both questions and answers—often answers which compete with religious truth claims. If we are to take our cultural situations seriously, we must hear *both* these questions and the answers. Otherwise, says Tracy, we are merely juxtaposing our religious answers with cultural questions, not genuinely correlating them.[4] Tracy thus calls for a "revised correlational analysis" in which the conversation involves *mutual correlation of both questions and answers*. Again, Tillich's correlational approach only allows half the dialogue. For instance, Tracy believes that Tillich did not adequately critically investigate the existentialist "answers" to human existence found in Karl Jaspers and Jean Paul Sartre.[5] Both of these philosophers thought they had discovered better answers to the problem of estrangement than Christianity offers. For genuine correlation to occur, argues Tracy, Tillich would have been forced to "compare answers" as well as simply answer questions.

There are other times, however, in which Tillich seems quite willing to do more than his own correlational method calls for. As we have seen in the New York Psychology Group discussions, Tillich both listened to and was quite critical of Fromm's "solution" to the problem of human estrangement. In this discussion, Tillich seemed quite willing to contrast what he considered to be the religious, and specifically Christian, answer to estrangement with what he thought was the utopian vision of Fromm. This is

---

the questions and answers of Fromm and Tillich.

[4]Hammond's work, *Man in Estrangement*, 46.

[5]Hammond's work, *Man in Estrangement*, 46.

perhaps the reason that Tracy can say the following of Tillich's correlational method.

> The fact is that Tillich does allow the answers (and not just the questions) of psychoanalysis, socialist theory, existentialism, and his own "self-transcending" naturalism to provide answers, not only questions, in his theology.... In sum, the method of correlation is better formulated not as he usually formulated it, but as he actually employed it: an interpretive correlation of the questions and answers of the message and the questions and answers of the situation.... This interpretation of Tillich's method is, I believe, not only more faithful to his own use of the method but also more in keeping with the hermeneutical character of much contemporary theology. What Tillich has given us is a general guiding theological method that expresses in explicit terms the hermeneutical character of all contemporary theology.[6]

In my view, Tillich's involvement in the New York Psychology Group reinforces the notion that he *practiced* a method closer to the revised correlational approach. Tillich engaged answers as well as questions. He did not assume a privileged position in which other people simply brought up their secular questions. He was quite aware, for instance, that Fromm held a competing worldview with its own answers and resolutions to the problems of human existence. Tillich did not simply "answer" Fromm's questions; instead, he disagreed with Fromm's solutions.

In describing the task of the revisionist theologian who employs the revised correlational method, Tracy thus says the following.

> In short, the revisionist theologian is committed to what seems clearly to be the central task of contemporary theology: the dramatic confrontation, the mutual illuminations and corrections, the possible basic reconciliation between the principal values, cognitive claims, and existential faiths of both a reinterpreted post-Christian consciousness and a reinterpreted Christianity.[7]

Or, stated differently, this expansion of Tillich's model involves critical philosophical reflection on both the meanings and faith of cultural experience and the meanings and faith of the Christian tradition. The Tillichian

---

[6]David Tracy, "Tillich and Contemporary Theology," in *The Thought of Paul Tillich*, ed. Adams, Pauck, and Shinn (San Francisco: Harper and Row, 1985) 266.
[7]Tracy, *Blessed Rage for Order*, 32.

influence can be seen in the notion that both culture and Christianity possess a faith. No one is "faithless" in this sense.

For Tillich, once again, a person can only criticize the notion of faith from the standpoint of another faith. This insight has become a pivotal feature of postmodern thought. It is both pretentious and impossible to declare that one can criticize faith from a standpoint of pure, objective, scientific observation. All theorizing begins somewhere; and the place it begins involves faith assumptions. Thus theology must not fall prey to the intimidating sense that it is built on faith while its critics start with purely objective, scientific data. As we shall later see, this has often occurred in theology's dialogue with psychology, and particularly psychotherapy. Many times, psychotherapy attempts to hide its extra-empirical assumptions and philosophical convictions behind the notion that it is scientific while religion operates only on faith. A closer look will reveal, however, the quasi-religious character of many psychotherapies.

This is the point that Don Browning and I try to make in *Religious Thought and the Modern Psychologies*.[8] Psychotherapy has its own view of human potential, sense of ethical obligation, and vision of the ultimate context of our lives. We do not criticize psychotherapy for "crossing over" into these larger philosophical issues. In fact, we welcome them as dialogue partners. The concerns of psychotherapy eventually deal with questions of purpose, meaning, and the overall scheme of life. Unlike other dimensions of psychology, which limit themselves to carefully controlled experiments, working with human lives inevitably brings up these larger questions of motivation and one's place in the overall scheme of things. Psychotherapy is welcomed to this discussion. We can indeed contrast both questions and answers. But psychotherapy should be consciously aware of the fact that it has crossed over into the world of philosophical reflection and practical reason. It cannot continue wearing its hardhat of science when it enters this new turf of dialogue. Stated simply, it's fine for psychology to raise faith concerns; just don't pretend to be doing so in the name of science. I will come back to this later.

Revisionist theology, then, is interested in the public character of theology. It attempts to involve itself in the conversations of the larger

---

[8]Don S. Browning and Terry D. Cooper, *Religious Thought and the Modern Psychologies*, 2nd ed.

culture, always looking for opportunities to demonstrate the relevance of Christian thought for today's world. Postliberal theology, by contrast, is more "confessional" in that it is interested primarily in a coherent description of the Christian faith which preserves the Christian vision. It is suspicious of apologetic attempts to correlate Christian beliefs with general aspects of human experience. If revisionist theology is in danger of excessive accommodation to cultural meanings and values, the postliberal danger concerns sectarianism.

Postliberals are concerned that revisionists are trying to reach some sort of "neutral" place between themselves and secularity. Many, they say, are looking for a universal religious experience, a prelinguistic experience which shows us the essence of religion.[9] Once they find this universal experience, they can show how Christian symbols address this experience shared by all. Postliberals, however, are very doubtful of any sort of universal religious experience. The reason for this is that human experience is not possible without a language and a tradition of shared meanings. In other words, we can't get back to some sort of prelinguistic world of direct, raw experience. Experience is always mediated by language and language always assumes a tradition. Therefore looking for some universal point of contact is futile. This point about language is a crucial one. Following the work of the later Wittgenstein, postliberals, as William Placher says, argue that we have reversed the experience and language connection. We do not first have an experience and then go looking for a language. Instead, a language comes first and makes experience possible.[10] Placher states this well.

> Therefore, prelinguistic experience can hardly provide the criterion for judging linguistic formulations. We cannot argue for Christianity by saying that it best captures the essence of universal religiousness since there is no coherent "religousness" prior to a particular tradition's language.[11]

---

[9]See Lindbeck, *The Nature of Doctrine*.

[10]Placher's work on contrasting a revisionist and postliberal model is outstanding and fair-minded. Though he leans toward the postliberal camp, he appreciates Tracy, in particular. In addition to his *Unapologetic Theology*, see also his chapter on "Postliberal Theology," in *The Modern Theologians: An Introduction to Christian Theology in the Twentieth Century*, ed. David F. Ford (Oxford: Blackwell Publishers, 1997) 343-56.

[11]Placher, *Unapologetic Theology*, 163.

Also, according to many postliberals, revisionists are often looking for some sort of Enlightenment standard of neutral reason, a place where all people can come together and share an epistemological foundation. This is why the pursuit of apologetics and public theology is fallacious. Revisionists assume that we still have one public. Instead, we have many "publics." There are a diversity of competing perspectives and we can't find a universally agreed upon epistemological mid-point where all parties feel comfortable. Revisionists keep wanting a neutral point of conversation when no such place exists. They have not given up their Enlighenment dream of universal knowledge.

Revisionists, on the other hand, believe that postliberals cannot simply appeal to Scripture or the Christian tradition without trying to also provide reasons for the plausibility of their positions. They must be willing to submit their claims to critical, philosophical reflection. Surely, argue the revisionists, we must at least attempt to show the relevance of Christianity and not simply say, "This is the Gospel, take it or leave it."

For Tracy, the very universality of the concept of God necessitates a public explanation of the meaning of this word.[12] We cannot simply rely, as the postliberals claim, on personal faith or beliefs. Instead, a philosophical argument must also be made. As he states, "the theologian should argue the case (pro or con) on strictly public grounds that are open to all rational persons."[13] Other revisionists might add that postliberals come dangerously close to encouraging a radical relativism, promoting sectarianism, and proclaiming a type of fideism in their retreat from public discussion.

> When challenged on an interpretation, do I have any evidence that my conversation partner could accept? Can we find those common places that constitute the right places for discussing our differences? Can we find common places on what constitutes argument itself? Or shall I simply retreat into announcements arising from my intuitive sense? I may be right, but no one else, in principle, will ever know it. I have become the Delphic oracle. I am reduced to solipsism, which is the enemy of conversation.[14]

---

[12]Tracy, *The Analogical Imagination*, 62.

[13]Tracy, *The Analogical Imagination*, 64.

[14]David Tracy, *Plurality and Ambiguity: Hermeneutics, Hope, and Religion* (San Francisco: Harper & Row, 1987) .

Tracy adds that to offer an interpretation is to make a claim and that one needs to be willing to defend such a claim when it is questioned or challenged. Otherwise, the conversation simply can't go forward.

Postliberals might then respond by saying that this so-called public standard for dialogue is a fiction. Again, there is no common ground to which we can all appeal. And the attempt to find this neutral place ends up subordinating the Gospel to the cultural standard one finds. The Christian tradition is then pushed and controlled by a standard foreign to its own tradition, language, and meaning. The Christian faith has its own internal logic and should not be forced to match the bar of some artificial epistemological midpoint. As soon as the Gospel submits to this external standard, it is usually "taken over" by this standard. And further, this standard looks strangely like the imperialistic norm of Enligtenment rationality.

Critical Hermeneutics: The Best of Both Worlds?

While he does not in any way denounce his 1975 work, *Blessed Rage for Order*, Tracy, in his later work *Plurality and Ambiguity*, seems to indicate a deepening of his hermeneutical approach, a development surely based on a greater appropriation of Ricoeur.[15] Also, this development seems to provide a greater appreciation of the narrative and linguistic approach of postliberals. I would like to suggest, then, that Tracy's more seasoned critical hermeneutical approach, as well as the later developments in Tillich's thought, offer the possibility of appropriating some of the wisdom of both traditions. Whether or not one can truly have one's theological cake and eat it too will be left to the judgment of the reader.

I would like to briefly examine Tracy's more hermeneutically oriented work and describe how it affects theology's dialogue with psychotherapy. Of particular help in this process will be the work of Don Browning, whom I have already mentioned.

Much of Tracy's work revolves around an analysis of what he calls "the classics" in Western culture. Classics refer to texts which perpetually demand our attention because they so deeply speak to the human condition. He discusses four important factors about "classics" in our culture. First, classics have shaped our preunderstanding even before we approach them. In other words, they have shaped the culture we inherit. Religious classics,

---

[15]Tracy, *Plurality and Ambiguity*.

for instance, are also cultural classics. In that sense, religious classics have influenced the preunderstanding of even those who claim to be thoroughly secular. Second, classics bear an excess or permanence of meaning and they cannot be interpreted in a once-and-for-all manner. They continually need to be reinterpreted. This excess fund of meanings requires ongoing attention. And according to Tracy, these classics *command* our attention. As he puts it, "the classics will not be so easily tamed."[16] Third, even though they are born out of particular locations, these classics have the potential to be universal. And finally, while these classics may be eclipsed during particular cultural periods, they will reappear and claim our attention.

Again, a major factor in all interpretation of classic texts is that they have *already influenced us before we begin the interpreting process*. This is another way of saying that no one approaches a classic from a neutral or completely objective place. Without a preunderstanding, the classic would not even make sense. We would have no frame of reference by which to interpret it. This is the illusion of all foundationalisms. They deny the need for an interpretive grid. Whether we are talking about scientific foundationalism or biblical foundationalism, the point is that we bring an orientation, a framework, an interpretive mechanism to the text. No one starts from scratch. To use a language is to have a preunderstanding. The Enlightenment notion of a completely autonomous, neutral consciousness is as impossible for Tracy as it is for postliberals.

> No human being is simply a passive recipient of texts. We inquire. We question. We converse. Just as there is no purely autonomous text, so there is no purely passive reader. There is only that interaction named conversation.[17]

For Tracy, only scientism denies its own hermeneutical character as it claims an ahistorical understanding of the world in spite of the fact that its own understanding is embedded in a socio-historical framework. These claims, for Tracy, deny the hermeneutical character of all thought and are no longer tenable.

Yet it is at this point that Ricoeur's influence becomes obvious in Tracy. While Enlightenment objectivity is no longer possible, this does not

---

[16]Tracy, *Plurality and Ambiguity*, 14.
[17]Tracy, *Plurality and Ambiguity*, 19.

have to lead to a complete relativism. The reason for this is that while objectivity is impossible, Ricoeur's term, "distanciation" is not.[18] Distanciation refers to the purposeful and critical distancing of ourselves from our own perspective in order to see it with greater objectivity. Notice that I did *not* say complete objectivity, which Riceour would deny as an impossible hangover from Enlightenment thinking. Yet we can distance ourselves from our own assumptions *without alienating ourselves from those assumptions*. Again, to deny total objectivity is not to deny distanciation. We can be self-critical without being self-alienating. We do not have to throw the baby out with the bath water.

If this moment of distancitation is not possible, then conversations are not really plausible. All we do is "story swapping" which involves talking *past* each other rather than *to* each other. Again, while Tracy clearly agrees with postliberals that all understanding is grounded in a cultural-linguistic framework, he does not believe that is the end of the story. Yes, all data is theory-laden, all inquiry is self-involved, and positivism is impossible. In fact, at times, Tracy sounds like a postliberal.

> We do not first experience or understand some reality and then find words to name that understanding. We understand in and through languages available to us, including the historical languages of the sciences.[19]

This comment indicates that Tracy does not really fall into the experiential-expressivist form of theology outlined by Lindbeck.[20] He does not think we first have some sort of universal experience then go looking for a language to describe it. We are language-saturated in our thinking. We are embedded creatures and our self-understanding "grows up" in a language system. Nevertheless, this does not mean that we cannot establish a degree of distance from our presuppositions, think critically about them, and offer public reasons as to why they make sense.

Browning's Development of Tracy and Ricoeur

Having been heavily influenced by his colleagues, Tracy and Ricoeur, Don Browning has provided a critical hermeneutical approach to the relationship

---

[18] Paul Ricoeur, *Hermeneutics and the Human Sciences*, ed. and trans. John B. Thomspon (Cambridge: Cambridge University Press, 1981) esp. chap. 4.

[19] Ricoeur, *Hermeneutics and the Human Sciences*, 48.

[20] George Lindbeck, *The Nature of Doctrine*.

between psychology and theology which has been well received. Working with Browning on his revised *Religious Thought and the Modern Psychologies* provided me with an opportunity to see critical hermeneutical thinking at its best. Also, his important book, *A Fundamental Practical Theology* lays out his method in detail.[21] Browning also follows the legacy of Tillich in that he has a masterful ability to smoke out the hidden ontological assumptions in various psychotherapeutic frameworks.

Browning is convinced that Tracy's approach "combines the best of the cultural-linguistic and the apologetic approaches."[22] Specific reasons for the attraction to Tracy's method include the following: (a) it is thoroughly hermeneutical, (b) it understands that the religious classics we interpret have *already* shaped us before we officially approach them, (c) while faith and confession precede reason, this does not mean that distanciation is not important, (d) our thought is historically and socially embedded *before* it becomes conscious, and (e) there is no unambiguous starting point because a plurality of confessional traditions exist.[23]

Browning's apologetic approach, influenced by both Tillich and Tracy, refuses to stop at simply proclaiming the Christian narrative and leaving it at that. He takes on the extra burden of setting forth reasons for the claims he makes, reasons he wishes to take to the public table of dialogue. Browning's perspective is similar to, though less Enlightenment-bound, than Jurgen Habermas's insistence on "validity claims."[24] Many postmodern thinkers, however broad in scope they may be, often identify Habermas as one who attempts to extend the Enlightenment, and thus a champion of modernity and an enemy of postmodernity. While that highly interesting debate is beyond the parameters of this book, it is important to say that Browning is more modest in his hopes for validity claims. Put simply, the possibility of certain, universally convincing arguments is no longer with us. Foundationalism is dead. Yet just because we can't have perfect reasons or all-convincing reasons does *not* mean that we cannot have *good* reasons. It is these good reasons which we must bring to the con-

---

[21]Don S. Browning, *A Fundamental Practical Theology* (Minneapolis: Fortress Press, 1991).

[22]Browning, *A Fundamental Practical Theology*, 45.

[23]Browning, *A Fundamental Practical Theology*, 45-46.

[24]Jurgen Habermas, *Communication and the Evolution of Society* (Boston: Beacon Press, 1979).

versation. Without them, conversation stops. It is here that we can see Browning's agreement with Richard Bernstein.

> For although all claims to truth are fallible and open to criticism, they still require validation—validation that can be realized only through offering the best reasons and arguments that can be given in support of them— reasons and arguments that are themselves embedded in the practices that have been developed in the course of history. We never escape from the obligation of seeking to validate claims to truth through argumentation and opening ourselves to the criticism of others.[25]

Thus, while all discourse *begins* in faith and is *embedded* in tradition, this does not mean that we should not step outside of our confessional communities and offer reasons for our convictions. The dialogue, for Browning, Tracy, and Tillich, should extend outward toward other communities and not just our own. This is, as we have seen, in fundamental disagreement with the postliberal claim that the truth of the Christian narrative can never be demonstrated by evidence outside its own language structure.

A revised correlational approach, then, is very important in psychology's dialogue with religion. We can state it sharply: If psychology *both* raises questions and makes claims about human nature, ethical obligations, and the ultimate context of our lives, then religion needs to view psychology as at least quasi-theological.[26] Psychology's assumptions often seem to extend beyond a philosophical anthropology and on into an implicit religious framework. Psychology does more than merely raise questions; it, too, interprets human life. And when any discipline starts to interpret human life, it eventually shifts to larger issues of purpose, meaning, ethics, and our "place" in the universe. One cannot address the issues of the human condition without examining basic needs, motivations, ethical convictions, personal meaning, and an image of human fulfillment. These investigations are incurably philosophical, and at least quasi-theological. Stated differently, there will be ontological baggage here.

While many psychologies want to make modest empirical claims about their own status, a closer look at their guiding assumptions, research frame-

---

[25]Richard Bernstein, *Beyond Objectivism and Relativism* (Philadelphia: University of Pennsylvania Press, 1983) 163.

[26]This is a central argument of Browning and Cooper, in *Religious Thought and the Modern Psychologies*.

works, and broader horizons, reveals that they are operating from meta-empirical grounds. They have assumptive worlds, stand in a particular social and historical context, and possess a preunderstanding which inevitably leads them to notice certain data while ignoring others. They have not established a land without bias, a world without prejudices, an Enlightenment vision of isolated, autonomous reason divorced from self-interest and historicity.

Granted, some types of psychological investigation may involve less influence from our preunderstanding than other types. Our own effective history, to use Gadamer's phrase, may not influence an investigation into neuroscience quite as much as it does the issue of motivation in personality theory. Yet as current philosophy of science reveals, even the so-called "hard" sciences *interpret* events. We bring our own conceptual equipment when we interpret anything. That conceptual equipment has been shaped by a fund of meanings, symbols, and ideas which are part of our social and historical context. Some of these meanings may be highly personal, but they were not developed in isolation. Instead, they are part of the conceptual community or "plausibility structure" out of which we operate.[27]

Tillich, of course, regularly recognized the philosophical underpinnings of various psychological theories. In fact, one could say that he was rather brilliant in linking contemporary ideas to their historic origins. The point, however, is that Tillich may not have fully grasped the manner in which psychologies were on their way to becoming competitive theologies. He at times gave theology a privileged status over them. Since that time, the various psychologies seem much more willing to engage the issues previously under the auspices of theology.

Beyond Existential Anthropology:
From the Individual to the Social

One of the central themes of pastoral and practical theology for the past two decades has been the need to expand beyond an individual model of care and move toward a more systemic view of persons in crisis. These changes have been well summarized by Nancy Ramsay and others in the recently

---

[27]I am indebted to Peter Berger for the concept "plausibility structure." It is used throughout his numerous writings.

released *Pastoral Care and Counseling: Redefining the Paradigms*.[28] Much of this discussion has focused on the movement against individualism, a protest we have already discussed in the last chapter. This priority of the individual over social context and larger social realities has been brought on, in part, by a love affair with psychology, and particularly the focus on intrapsychic dynamics. The problem with this "inward look" is that it has assumed an ahistorical, asocial, apolitical framework which has ignored important influences on the emergence of the "self." Rather than emphasizing individual autonomy, many theorists are now stressing the social, historical, and political location of all thought. Further, issues of race, gender, and other cultural factors are taken into consideration. As Ramsay puts it, "rather than focusing on the particular pain of individuals, attention shifts to naming dominant norms and practices such as patriarchy, racism, classism, and ethnocentrism as major barriers to human well-being."[29] This shift from the clinical, individual focus to a more socio-economic and political concern is what John Patton calls a movement from the "clinical pastoral paradigm" to the "community-contextual paradigm."[30]

Larry Graham's *Care of Persons, Care of Worlds: A Psychosystems Approach to Pastoral Care and Counseling*, has had wide influence in its critique of what he calls the "existential-anthropological" focus in pastoral theology and care.[31] He describes this model as follows:

> This model focuses upon intrapsychic dynamics, with autonomy and self-realization as its primary goals. It is assumed that persons and their primary groups may go about the task of fashioning fulfilling lives largely in spite of "external" realities such as culture, society, and nature. These realities are only secondarily regarded as arenas of ethical responsibility requiring strategic intervention and change if care is to be possible for individuals and their families in the first place.[32]

---

[28]Nancy J. Ramsay, ed., *Pastoral Care and Counseling: Redefining the Paradigms* (Nashville: Abingdon, 2004).

[29]Nancy J. Ramsay, "A Time of Ferment and Redefinition," in Ramsay, *Pastoral Care and Counseling*, 16.

[30]John Patton, *Pastoral Care in Context: An Introduction to Pastoral Care* (Louisville: Westminster/John Knox Press, 1993).

[31]Larry Kent Graham, *Care of Persons, Care of Worlds: A Psychosystems Approach to Pastoral Care and Counseling* (Nashville: Abingdon, 1992).

[32]Graham, *Care of Persons, Care of Worlds*, 14.

For Graham, this existential-anthropological approach has been entirely too influenced by existential philosophy and theology, along with a fixation on intrapsychic processes. It misses the crucial point that the "self" is socially constructed in a particular context. It encourages individuals to become more and more concerned with what they feel and need as it assumes the ultimate goal of life is self-realization. "Personal growth" is perceived as something which somehow transcends one's particular social and historical location. It operates out of a psychology divorced from social and communal dimensions. It also supports the individual in his or her attempt to transcend all contextual limitations and achieve self-fulfillment.

Graham faults many pastoral theologians for falling prey to this self-realization model. Even theorists who seem interested in community and ecological issues such as Howard Clinebell, John Patton, and Charles Gerkin, do not sustain an adequate social emphasis, but instead, fall back into individual psychological concerns. Reinhold Niebuhr, also, according to Graham, is guilty of thinking negatively about social groups and overvaluing an individual's capacity to transcend social and historical influences.[33] Niebuhr advocates the moral superiority of individuals over groups because groups often develop a self-serving bias as they reinforce egoistic impulses among their members.

This change of focus in recent pastoral theology has incorporated many key themes of postmodernity. For instance, there is a definite movement away from an Enlightenment view of universal rationality. The reason for this is that this so-called universal reason has all-too-often simply been the voice of those dominant in culture—normally, white, male European and American intellectuals in positions of power. This preoccupation with a metanarrative capable of accounting for *all* human experience has inevitably marginalized and even silenced those who are in the cognitive minority. A privileged, white male standard of reality has set the bar for everyone else. Considerations of difference have been lost. This universal discourse has been imposed on groups whose experiences do not match these all-inclusive claims. Ideological genocide has occurred as certain powerful groups have a monopoly on the business of defining worldviews.

Joretta Marshall, another contributor to the shifting paradigm in pastoral theology, makes this observation:

---

[33]Graham, *Care of Persons, Care of Worlds*, 71.

> What is important in postmodernity is not to move too quickly into assuming that one's own story or vantage point is the single most important guiding principle in the development of pastoral theology, care, and counseling. Instead, it seems wiser to move into a process of allowing a larger diversity of stories to shape and form our theological reflections....
> It is not enough to appreciate multicultural competencies; rather pastoral caregivers must carry a deeper awareness of the epistemological differences of our experience.[34]

Marshall is "softer" in this comment than many postmodern thinkers. Some would argue that totalizing narratives are violent, and even terrorist, in their attempts to "kill" or stamp out unpopular, minority perspectives. For some thinkers, power always ends up defining reality. This power is epistemologically oppressive. The price paid for not accommodating to the dominant worldview is marginalization. The vital point here is that multiculturalism doesn't merely bring a difference in customs, social habits, or ideological orientation. Instead, it brings with it a diversity of epistemologies. Individuals "know" differently. Intellectual claims, in some groups, simply emerge from different cognitive "styles."

This link between wealth, power, and normative claims has been especially challenged by liberation theology, which in turn, has influenced much of contemporary pastoral theology. Dominantly white, male theologians have spoken to a very small percentage of the world's population. Liberation theology wants to "speak to" and "hear from" those who have not had a voice until now. It chastises much of academic theology for its insular conversations. Rather than simply speaking to each other, it challenges professors in the academy to take into consideration the perspectives of the intellectually underprivileged—those whose claims to reality have been pushed to the side.

This new emphasis in pastoral theology, based in part on liberation theology, has moved from a focus on healing to a concern with liberation. While both of these terms have been connected, the new paradigm stresses not just intrapsychic liberation from oppressive thinking but social, political, and economic liberation from external forces also. Practical, grassroots strategies and involvement in public policy mark a significant

---

[34]Joretta L. Marshall, "Methods in Pastoral Theology, Care, and Counseling," in *Pastoral Care and Counseling: Redefining the Paradigms*, ed. Ramsay, 153.

change from a relatively sedate counseling focus. Personal healing is not enough; empowerment is sought. Pastoral care is societal care.

An interesting, and somewhat self-contradictory thesis of some thinkers, particularly Graham, is that while they greatly emphasize the importance of the social and cultural conditioning of all thought, they do not seem very sympathetic to the social and cultural factors that contributed to the existential-anthropological model. For instance, it can easily be pointed out that someone like Erich Fromm spent too much time and effort exaggerating individual autonomy and its fight against all forms of authoritarianism. Fromm, in other words, was too concerned with self-realization. But when one contextualizes Fromm's thought and understands the horrific conformity, lack of individuality, and "escape from freedom" in his own experience, it is easy to understand why he emphasized the importance of personal autonomy.[35] The same can be said for individuals such as Carl Rogers who came out of a social matrix in which many persons were discouraged from any form of self-discovery and instead pushed toward a blind conformity to cultural standards. It is easy, *from our own intellectual location*, to criticize the apolitical, asocial, and ahistorical tone of their thinking. But we do not inhabit the world they inherited, a world in which personal autonomy may have seemed as foreign to their clients as the community-contextual paradigm seems to our own.

Graham, while writing a very comprehensive book, comes dangerously close to a lop-sided social focus which ends up ignoring the *very real* psychological needs of individuals. Again, I agree with him that themes of individuality have run amok in psychology and pastoral counseling, but if the social and contextual dimension is overplayed at the expense of any sort of focus on interiority, I suspect that future generations will say the same thing that Kierkegaard said to Hegel, namely, the self has been lost in the system. It's one thing to say that the personal, psychological end of pastoral care has been overdeveloped at the expense of the communal and contextual dimensions. But Graham comes close to saying that this personal dimension is an unnecessary fixation along the way to where the *real* problems are—the social, political, and ecological dimensions. While he offers a very well-developed and helpful interpretation of the unfortunate

---

[35] Also, I would suggest that Fromm's concern with human autonomy was matched by his equal interest in social character, thus indicating a dual focus on individuality and context.

excessive individualism of much of contemporary psychotherapy—an individualism I also examined in the last chapter—Graham's proposal may swing the pendulum too far in the direction of systemic thinking. The cure for pastoral *psychology* is not pastoral *sociology*. Again, it is very true that one can run away from social responsibilities through a retreat to the inner world. Yet it is also true that one can run away from one's own interiority through a preoccupation with social systems.

Also, as one reads many current discussions of the methods, role, and paradigms within pastoral theology, one wonders if there is not an uncritical appropriation of many postmodern themes. For instance, the problem seems to revolve around the master narrative that has been forced onto everyone. Instead, we are told, we need a celebration of beliefs and the emancipation of multiple epistemological "styles." Yet there seems to be lacking a concern for the equally difficult problem of radical relativism. Throughout much of this literature, and particularly those deeply influenced by liberationist themes, there seems to be only one epistemological danger—the danger of forcing a universal standard onto marginalized, under-represented individuals. Point granted. But what about the other enormous epistemological challenge, namely, the easy step from diversity to complete relativism. In this world, one's belief system becomes very much like one's personal taste in clothing or food. My response to a validity claim can simply be dismissed because it doesn't fit my epistemological "style."

Some aspects of postmodernity seem to confuse contextualism with radical relativism. Contextualism indeed states that all thought is historically and socially located. One's "plausibility structure," to once again use Peter Berger's frequent phrase, is dependent on the social world one inhabits. Perpsectives are planted in concrete situations and not freefloating ahistorical, asocial, and apolitical "pure" thoughts. However, this limitation of context does not necessarily mean that all concepts have equal value and are reducible to mere opinions from various social locations. Certainly not all theories of the world handle the complexities of life with equal finesse. Also, isn't the announcement that all grand narratives are impossible *itself a grand narrative*? It is one thing to recognize the plurality of worldviews available, but it is another thing to say that none of these definitions of reality could possibly be more adequate than another.

Van Harvey offers an important point on this issue as he describes sociologist of knowledge, Karl Mannheim:

> He coined the term "relationism" (in contradistinction to "relativism") to denote the epistemological perspective of his sociology of knowledge—not a capitulation of thought before sociohistorical relativities, but a sober recognition that knowledge must always be knowledge from a certain position.... Mannheim believed that ideologizing influences, while they could not be eradicated completely, could be mitigated by the systemic analysis of as many as possible of the varying socially grounded positions.[36]

Again, recognizing the sociohistorical limitations of one's thought does not mean that all thought is of equal value. Or to put it in the terms of Tracy and Riceour, the impossibility of complete objectivity does not eliminate the possibility of distanciation, a critical distancing from one's cognitive home-world or preunderstanding. It is intellectually hazardous to leap from the notion of a limited epistemology to the conclusion that all perspectives have equal validity. In fact, radical relativism quickly turns into nihilism. What's the point of *any* conversation if our narratives simply talk past each other and are all of equal value? If the university, at its best, represents a very large conversation, then there is no conversation-stopper as potent as radical relativism. Again, giving up and grieving our Enlightenment hopes for finding a universally agreed-upon definition of Reality should not mean that we cease offering "good" reasons for perspectives. The notion that various discourses can find absolutely no point of contact whatsoever seems to be an exaggeration of human differences.

Tillich's Ongoing Relevance

To conclude this study, I would like to list what I consider to be the most significant contributions that Tillich still offers theology's dialogue with psychology. One of the most abiding values of Tillich's work is his insistence upon pushing psychotherapy to expose its hidden philosophical, and particularly, ontological assumptions. This has had an enormous impact on pastoral counseling and theology. As I have indicated throughout this book, Tillich insisted that beneath practical aspects of care are assumptive worldviews about human nature and the structure of existence. Tillich was a pioneer and model of pushing psychotherapy to reveal its less-than-scientific vision of the world. This emphasis pushed "psychological

---

[36]Van A. Harvey, "Religious Faith and the Sociology of Knowledge: The Unburdening of Peter Berger," *Religious Studies Review* 5/1 (January 1979).

scientists" to confess that they were also philosophers, and in many cases, implicit theologians. A critique of psychology's ontological assumptions has become second-nature to many pastoral counselors and theologians, and we owe this debt to Tillich.

Related to this, Tillich needs to be credited with showing that while many claim to attack religious faith on strictly empirical grounds, they actually attack it *in the name of another faith*. No one is without an ultimate concern. Something is always functioning as sacred even in the most secular existence. By pointing out the "faith dimension" of all thought, Tillich, in many ways, anticipated the postmodern reaction against the possibility of pure science and objective reason. In *Dynamics of Faith*, Tillich makes the following point.

> [E]ven in the scientific view of reality an element of faith is effective. Scientists rightly try to prevent these elements of faith and philosophical truth from interfering with their actual research. This is possible to a great extent; but even the most protected experiment is not absolutely "pure"—pure in the sense of the exclusion of interfering factors such as the observer, as the interest which determines the kind of question asked of nature in an experiment. What we said about the philosopher must also be said about the scientist. Even in his scientific work he is a human being, grasped by an ultimate concern, and he asks the question of the universe, as such, the philosophical question.[37]

Regardless of how detached one's investigation attempts to be, the investigating subject brings an existential investment in the pursuit of knowledge. Again, the traditional objective detachment of Enlightenment scientific inquiry does not match the actual work of the scientist.

Tillich, as I mentioned in chapter 1, greatly revived the meaning and "gut reality" of Luther's "justification by grace through faith" by relating it to psychotherapeutic acceptance. Countless articles, sermons, and books have emphasized this "theology of acceptance." Tillich's brilliant exploration of Luther, as we have seen, revealed not just an existential theologian but a depth psychologist. Tillich was the first in a long line of people who argued that psychotherapy *assumes* an ontological acceptance based on far more than psychology can uncover. This ontological acceptance is ultimately grounded not in the therapist or the society, but in God. The

---

[37]Paul Tillich, *Dynamics of Faith*, 93.

therapist or minister represents this reality but cannot create it. Who are *we* to announce that clients or parishioners are ontologically acceptable? Yet we can rest in the assurance that a Source far greater than the therapist or the therapeutic community has declared this acceptability.

This acceptance is particularly powerful because Tillich refused to reduce the reality of guilt to mere "guilt feelings." For Tillich, our brokenness, our separation, our guilt is quite real. It cannot be psychologically reduced and therefore clinically removed. Instead, any genuine sense of acceptance is always an acceptance "in-spite-of" our guilt. This awareness guards against both cheap grace and artificial psychotherapy. For Tillich, as we have seen, *there is no genuine sense of acceptance without an acknowledgment of estrangement and guilt.* This is an important point for psychotherapists who continue to minimize guilt or even say that *all guilt feelings are neurotic.* As we saw in the New York Psychology Group, some members asserted that we are guilty of nothing and hence do not need forgiveness. Tillich points us back to the reality that *a transformative experience of grace presupposes an acknowledgment of our guilt.*

Tillich also modeled a balance between concerns for the individual and concerns for the social network that affects the individual. While he is obviously associated with existentialism and an interest in the private world of psychotherapy, Tillich also carried with him an interest in the social context out of which individuals operate. His early association with the Frankfurt School, in my mind, was never completely lost. An excellent example of Tillich's wholistic concern for the psychological, economic, and social plights of people was his involvement in what was called "The Self-Help for Emigrants from Central Europe." Tillich became the first chairperson of this group, a group devoted to helping emigrants find housing, employment, and other resources. Tillich maintained this position for fifteen years. Many of his friends from Frankfurt, such as Theodore Adorno, came straight to Tillich's home when they arrived in the United States.[38] Tillich later described the group as follows.

> [W]e wanted to help a larger self than our own, the community of those who were the first victims of national socialism. We felt united in this group, not by clever devices of mutuality, not by sentimental feelings of

---

[38]Wilhelm Pauck and Marion Pauck, *Paul Tillich: His Life and Thought* (San Francisco: Harper & Row, 1976).

pity, but by the experience of an embracing "we" based on a common catastrophe, a common wrath against those who brought about the ruins of our past, and a common resolute will to create something new out of these ruins. This experience of a higher self has given rise to self-help, its name and its reality.[39]

According to the Paucks, Tillich received a steady flow of visitors to his Union Seminary office. Many of these emigrants were nonacademics who felt greatly comforted by Tillich's warmth and helpful advice. As chair of the self-help group, Tillich offered consolation, referrals, and job connections for many persons.

Tillich has also provided an ongoing contribution to an understanding of anxiety, and particularly, the difference between existential and neurotic anxiety. Tillich, more clearly than anyone else, pointed toward a type of anxiety that simply cannot be "therapized" away. This is the anxiety of non-being, the constant threat which can only be met through the courage to be. A perpetual theme in Tillich's thought was that all attempts to flee from this *ontological* anxiety result in *neurotic* anxiety. Just as we must face our genuine guilt, so we must face our genuine anxiety. This ontological anxiety is not based on a faulty interpretation of life or an over-reaction to stress. Instead, it is part of the human condition. We may attempt to transfer this ontological anxiety into a manageable fear, but this cannot be done.

While Tillich is widely known for showing the ontological roots of anxiety, he matches this philosophical analysis with a very keen clinical understanding. For instance, his discussion, which we explored in chapter 2, of how anxiety pushes us toward a limited self-affirmation, offers a vivid portrait of the person who runs away from his or her own depths. Tillich's insights here are very instructive for psychotherapists working with anxiety-ridden patients who can only affirm part of their being.

Also, in spite of the enormous disfavor of the word "conformity" after World War II, Tillich, as we observed in *The Courage to Be*, insisted that the "courage to be a part of," or the courage to participate, is a major part of the courage to be. This concept of participation is often overlooked as readers only focus on Tillich's individualized, existential courage in the face of anxiety. Yet Tillich balanced this individual emphasis on the courage to be oneself with the the courage to be a part of the community.

---

[39]Quoted in Pauck and Pauck, *Paul Tilich*, 157.

This is another reason that he offers balance between individual and social concerns.

Tillich also offers an ongoing resource against the battle with psychological Pelagianism. As we have witnessed in his critique of Fromm's utopianism, Tillich's Augustinian and Lutheran roots can be seen time and time again when he asserts that humanity cannot resolve its own ultimate dilemma. We cannot accept ourselves, forgive ourselves, cognitively heal ourselves, or provide any method of self-salvation. The finite cannot resolve infinite questions. As conditioned human beings, we cannot provide ourselves with "unconditioned" solutions. Will power, human reason, and moral intention will not deliver us from our ontological plight. Our estrangement from our Ground and Source cannot be remedied by our own efforts. In this sense, Tillich's understanding of sin is profoundly neoorthodox and clearly against the tide of classical liberalism.

And finally, in a current situation which at times seems so dizzy with pluralism that it insists that all truth is radically relative and that all we can ever voice is our own local narrative, Tillich still offers a refreshing invitation to examine universal dimensions of the human condition. He encourages us to look at those structures and realities which do indeed make us human. Granted, this should not be done at the expense of our genuine differences, and all voices should be heard rather controlled by an oppressive singular voice. But the search for a common humanity set against the backdrop of the Ultimate should still gain our attention. In a reaction against a monopolizing metanarrative which has seemed to silence the cognitively underprivileged, we should not give up a concern for what binds us together in the face of our Source and Creator.

It is my hope that this book, even in a small way, will help further a discussion of theology's relationship to psychology, and particularly Paul Tillich's contribution to that discussion. As my friend and mentor Don Browning has often suggested, the point is not to say something which is ultimately definitive, but to contribute to and further the conversation. That is what I have attempted to do.

Index

Adams, James Luther, 7
addiction, 93
Adler, Alfred, 61
Adorno, Theodore, 216
American Psychological Association, 16
Aquinas, Thomas, 66
Aristotle, 9
Arther, Don, 40, 41
atheism, 138, 144, 181, 184
Augustine, 10, 13, 71, 72, 73, 93, 112, 116, 142, 218

Barth, Karl (and Barthian), 25-31, 40, 102, 115
  postliberal theology, 195-203
Beck, Aaron, 55-57
Becker, Ernest, 37, 39
Bellah, Robert N., 189
Benedict, Ruth, 99, 100, 114, 133-34
Berger, Peter, 208, 213
Bergson, Henri, 95
Bernstein, Richard, 207
Biel, Gabriel, 8-9
Bigham, Thomas J., 100, 125, 139, 156-57, 184
Bone, Harry, 100, 105, 106, 107, 139, 155-56, 158, 159, 160, 171-76, 178, 186-87, 188-89, 192
Booth, Gotthard, 100, 132-33, 164
Bowen, Murray, 61
Browning, Don, 23, 58, 203, 218
  ethical context of psychotherapy, 189-94
  personal language and Ground of Being, 32-35, 36
  ontological acceptance, 6, 12, 31
  ontological assumptions in psychology, 6, 28-29, 29, 200, 205-207
Buddhism, 78
Bultmann, Rudolf Karl, 125

Calvin, John, 9, 119, 141
Clinebell, Howard, 181-82, 210
Clinical Pastoral Education, 1

cognitive therapy, 55-60
community, 60-62, 185, 208-14
concupiscence, 18, 68, 77, 9293
Cooke, Joseph, 28
Cooper, Terry, 23, 28-9, 29, 58, 142, 189, 200
  ontological assumptions in psychology, 20, 207-208

De Laszlo, Violet, 100, 154-55
"demonic," the, 12, 21-25, 35, 59, 126
Descartes, René, 66
Doherty, William, 189, 192ff.
Dunfee, Susan Nelson, 142

Emery, Gary, 55-57
Elliott, Harrison 100, 136, 162, 176, 177
Elliott, Grace, 184-86
Ellis, Albert, 57, 58
Erasmus, dispute with Luther, 9-11, 66
Erikson, Erik, 38
estrangement, Fromm's and Tillich's concepts of, 84-98
evil, 71, 72, 58, 84ff.
existentialism, 65-67, 94-95

"Fall," the, 69-75, 80-84, 167
father,
  Freudian role of, 89, 123, 148-49
  God as, 79, 123, 136, 159
  Tillich's, 39-40
female image of divine (see also "mother"), 31, 79-80
Feming, E. McClung, 100
feminist theology, 77-80, 142
Feuerbach, Ludwig, 97, 101, 117, 121-22
Fox, George, 153
Frankley, Greta, 100
Frei, Hans, 197
Freud, Sigmund, 13, 15, 16, 21-22, 25, 43, 63, 66, 67, 82, 86, 89, 91, 95, 97, 118, 123, 129-30, 141, 191, 193
  neo-Freudian, 25, 65, 69
  libido and concupiscence, 68

sin, 149
conscience, 148, 154
Fromm, Eric, 3, 46, 63, 64, 68, 69, 70, 99, 100, 128ff., 133, 137, 139, 140, 177, 212
  anthropocentric ethics, 147-50, 157-64
  Calvin, 119-20
  doubt, 107-108
  estrangement 84-91
  faith, 102-103, 109-10. 115-14
  God as symbol, 97, 101, 105, 107, 111, 114, 116, 159
  human condition, evolution of, 93-98
  Luther, 119-20
  Marxist influence on, 82-93
  productive orientation, 96, 129-30
  psychological help, 168-70, 174
  self-love, 128, 141ff.
  syndrome of decay, 84-91
  transcendence, 157-58, 163, 183-84

Gerkin, Charles, 210
Gilkey, Langdon, 70-75, 197
Glen, J. Stanley, 121-22
Glickman, Martha, 100, 104, 139-40, 142
"God" concept of, 97, 101-102, 105, 107, 111, 114, 116-17, 125, 135ff., 144-45
Graham, Larry Kent, 209-10, 212
Grenz, Stanley, 144
Gross, Martin, 189

Habermas, Jurgen, 206
Hammond, Guy, 63, 64, 83, 94, 98, 127, 197
Hampson, Daphne, 142
Harvey, Van A., 213-14
Hegel, Georg Wilhelm Friedrich, 66, 121, 212
Heidegger, Martin, 95, 167
Henderson, Valerie Land, 3, 22, 23, 24
Hiltner, Seward, 99, 10, 103, 127, 165, 170-71
Holifield, Brooks, 16-17
Hordern, William, 13
Horney, Karen, 53, 61, 68, 69, 129, 141, 142

humanism, secular (see also Fromm), 63, 101, 106-107, 125-26, 160
Husinger, Deborah van Deusen, relation of psychological and theological terms, 25-31, 35

James, William, 123
Jaspers, Karl Theodor, 95, 198
Jesus, 21, 112, 136
Jones, Ernest, 17
Jung, Carl (and Jungian), 4, 31, 54, 60, 67, 95, 130ff., 14, 142,
  on conscience, 154-55

Kafka, Franz, 110
Kaminer, Wendy, 189
Kant, Immanuel, 166
Kierkegaard, Søren, 23, 37, 66, 72, 110-11, 212
Kirschenbaum, Howard, 3, 22, 23, 24
Klass, Dennis, 39
Kohlberg, Lawrence, 165
Kopp, Sheldon, 4
Kotschnig, Elined Prys, 100, 103, 104, 105, 132
Kotschnig, Walter Maria, 100

Lasch, Christopher, 189ff
LeFevre, Perry, 1
Lerner, Michael, 189
Lindbeck, George, 196, 197, 201, 205
Luther, Martin, 1, 4, 7-15, 35, 38, 48, 72, 116, 119-20, 123, 152, 165, 215, 218
  and Freud, 13, 15
  disputation with Erasmus, 9-11, 66

Manichaean, 10, 71
Mannheim, Karl, 213-14
Marshall, Joretta L., 210f
Marx, Karl, 21, 63, 65, 66, 97, 190
  the "Fall," 80-84
Maslow, Abraham, 43, 86, 103
May, Rollo, 16, 24, 35, 38, 99, 100, 116
mother,
  Fromm's concept of mother-fixation, 89-91, 130
  Great Mother, 79-80

negative mother complex, 27-28
Tillich's mother, 38-39
Muentzer, Thomas, 153

Nazi Germany, 60, 63, 91, 118, 154
Neumann, Erich, 79
New York Psychology Group, 17, 35, 63, 64, 98, 99-194, 198-99, 216
   conscience (ethics), psychology of (1943–1944), 147-68, 188-94
   community context, 189-94
   faith, psychology of (1941–1942), 100-27
   helping (therapy), psychology of (1944–1945), 168-88, 188-94
   relation of psychology to theology, 178-84
   love, psychology of (1942–1943), 127-45
   self-love, 131ff., 138ff., 141ff.
   analogy to divine love, 135ff., 143ff.
Nicol, Helen, 100
Niebuhr, H. Richard, 17
Niebuhr, Reinhold, 60, 64, 67, 70-75, 76, 77, 142, 210
Nietzsche, Friedrich, 37, 66, 95

Oberman, Heiko, 8
Occam, William of, 8
Oden, Thomas, 6, 12, 29-31
Olson, Roger, 144
Origen, 71
Otto, Rudolph, 112
Ozment, Steven, 10

pantheism, 90
Pascal, Blaise, 66
Patton, John, 209, 210
Pauck, Wilhelm and Marion, 38, 40, 41, 216-17
Paul (New Testament), 73, 112-13, 151, 153
Pelagian controversy (self-salvation), 4, 9-10, 58, 59, 62, 71, 116, 123, 158, 218
Perls, Fritz, 53, 54
Placher, William, 197, 201
Philo, 151
Plaskow, Judith, 76-80, 142

Plato, 173

Ramsay, Nancy J., 208-209
Rank, Otto, 61
Rice, Otis, 100, 176-77
Richardson, Cyril, 135ff.
Ricoeur, Paul, 5, 164, 195, 203ff.
   distanciation, 29, 205, 214
Roberts, David, 2, 99, 100, 106, 108, 110, 111, 116, 135, 136, 139, 150, 160ff., 178, 188
   relationship of psychology to theology, 178-84
Rogers, Carl, 1, 3, 12, 15-25, 29-31, 35, 86, 99, 100, 103, 143, 177, 178, 191, 212
   actualizing tendency, 20, 23, 24
   client-centered therapy, 187
   the "demonic, 21-25, 35
   empathy, 20
   incongruence, 17-21, 53
   unconditional positive regard, 20, 187
Rohrbach, Elizabeth, 100
Rousseau, Jean-Jacques, 20

Sanders, John, 144
Sartre, Jean Paul, 66, 95, 198
Saiving, Valerie, 142
Schachtel, Anna Hartoch, 134
Schachtel, Ernest, 100, 110, 116, 134, 135, 136
Schelling, Friedrich Wilhelm Joseph von, 66
scholasticism, 151
Schur, Edwin, 189ff.
Scott, Nathan, 67
Scotus, Duns, 66
sin, 2, 18, 63, 68, 72-73, 84ff., 111
   feminist concept of 77-78
   Marxist concept of, 80-84
   and therapy (H. Bone), 172
social context, see community
Staupitz, 14
Steinmetz, David, 8
stoicism and cognitive therapy, 58
Stokes, Allison, 99-100

Thelan, Mary Frances, 81-82
theology,

feminist, 77-80, 142
liberation, 211-12, 213
postliberal (e.g., Barthian) and revisionist (apologetic) debates, 195-203
Thomism, 34
Tillich, Hannah, 100
Tillich, Mutie, 41
Tillich, Paul,
  acceptance, 2-7, 31-35, 214,
  anxiety, 45-48, 51-55
    and fear 43-45, 56
    neurotic and ontological, 50-51, 217
    own experience, 38-41
    positive aspects, 48ff.
  chaplain, 40-41
  concupiscence, 18, 68, 92-93
  conscience, 150-54, 165-68, 174-75
  correlational method, 197-200
  courage, 41-42, 217
  "demonic," 21-25
  essential being, 166ff.
  estrangement, 3, 17-21, 64-65, 69-75, 91-93
  faith, 112-14, 123-127, 199-200
  guilt, 5, 44, 47
  grace, 3
  Ground of Being,
    and acceptance, 18, 31-35
    and personal language, 32-35, 144-45
    "God" as symbol, 105-106, 122, 135, 138
    transcendence, 158
  hubris, 77, 92
  love, ontology of, 137-38
  Luther, 7-15
  myth, 125
  self-acceptance, (limited) 52-55, 217
  self-love, 3-4, 138, 143
  separation, 2
  sin, 2, 18
  theology-psychology dialogue, contributions to, 214-18
  unbelief (unfaith), 18, 91-92
Tracy, David, 64, 195, 196,
  mutual correlation, 197-99
  recent hermeneutics, 203-206

Wallach, Lise, 189
Wallach, Michael A., 189
Wickes, Frances G., 100, 104-105, 130-32, 178
will, Luther and Erasmus on, 9-11
Wittgenstein, Ludwig, 201

www.ingramcontent.com/pod-product-compliance
Lightning Source LLC
Chambersburg PA
CBHW021808220426
43662CB00006B/233